# the art
*of*
## WOO

# the art
## *of*
# WOO

Using Persuasion to Sell Your Ideas

G. Richard Shell

Mario Moussa

CAPSTONE
*be inspired!*
™

*For Robbie, always.*

*For Robin, Ella, Miles, and Bix.*

# Contents

# introduction

# Woo?

What's Woo?

We're glad you asked.

Marcus Buckingham and Donald Clifton, in their best-selling book *Now, Discover Your Strengths,* tell us that "woo" is a talent for "**Wi**n-ning **O**thers **O**ver." The *Wall Street Journal* recently reported that Barbara Broccoli and her half brother Michael Wilson, part-owners of the James Bond movie franchise, "wooed" business tycoon Sir Richard Branson to be a partner in their latest James Bond film. On that same day, according to other news reports, President Hu of China arrived in India to "woo" officials there on his plans for regional cooperation, and the Central Kenya Initiative was formed to "woo" voters in that African region. Meanwhile, officials from a small southern city traveled to Las Vegas, Nevada, to "woo" shopping center developers into locating a mall in their city, and a major British university introduced a new program to "woo" corporate recruiters to its campus. Around the world, in places too numerous to name, people were wooing their bosses, town councils, colleagues, and spouses to adopt their latest plans to improve lives and solve difficult problems.

So what is Woo? It is relationship-based persuasion, a strategic process for getting people's attention, pitching your ideas, and obtaining approval for your plans and projects. It is, in short, one of the most important skills in the repertoire of any entrepreneur, employee, or professional manager whose work requires them to rely on influence and persuasion rather than coercion and force.

Woo. Simple to say. Hard to do.

A manager we know once lobbied for a bigger-than-normal raise by sending his boss a detailed e-mail listing all his recent accomplishments.

The boss circulated the e-mail to the senior staff and asked for comments. One of the executives copied on the e-mail was offended by what he saw. It appeared to him that the manager was taking the credit for a major project that the executive thought *he* should get the credit for. A flurry of e-mails followed. Long story short: our friend did not get his raise. Instead, he was fired for not being a "team player."

He lost his job because he ignored the ever-present danger of office politics and forgot that idea-selling campaigns begin with relationships, not e-mails. Lacking tone and context, e-mail messages are easy to misinterpret. You cannot control who will see them, and they are never deleted. If you want to get people on your side, go meet with them face-to-face and see firsthand how they react to your ideas. Then use e-mail later, after they are already on your team.

Woo is about people, not saving time.

## Woo and You

Woo starts with a look in the mirror. If you do not know your own goals, biases, emotions, and preferences, you cannot hope to see your audience clearly. With this self-awareness as a foundation, you gain the perspective needed to focus on the people you are trying to persuade. If you look up the word *woo* in the dictionary, you will find that the first definition relates to romantic courtship, as in "Charles wooed Victoria, hoping she would marry him." Indeed, the root of the word *persuasion* is "Suada," a Roman goddess who attended Venus, the goddess of romantic love. You persuade others that you love them by showing that you care deeply about their interests and needs. You demonstrate in unique, personal ways that you "get" who they are, how they are unique, and why that uniqueness attracts you.

But woo also has a more general meaning as we saw in the news stories about everyone from James Bond's Barbara Broccoli to China's President Hu. That meaning is "seeking favour and support." Once again, woo carries a connotation of focusing on others—the people being wooed.

The best books on management also emphasize this value. The fifth of Stephen Covey's seven habits of "highly effective people" is:

"Seek first to understand, then to be understood." By understanding your audiences, Covey argues, you have a better chance of being understood by them. And, as we noted above, Marcus Buckingham and Donald Clifton actually use the word *woo* in *Now, Discover Your Strengths* to describe one of thirty-four personality "themes" that people use to succeed at work. They define *woo* as a special talent for establishing rapport quickly and easily with strangers by finding "some area of common interest so that you can strike up a conversation." Their definition of *woo* is much narrower than ours, but it points in the same direction.

This all sounds fine. But what is the "art" of Woo?

The art comes in the balance you strike, each time you persuade, between what we call the "self-oriented" perspective emphasizing your own credibility, point of view, and level of commitment, and the other-oriented perspective that focuses on your audience's needs, perceptions, and feelings. On the one hand, you have your own passions and perspectives. On the other hand, your audiences may not be able to hear you unless you speak in terms they can understand and in ways that make your message attractive to them. How should you balance your own need for authenticity with your audience's need for a tailor-made message?

Two problems make this balance especially hard to strike in many organizational settings. The first is familiarity. People often have personal knowledge of (and, on occasion, animosity toward) those they work with. Such familiarity breeds lazy habits when it comes to persuasion. The second problem is formality. People fall into the trap of thinking that all they need to know about those they are trying to persuade are their job titles. They forget that persuasion involves personalities as well as positions. These assumptions prompt idea sellers to make careless moves, and this carelessness is what generally gets them into trouble.

With Woo, you approach each persuasion moment as a fresh event, even if it is happening with someone you have encountered a hundred times. You come prepared with a plan, then improvise and adjust as you go along.

That takes art.

## How It All Began

This book came out of our experiences teaching negotiation to business and nonprofit executives. Richard is the author of an award-winning book on negotiation called *Bargaining for Advantage: Negotiation Strategies for Reasonable People* and a professor at the Wharton School of Business. He cofounded and directs (with colleague Stuart Diamond) the Wharton Executive Negotiation Workshop. Mario teaches organizational change in Wharton's executive programs and heads up the Negotiation Practice Group at CFAR (The Center for Applied Research)—a consulting firm that started as a Wharton research center.

In our respective seminars, we always ask participants to help us make the class more relevant by telling us about the real-world problems they face that require enhanced negotiation skills. As you might expect, many are working on classic bargaining problems: acquisitions, asking for lower prices from their vendors, or trying to get higher prices from their customers. But a surprising number of people (nearly 50 percent) report problems that do not look, at first glance, to be negotiation problems at all. In a recent running of the Wharton Executive Negotiation Workshop, for example, participants gave the following reasons for attending:

- William (a vice president at an international bank): "I am here because my unit has been so successful that my boss wants to reassign 30 percent of my staff to other bank units that are not performing as well. He says that, given our performance, we can meet our goals without these people and that the other units need the help. I think this is crazy and want to figure out how to preserve what has been a remarkable team."

- Martha (dean of a major graduate school at a large American university): "I am trying to obtain budget authorization from the provost at my university for an important new initiative. He charged me with raising the profile of the school a year ago when he appointed me to this position, but I now find that the administration is reluctant to give me the resources to make that happen."

- Ken (litigator for a major insurance company): "We want to institute a new program to encourage early settlement of lawsuits, but many of the outside law firms we partner with are reluctant to sign on. I need to figure out a way to sell this idea to them without ruining what are very good working relationships."

Our workshops address problems such as these along with more traditional bargaining issues, but we have found that the language and tactics of negotiation are not always the best means to analyze and discuss these organizational matters. Negotiation skills are a key part of the influence and persuasion process when you are allocating resources, asking for money to implement a strategy, and trying to get your strategic partners to go along with new programs. But negotiation is not the whole story—or even the biggest part of it.

To capture the richness of relationship-based persuasion—without getting lost in the sea of psychological research on all forms of social interaction—we decided to focus our efforts. First, we zeroed in on the most important influence moments people face: the moments when they are trying to sell major proposals, ideas, programs, and initiatives to others. We targeted, in short, the process of *selling ideas*. As you will see in chapter 1, this process follows a simple, four-step pattern that you can repeat each time you want to advance a proposal.

Second, we focused squarely on you, the reader, rather than on abstract psychological topics or organizational designs. You are, after all, the center of your own organizational chart. The book therefore features two personalized, tested diagnostic surveys to help you discover your unique persuasion styles and preferences. These assessments will give you personal points of reference for the entire book.

Third, we anchored our research on real-world examples culled from literally hundreds of articles and biographies about the lives of some of the most skilled persuaders in history. Our own personal experiences with top leaders and companies also came into play. These stories mean that you will be learning from some great idea salesmen, including Abraham Lincoln, Andrew Carnegie, J. P. Morgan, Charles Lindbergh, Frances Perkins, Nelson Mandela, and Bono, among others.

Fourth, we built our ideas on a solid research foundation grounded in social science, with references at the end of the book for those who want to dig deeper.

Finally, our attention in this book is squarely on the problems you face when you must persuade others who are, at least nominally, on your team—your own firm, your clients, your long-term customers and suppliers, and even your own family.

## How the Book Is Organized

The book begins in chapter 1 by defining our target. What does it mean to use Woo to "sell an idea"? We are not talking about selling cars or marketing to a mass audience. In the encounters we will discuss in this book, the other party will be listening and the ideas will have weight. To succeed in such situations, you need to be persuasive, not slick. This chapter introduces and summarizes the four-step Woo process.

Next, chapter 2 helps you see exactly what persuasion skills and aptitudes you bring to the table. Extensive research reveals that, regardless of the positions people occupy, they rely on six main channels of influence—authority, rationality, vision, relationships, interests, and politics—to solve problems. Most people mix several of these modes in important influence encounters. An administrative assistant who is charged with enforcing paperwork requirements for the office, for example, may use a combination of authority and relationship skills in carrying out this responsibility.

This leads us to one of our overall points in chapter 2: we think most people tend to rely on certain *preferred* persuasion channels and that it helps a great deal to know which ones they prefer and which ones they do not. Our first self-assessment tool, the Six Channels Survey presented in Appendix A, will help you investigate which of the channels you feel compelled to use most often at work and which of the six you would actually prefer to use if you had your choice in the matter.

In addition, people have different *styles* of using the six influence channels, just as different musicians have different styles for playing the notes on a musical instrument. In social situations, do you tend to be bold and brassy or restrained and thoughtful? Do you speak up and lead the discussion or do you prefer to hear others out and then quietly make your views known? When you walk into a room full of strangers, is your first thought "Who do these people want me to be?" or "How can I communicate to these people who I am?" Our second profiler, the Persuasion Styles Assessment in Appendix B, will help you tease out which of five distinct persuasion roles you prefer to play: Driver (a highly assertive person who speaks his or her mind without much concern for the audience), Commander (quieter use of the self-oriented mode), Promoter (an assertive, gregarious person who tends to approach persuasion more from the audience's point of view), Chess Player (quieter use of the other-directed mode), and Advocate (moderately assertive person who is balanced between the self- and other-oriented modes).

Chapters 3 through 9 present the balance of our systematic planning process for practicing Woo. These chapters ask the key questions you should address whenever you are trying to sell an important idea:

- What decision-making process do you face and whom should you target first?

- What relationship and credibility problems might you encounter and how can you overcome them?

- Does your audience want you to use a special language, such as data-based analysis or inspirational appeals?

- What values and beliefs does your audience bring to the table that may affect how it will hear your pitch?

- Are your interests aligned or conflicting?

- How should you organize your pitch for maximum impact and what forms of evidence do other parties need to persuade them?

- What devices can make your proposal truly memorable and effective?

- How can you overcome organizational politics to secure ongoing commitment and translate your idea into action?

As you answer each of these questions, you identify the principal barriers to persuasion and build your case. Chapter 10 concludes with a deeper look at one of our most important themes: the role of personal character in persuasion.

As you read through the book, you will notice an underlying structure: Woo represents a step-by-step movement from you and your ideas toward your audience and its needs. When you succeed, your audience stops being "the other" and starts being your partner-in-persuasion. That is because, when relationships matter, you cannot force anyone to accept anything you say. You can only help people to persuade themselves.

We need to make one disclaimer before we start. Woo is not about setting high-level strategies to defeat opponents in a competitive world. If you need advice on such strategy, you ought to consult one of our favorite books, Sun Tzu's *The Art of War*.

But if you are trying to win people over rather than defeat them, we offer *The Art of Woo*.

## chapter one

# Selling Ideas:
# How Woo Works

You can have brilliant ideas, but if you can't get them across,
your ideas won't get you anywhere . . .
—Former Chrysler Chairman and CEO Lee Iacocca

To just invent something and have a great idea is a lot of
work, but it is not enough. [You need to know] how to get
people excited.
—Larry Page, Cofounder of Google Inc.

We once met a thirty-one-year-old technology manager on the West
Coast named Kumar Chandra. He moved to the United States from
India several years ago to work for a major pharmaceutical firm.
With an advanced degree in computer science, he was an expert on
improving the information systems at his company. But he could not
get support for his initiatives. After telling us a sad story about how a
coworker had stolen his best proposal and gotten it adopted, Kumar
summed up his problem with stunning simplicity: "I just can't seem
to sell my ideas."

Kumar is not alone.

Companies sell their products and services. People in organizations
sell their ideas.

Your success depends on how well you sell.

The president and chairman of the board of a large bank in the
Northeast once was asked how he thought about his job. "I am a
salesman," he replied. "I have to sell policy changes and new ideas. I

sell to the board of directors, the stockholders, the branch managers, the tellers, the cleaning crew, and the customers all at the same time."

But selling ideas—especially the kind of ideas that make organizations work—is a skill shrouded in mystery. Classical geniuses from Aristotle to Cicero considered idea selling (they called it "rhetoric") to be one of the most critical subjects an educated person could learn. Yet two thousand years later, most schools have stopped teaching it. Rhetoric is seen as a dark art practiced by the wizards of political spin, and selling is viewed as something people can learn once they start work.

Yet out in the real world, there are few sales classes teaching the type of selling that would help Kumar. Sales training focuses on buyers and customers—parting people from their money—not pushing initiatives through a dense network of relationships.

Result? This critical part of life's curriculum, for students at the best business schools as well as for everyone else, is left to the individual. It's up to you to learn on the fly.

## "It's Only Seven Letters"

Let's start with a simple example of what selling an idea looks like.

When the young Sam Walton was trying to figure out what to call his first large discount store in Rogers, Arkansas, one of his key employees, store manager Bob Bogle, had a great idea for a name—"Walmart" (the hyphen in Wal-Mart came later in the company's history). Walton had started out running a Ben Franklin variety store in Bentonville and eventually turned it into "Walton's Five and Dime." Now it was time to come up with a name for Sam's new big-store concept. Most of the names Walton was considering, like the old Walton's Five and Dime, had three or four words.

Bob came up with his "Walmart" idea by combining the first syllable from Sam's last name with a shorthand word for "market." It was a pretty good idea, but pitching his boss on it was tricky.

Bob figured Sam would be flattered to have a store that alluded, however indirectly, to his name. But Sam Walton did not like to parade his ego. So Bogle decided to sell his idea by appealing to one of Sam Walton's most fundamental core values: saving money. Listen as Bob Bogle tells his simple story (as recounted in Sam Walton's autobiography *Made in America*):

> I scribbled W-A-L-M-A-R-T on the bottom of [a] card, and said [to Sam] "To begin with, there's not as many letters to buy." I had bought the letters that said "Ben Franklin," and I knew how much it cost to put them up and to light them and repair the neon, so I said, "This is just seven letters." He didn't say anything, and I dropped the subject. A few days later I went by to see when we could start setting the fixtures in the building, and I saw that our sign maker . . . already had the W-A-L up there and was headed up the ladder with an M. . . . I just smiled and went on.

Bob Bogle's sale of the name "Walmart" to his boss is as straightforward as idea selling gets. But even this simple example illustrates some basic principles of effective persuasion.

First, Bob had a specific goal: persuade his boss to adopt the "Walmart" name for the new store.

Second, Bob identified the decision maker—Sam Walton—and presented his idea directly to this person.

Third, Bogle drew on his credibility as one of Walton's key employees. You don't need to be a key employee to sell an idea. But you do need to have credibility.

Fourth, Bob Bogle appealed to one of Sam's core interests—a single-minded focus on cost. Low cost was a value that Sam Walton saluted every day, so pitching the "Walmart" idea in terms of cost was exactly the right way to get Sam's attention.

Fifth, Bogle used his knowledge of Walton as a person. Sam solved problems as they came up, so Bob picked his moment to pitch his idea. That moment came during a trip the two men were taking together just days before a sign would be needed to go on the front of the new store. And because the sign was something the public would see, Bob wrote it out for Sam to visualize.

Walton also liked to mull things over. So Bogle resisted the temptation to oversell. He put his justification out there and then stopped talking.

Finally, all of this took place as part of a relationship. Bogle and Walton were working together to solve problems. They trusted each other. So Bob "just smiled and went on" when Sam decided to use the Walmart name. And Walton put Bogle's story in his autobiography after he became a billionaire. Both men, in short, did very, very well in this relationship. We will be emphasizing the importance of relationships, communication channels, and presentation strategies throughout the book.

With this example in mind, it may be easier to understand what makes selling ideas different. It's not about tricking people into buying things they do not need. It's about helping people see things your way—engaging their minds and imaginations, then getting them to take action on the idea you recommend.

## How Woo Works: The Four Steps

As the book progresses, you will discover that relationship-based persuasion follows a distinctive, repeatable four-step process that you can master to achieve your influence goals.

- Step 1—*Survey Your Situation*
- Step 2—*Confront the Five Barriers*
- Step 3—*Make Your Pitch,* and
- Step 4—*Secure Your Commitments.*

Below, we trace each of these steps in detail, forecasting what is to come in the chapters ahead.

### Step 1: Survey Your Situation (Chapters 2 and 3)

Step 1 requires you to see yourself, your idea, your goals, and your organizational challenges with crystal clarity. What is distinctive about the idea you are trying to sell? What is your idea-selling strategy—whom should you speak with and in what order? What communication preferences and biases will you bring to each persuasion encounter? What level of commitment and purpose can you summon for your idea?

Later in the book we will tell the story of how Charles Lindbergh planned and executed one of the most compelling idea sales of the twentieth century—the first nonstop flight across the Atlantic Ocean in 1927. As you will see, Lindbergh—who had few assets, no plane, and no backers—took particular care with his initial steps in this campaign. The inspiration for the flight came to him one evening while he was flying his mail route between St. Louis and Chicago. He quickly seized on its distinctive quality—he wanted to make the flight alone in a single-engine plane—and became passionately committed to his plan. He then set in motion a careful strategy for turning his idea into reality. Lindbergh studied the social environment in his hometown of St. Louis to determine exactly whom he should approach for support and in what order. And as he approached each person, Lindbergh assessed his own strengths and weaknesses as a persuader and adjusted his style to maximize his chances for making a successful pitch. We will review exactly how and why he succeeded in this historic quest—which illustrates the vital importance of each step in the Woo process.

### Step 2: Confront the Five Barriers (Chapters 4, 5, and 6)

Step 2 forces you to consider the obstacles that pose the greatest risks to a successful influence encounter. These are: negative or ambiguous relationships, poor credibility, communication mismatches, hostile belief systems, and conflicting interests. The first two of these barriers relate to how people see you personally. The final three make it harder for people to hear your idea clearly.

Each of the five barriers has the potential to become a valuable asset in your idea pitch if you do your homework well. But, at a minimum, your goal should always be to clear as many of these obstacles as possible out of your path so you give the other person a chance to objectively evaluate the merits of your proposal.

**Potential Barrier number 1: Relationships.** The first potential barrier is often the one that colors all the rest: How will the other person view your relationship to him or her? Will they know you? Like you? Best of all, trust you?

As Bogle's sale of the Walmart name shows, persuasion at work always takes place within a network of relationships. A relationship with someone, somewhere will be the starting point for putting your idea "in play," and relationships with and between people you may not even know will often be the end point for getting it adopted. You need a circle of influence, a network of people who know people who know people. And it may be too late to form such a circle when you are ready to make your sale. The relationships must already be in place. The biggest barriers, of course, arise when you face negative or hostile relationships in the pathway of your idea.

**Potential Barrier number 2: Credibility.** Next, you need to think about whether the other person will see you as a credible advocate for your idea. Will they view you as competent? Reliable? Someone with special expertise? This factor explains why trying to manipulate other people does not work when you are selling important ideas.

We have a friend who is the regional sales manager for a large franchise organization. He is fascinated by books that explore the "hidden psychology" of persuasion—the kind of books that promise to make you an expert in "instant influence" so you can close deals "in ninety seconds."

Our friend learned about the importance of credibility when he tried the "Door in the Face" technique on his boss at raise time. The gambit works (when it does) by making a request that the other party is sure to reject (he slams "the door in your face"). Then you immediately back down to a much more modest suggestion. Your second request looks so reasonable by comparison with the first one that people are more inclined to say "OK." Research on the "Door in the Face" technique has shown that people raising money for charities can get more ten-dollar donations if they start by asking for fifty dollars and shifting quickly down to ten dollars (after the target donor says "no") than they can by asking for ten dollars in the first place.

Our friend decided he would try this with his boss. He asked for a raise that was three times what anyone in their right mind would have requested. When the boss looked at him in shock, he backed down to the regular raise he had planned to ask for.

The boss was still in shock. "You are being completely unreasonable," he said. Our friend tried to recover by making a joke of it, but nobody was laughing. Our friend got no raise because he had, temporarily at least, lost his credibility.

An important part of credibility is character, a point emphasized by the ancients who studied rhetoric and persuasion. Aristotle, in particular, underlined character—one's *ethos*—as the antidote to becoming overly focused (as the Greek "sophists" eventually became) on pandering to particular audiences. He argued that character was the most important persuasion tool of them all.

So will we. If you want to be truly persuasive within your organization, you must develop your own ethos and endorse character as a value. This attitude was summed up well by the banking mogul J. P. Morgan in a short interchange he had with a congressional committee in the early 1900s. The committee was investigating possible financial manipulations in a deal Morgan was associated with (the committee eventually exonerated him). In the course of the hearings, the following exchange took place:

> *Committee Member:* Is not commercial credit based primarily on money or property?
> *J. P. Morgan:* No, sir. The first thing is character.
> *Committee Member:* Before money or property?
> *J. P. Morgan:* Before money or anything else. Money cannot buy it.

Chapter 10 will investigate the issue of character in more detail.

**Potential Barrier number 3: Communication Mismatches.** With both the relationship and credibility issues addressed, you are ready to encounter the third barrier: your audience's preferred style or channel of communication. Your natural enthusiasm and humor may be effective for selling an idea to your marketing group. But the company's straitlaced executive committee may not appreciate that style. You may need to adjust. Chapter 5 explores this critical variable.

For example, Jeffrey Katzenberg, the legendary media mogul who founded the studio DreamWorks and then took it public, once made this sort of mistake. Like many in Hollywood, he is a natural-born user of visionary influence, wooing audiences with enthusiasm, snap, and passion. But on this occasion, he got carried away with his own message and forgot to see it from his audience's point of view. It was a costly lesson.

One of the first movies DreamWorks launched after going public was a cartoon feature called *Madagascar*. Following his usual style, Katzenberg aggressively hyped the film in the media. When the production met DreamWorks' projections by pulling in £47 million at domestic theaters over its opening weekend, everyone inside the company was pleased. But DreamWorks' stock price took a dive. Why? Katzenberg had failed to recognize that, as CEO of a public company, he was now speaking to an audience of stock analysts. Addressing these number-crunchers required a prudent rather than a passionate approach. They read Katzenberg's prelaunch hype as a signal that the movie would hit a much higher number. As one analyst explained the stock-price dip, "Credibility has not been helped by 'talking up' *Madagascar* only to have the film [merely] meet expectations." Katzenberg's blunder was costly for his stockholders, and he quickly learned to adopt a more audience-sensitive persuasion style (in this case a data-driven, reason-and-logic mode) in public statements about future films.

**Potential Barrier number 4: Belief Systems.** If your organization is committed to diversity in hiring, a proposal to save money by focusing only on Ivy League universities during recruiting season will be a tough sale. Asking people to buy an idea that violates one of their basic values or beliefs—or the written standards and policies that sometimes give concrete expression to these beliefs—puts people in an uncomfortable position: either they buy your idea and give up the core value or reject your idea and keep their value.

They will usually find it easier to reject your idea. Effective idea selling, therefore, requires you to position your idea as consistent with (or better yet, furthering) your audience's important beliefs and values. Bogle's pitch for "Walmart" saluted his company's core mission of "low cost." Chapter 5 takes up this subject.

**Potential Barrier number 5: Interests and Needs.** Fifth and finally, effective idea sellers focus on the other party's interests. For example, when Napoleon was a young officer in the French army, he established an artillery battery at the siege of Toulon in such an exposed position that his superiors told him he would never get soldiers to man it. Had he ordered his men to take on this duty, his superiors would probably have been right. It was close to being a suicide mission. But Napoleon showed his skill as a persuader by finding and appealing to a fundamental interest—his soldiers' pride and their desire to be seen as men of courage.

He created a large placard to put on the battery. On it, the following words were printed in bold letters: THE BATTERY OF THE MEN WITHOUT FEAR. Instead of shying from a life-threatening assignment, Napoleon's men competed for the honor of being known as the members of this fearless band. The position was manned day and night.

As this story shows, understanding what is really motivating other people opens up a host of options for influencing them. It is also important to pay attention to interests because conflicts related to control over resources, credit for initiatives, and career advancement can be the source of political disputes. The more people who have interests that conflict with your idea, the more potential enemies you have.

## Step 3: Make Your Pitch (Chapters 7 and 8)

Your insights into the five potential barriers discussed above will give you valuable information, helping you gain the perspective you need to frame your ideas in the most effective way. This sets the stage for the third step in the Woo process—making your pitch.

The pitch is an especially important part of selling ideas because there are few "impulse buys" in the market for ideas. Careful deliberation—or at least the appearance of careful deliberation—is the norm. This raises a question: How do rationality, emotion, and intuition balance out when people buy an idea? What exactly went through Sam Walton's mind when he decided to take Bogle's advice and name his store Walmart? Which factor dominated: his thrift or his ego?

Research confirms that rationality is critical in the idea-buying process, but not in the way you would expect. For important, complex decisions, such as whether to take a new job, hire a new employee, or select one of several competing business strategies, people arrive at better decisions when they load up on as much data and reflection as possible, and then set all that aside and decide with their gut feelings.

Some great decision makers have confirmed this.

Andy Grove, former CEO of Intel: "Drive deep into the data, then trust your gut."

Alfred Sloan, CEO of General Motors in the 1920s and founder of the modern corporation: "The final act of business judgment is . . . intuitive."

Akio Morita, cofounder and former CEO of Sony Corporation: "[I]nstead of putting one fact together with another, [the best managers] grasp a general idea as a whole . . . in making decisions. This [is better] than one can get only through careful reasoning."

Malcolm Gladwell's book *Blink* summarizes the research on how this process works. The unconscious, which is the source of most new, creative ideas, also seems to do a better job than the conscious mind of processing lots of data, finding the patterns in the data, and folding all those patterns into our underlying preferences and experience to come up with a wise decision. Thus, however long and involved the process of thinking about a problem may be, the final act of deciding seems to reside in the realm of intuition.

But that is not the end of the story. Once they make their decision, people have to explain it to themselves and, more important, to others. And it may not be good enough to say "because that is what felt right, all things considered." People need good, solid reasons to justify important decisions, even if, truth be told, they are not sure exactly why they shifted from "no" to "yes."

In other words, people are not just "reasonable," they are also "rationalizing." As Benjamin Franklin once said (after deciding as a young man to call off his vegetarian diet), "So convenient a thing it is to be a Reasonable creature, since it enables one to find or make a Reason for everything one has a mind to do."

J. P. Morgan once noted that people generally have two reasons for everything they do, "a good reason and the real reason." A very important part of selling ideas, therefore, is providing your audience with good reasons—both because they *are* good and truly justify what you propose, and because they give your audience ways to explain their decision when their real motives may be either self-serving or hard to articulate. As a part of our treatment of what evidence and arguments to use in your sales pitch, we will examine how one of the most innovative companies in the world—Google—vets ideas.

We will also give you eight specific techniques you can use to grab and hold your audience's attention in presentating your idea— none of which involve the use of PowerPoint or similar software. The unconscious mind of your audience—which will be making the final decision on your idea—likes things to be clear, memorable, and personal. Thus, how you state your case can be as important as the idea you are selling. Timing matters. Sequencing matters. Stories and metaphors can help. Any device that makes your idea vivid and easy to recall, provided it is acceptable within the corporate culture, facilitates persuasion.

Consider a document called "The Peanut Butter Manifesto," which showed up recently on the front page of the *Wall Street Journal*. The Peanut Butter Manifesto was written by a senior vice president of Yahoo Inc. named Brad Garlinghouse. In it, he pitched his ideas for changing his company's business strategy.

Garlinghouse was in charge of Yahoo's e-mail service and the Yahoo.com home page. At the time he wrote his memo, the company had the most visited Web site in America. But rival Google was catching up fast in terms of Web traffic. Google had also demonstrated more imagination in its Web offerings, better focus in its strategy, and a much better way of making money from online advertising. Meanwhile, Yahoo's share price was down, its revenue growth was slowing, staff members were defecting, and a high-priority project designed to boost online advertising sales was behind schedule. Yet nobody in the top executive suite seemed to be aware that there was a crisis. Garlinghouse had specific ideas for turning the situation at Yahoo around, including a radical restructuring. But he needed to get people's attention.

To sell his ideas, he drafted a four-page memo, gave it the catchy "Peanut Butter Manifesto" title, circulated it to his internal network of contacts, and got his network to bring it to the attention of Yahoo's top decision maker, CEO Terry Semel. The memo is not exactly Shakespeare, but it grabbed attention within the world of Yahoo because it spoke in "Yahoo-ese" and presented its thesis in a compelling way.

The memo is too long to reprint here. But we'll break down the parts in terms of Woo.

First, Garlinghouse, like Bob Bogle, had a clear goal. He wanted to light a fire under senior management so they would see Yahoo's business situation in a new light and start taking action to fix its many urgent problems. Everything about the Peanut Butter Manifesto focused on this goal.

Second, he took pains in the Manifesto to establish his credibility within the Yahoo culture. When you don't have a personal relationship with the decision maker, you need to establish credibility in other ways. One good way is to demonstrate your loyalty to the organization and its goals.

The opening lines of Garlinghouse's memo positioned him as a Yahoo Guy, through and through. "Three and a half years ago, I enthusiastically joined Yahoo," he wrote. "It has been a profound experience . . . I proudly bleed purple and yellow [Yahoo's corporate colors] every day! And like so many people, I love this company." His loyalty ran even deeper than most: "I'm proud to admit that I shaved a Y [on] the back of my head," he went on. "I want to be part of the solution rather than part of the problem."

Next, he engaged his audience with a crisp summary of the problem as he saw it using an easy-to-grasp metaphor—peanut butter. "All is not well," he wrote. "We lack a focused, cohesive vision for our company. We want to do everything and be everything—to everyone. . . . We are scared to be left out. . . . We are separated into silos that far too frequently don't talk to each other. And when we do talk, it isn't to collaborate on a clearly focused strategy, but rather to argue and fight about ownership, strategies, and tactics."

The company's current strategy, he lamented, amounted to "spreading peanut butter across the myriad opportunities that continue to evolve in the online world. The result: a thin layer of investment spread across everything we do and thus we focus on nothing in particular."

"I hate peanut butter," he went on. "We all should."

After presenting this and several other, related problems, Garlinghouse's Manifesto proposed three specific solutions: focusing the strategy by selling or closing some noncore business units (getting rid of the "peanut butter"), restoring accountability in leadership positions (requiring that "heads must roll"), and radically reorganizing the firm (meaning that Yahoo had to "blow up the matrix" and "reduce head-count by 15–20%"). He included details for each of his proposals.

Finally, he acknowledged that he did not have all the answers—another way to gain credibility when you are not known as an expert—but asserted that doing anything at this point was better than continuing with the status quo. "The plan here is not perfect," he concluded. "It is, however, FAR better than no action at all." He invited others to come up with better ideas if they agreed with his peanut butter thesis.

We do not know anything about Yahoo's strategy problems. But we like Garlinghouse's way of selling his change initiative to the company. He made his ideas memorable. The image of peanut butter spreading thin is something anyone can visualize. And his care in getting the memo to the right people, establishing his credibility, embracing the Yahoo culture, explaining the problem, identifying its causes, and arguing vigorously (but modestly) is a model of Woo in action.

Moreover, the memo had its desired effect. Semel appointed Garlinghouse to a major task force to review Yahoo's strategy and make recommendations on what to do. And a few months later, Yahoo announced major changes—including the departure of its chief operating officer and the reorganization of the company into three operating units. Announcing the changes, Semel said he hoped the new structure would "increase accountability, . . . reduce bottlenecks, and speed decision-making." Not long after that, Semel himself departed and was replaced by one of Yahoo's founders, Jerry Yang.

### Step 4: Secure Your Commitments (Chapter 9)

The final step in the Woo process completes the cycle by taking you from the agreement stage to the concrete commitments you need to turn your ideas into action. Just because a decision maker says yes does not mean your job is over. Perhaps your initiative challenges one of the organization's core values. If so, your proposal may arouse political opposition. Perhaps your ideas run counter to an important constituency's interests. Members of that group may try to protect their turf.

Consider the Peanut Butter Manifesto. Why do you think this document was leaked to the *Wall Street Journal*? The circumstances suggest it may have been a political move by Brad's supporters (or Brad himself) because it brought millions of stock analysts, consultants, and Yahoo investors into this idea sale. Public companies do not like having their internal deliberations aired to the general public, so this was risky. But publication of the Manifesto gave momentum to Garlinghouse's ideas within the company and political protection to its author. When you are advocating that 15 to 20 percent of your fellow employees be laid off and that the heads of other senior managers "roll," you are sure to make some powerful enemies. The publicity in the *Wall Street Journal* assured that Brad's opponents within Yahoo would have a very difficult time launching a secret purge to get rid of him. And the investment community was now watching to see what would come out of Garlinghouse's task force—whether, in effect, Yahoo would stop eating peanut butter. The leaking of this memo to the press could have been the final step in this idea sale.

## A Word on Authority

Authority plays an important background role in almost every story you will read in this book. But there is no separate chapter that deals with it. We thought we should explain why.

A Nobel Prize–winning expert on business organizations, Herbert A. Simon, once explained that "of all the modes of influence, authority is the one that chiefly distinguishes the behavior of individuals as participants in organizations, from their behavior outside such organizations. It is authority that gives an organization its formal structure." Research confirms Simon's insight. Even in an era of "flat" organizations and collaborative teamwork, formal authority serves as the basis for more influence moves at work than any other influence foundation. People in higher positions tell people in lower positions to "just do it." And they do. So isn't this the real secret of success at work: get authority, then give orders?

Authority is good. Authority gives you credibility. But authority alone isn't enough to sell important ideas because big ideas always have multiple stakeholders. And those stakeholders also have authority. Think of a chessboard. Each piece has a unique position on the board and special moves it can make; you need them all to win the game.

The formal roles people occupy are the starting positions for a complex dance of organizational influence. Each role offers influence options, constraints, opportunities, and risks. Research shows that an average of twenty people inside an organization are involved in the approval of most important new ideas. And each of those twenty people will likely have some effect on the final outcome. Even relatively simple ideas require input and approval from an average of eight people. Thus, although someone in a high position may eventually be called upon to make the "go–no go" decision on a new idea, it is rare that authority alone dictates the shape, size, and scope of a new initiative.

Some people may think of their authority as a kind of club that they swing, driving people toward the solutions they prefer. We all know the office bullies. And they get away with that attitude some of the time, with some of their staff. But the truth is usually more complex. People in high positions "possess" authority *if and only if* the people in the lower positions cede it (implicitly or explicitly) to them. In general, the people who forget that they have only as much authority as others are willing to give them are the ones who make the most mistakes in selling ideas.

Remember what the bank president said about his job: "I am a salesman." Of course, he can force his ideas down people's throats and sometimes he probably has to do that. But that's a failure story, not a success story. He succeeds by selling his ideas.

In fact, the higher you go in a corporate hierarchy, the less position alone determines what ideas get adopted and the more relationship and persuasion skills determine what gets done.

## The Ideal: A Culture of Selling Ideas

A large body of evidence suggests that creating a culture built on the foundation of selling ideas—rather than authority—is a competitive advantage for firms that can do it. In one of the most influential management books ever written, *My Years with General Motors*, GM leader Alfred Sloan described his dedication to selling ideas (and the birth of the modern corporation) this way:

The practice of selling major proposals is an important feature of General Motors' management. Any proposal must be sold to central management and if it affects other divisions it must be sold to them as well. Sound management also requires that the central office should in most cases sell its proposals to the divisions, which it does through the policy groups and group executives. The selling approach provides an important safeguard . . . against ill-considered decisions. It assures that any basic decision is made only after thorough consideration by all parties concerned. . . . The manager who would like to operate on a hunch will usually find it hard to sell his ideas to others on this basis. But, in general, whatever sacrifice might be entailed in ruling out a possibly brilliant hunch is compensated for by the better-than-average results which can be expected from a policy that can be strongly defended against well-informed and sympathetic criticism.

A final example from Wal-Mart's early history provides a glimpse of what a corporate culture committed to selling ideas looks like. Wal-Mart has always been known for its cutting-edge use of technology to track inventory and manage supplier relations. But for years, people at the company thought Sam was opposed to these high-tech solutions. "All these guys [at Wal-Mart] loved to talk about how I never wanted any of this technology, and how they had to lay down their life to get it," Walton later wrote. But the truth was otherwise. "I did want it, I knew we needed it . . . but I always questioned everything. It was important to me to make them think that maybe the technology wasn't as good as they thought it was, or maybe it really wasn't the end-all they promised it would be. It seems to me they try just a little harder to check into things a little bit closer if they think they might have a chance to prove me wrong. If I hadn't wanted the technology, I wouldn't have sprung the money loose to pay for it."

Contrast this with one of the most famous—or infamous—missteps in marketing history: the introduction of New Coke in 1985. Its champion, CEO Roberto Goizueta, might have saved the Coca-Cola Company a lot of money and embarrassment if he had encouraged an open debate about replacing the one-hundred-year-old formula for the carbonated brown drink that consumers had grown to love with an almost religious fervor.

Instead, Goizueta, alarmed that Coke appeared to be losing the high-profile "Cola Wars" to arch-rival Pepsi, made a virtually unilateral decision to retire the old formula for a new concoction that was sweeter and less fizzy. "The best just got better," he declared at a news conference in New York. Others begged to differ—at first in secret, and then later in a torrent of angry letters and enraged phone messages. At an early tasting, a bottler's wife took a sip and exclaimed: "Goddamn! This'll *never* sell!"

Pepsi CEO Roger Enrico recalls first sipping New Coke with a bunch of his senior executives: "God knows how they did it, but they had blown it."

Consumer reactions were almost universally negative. Seventy-eight days after the introduction of New Coke, the old version, under the name Coca-Cola Classic, came roaring back. New Coke disappeared into oblivion, becoming a novelty offering that only one or two bottlers continued to carry.

Goizueta had violated a basic law of business: listen to the customer. Because Coke lacked a culture of selling ideas, the boss was free to dictate this decision without the benefit of an open debate where people could set aside job titles and speak their minds. This enabled Goizueta to make one of the most spectacular mistakes in business history.

## Conclusion

*The Art of Woo* provides tools for a critically important activity in professional life: selling your ideas to people within the context of ongoing, important relationships. If you want to be a player in your organization, a successful partner with your customers or suppliers, a leader in your community, or even a good parent, you need to woo people to your point of view by putting your ideas across in convincing, relationship-friendly ways.

This chapter introduced the basic concept of selling ideas. You saw how this skill can advance your goals in both simple and complex situations. At one end of the scale, Bob Bogle used a direct approach to pitch his boss, Sam Walton, on his idea for naming Sam's new store "Walmart." At the other end, Brad Garlinghouse at Yahoo wrote a carefully structured, politically sophisticated memo, the Peanut Butter Manifesto, to sell his agenda for changing Yahoo's corporate strategy.

Regardless of the context for your idea sale, the four-step Woo process, which we will elaborate in the chapters to come, constitutes the best practice for this art.

These steps are:

Step 1: *Survey Your Situation,* that is
- Forge and polish your idea,
- Map the decision process you face by understanding the social networks within the organization,
- Assess your persuasion styles, and
- Confirm your own level of passion for the proposal.

Step 2: *Confront the Five Barriers,* including
- Negative relationships,
- Poor credibility,
- Communication mismatches,
- Contrary belief systems, and
- Conflicting interests.

*Then transform these five barriers into assets.*

Step 3: *Make Your Pitch* by
- Presenting solid evidence and arguments and
- Using devices to give your idea a personal touch.

Step 4: *Secure Your Commitments* by dealing with politics at both
- The individual level and
- Within the organization.

To start using this process, you must master the main influence channels people use at work—and gain a sense of your own biases in communicating on these channels. Are you a soft-spoken relationship manager or a hard-driving task master?

Woo starts with a look in the mirror. You'll find one in the next chapter.

chapter two

## Start with You: Persuasion Styles

Management cannot be expected to recognize a good idea
unless it is presented to them by a good salesman.
—David M. Ogilvy, advertising pioneer

Just after Abraham Lincoln won the hotly contested presidential election of 1860, he faced one of the most important problems of his career: selling William H. Seward, the former governor of New York, on joining his cabinet. Seward had been the Republican favorite going into the party's convention. But he had seriously underestimated Lincoln and paid for his misjudgment with a stinging political defeat. Lincoln needed to recruit this former rival to his administration to unify his Republican base.

Lincoln was a visionary leader famous for his homespun stories and quiet, plain manner. He was at his best, historians say, in one-on-one encounters. Had he been a less gifted persuader, he would have relied on his favoured, folksy style to woo Seward. But Lincoln recognized that this was a politically sensitive moment. Seward and his allies were worried about status, appearances, and pride—not helping the party or fulfilling their patriotic duty. Lincoln drew on his diplomatic skills and political insights to adjust his message to suit the situation.

Lincoln's first step was to acknowledge Seward's need for status. He decided to offer Seward the most coveted job in the cabinet, secretary of state. Next, Lincoln showed his concern for Seward's reputation by quietly forwarding his offer through his vice president–elect,

Hannibal Hamlin, rather than making a public spectacle by presenting it himself or leaking it to the press. Third, and most important, Lincoln addressed Seward's delicate, injured ego by drafting two letters for Hamlin to carry to Seward.

The first letter conveyed the formal offer to be secretary of state. The second letter, marked "private and confidential," addressed the possibility that Seward might reject the post. Lincoln had heard political gossip that Seward might think this offer was motivated by a desire to placate Seward's allies rather than to gain Seward's services. Lincoln feared that this would make the actual offer deeply offensive to Seward.

As Doris Kearns Goodwin tells the story in her authoritative study of Lincoln's cabinet, *Team of Rivals,* events unfolded just as Lincoln had anticipated. Seward responded coldly to Hamlin's query regarding his interest in the job. Hamlin then handed over the two letters and watched as Seward opened them. Seward was agitated as he opened Letter number 1—the formal offer. Then he opened Letter number 2, which read as follows:

> Rumors have got into the newspapers to the effect that the Department, named above, would be tendered you as a compliment, and with the expectation that you would decline it. I beg you to be assured that I have said nothing to justify these rumors. On the contrary, it has been my purpose, from the day of the nomination at Chicago, to assign you, by your leave, this place in the administration. . . . I now offer you the place, in the hope that you will accept it, and with the belief that your position in the public eye, your integrity, ability, learning, and great experience, all combine to render it an appointment pre-eminently fit to be made.

According to Hamlin's personal account of this meeting, Seward's face became "pale with excitement" after reading this second letter, and he grasped Hamlin's hand. "This is remarkable, Mr. Hamlin," he said, marveling at Lincoln's ability to so accurately read the situation. After consulting with his political advisers, Seward accepted the job and helped Lincoln recruit the balance of the cabinet. Indeed, under

Lincoln's influence, Seward became his most trusted and effective political ally throughout the Civil War. The two men became so closely associated that both were targets of assassination attempts by members of the John Wilkes Booth conspiracy on April 14, 1865. Seward survived.

## To Understand Others, Start with Yourself

Lincoln succeeded in selling his idea to Seward because he had acquired the ability to get outside of his own frame of reference and see situations from other people's standpoints. That gave him insights into Seward's feelings and allowed him to communicate on Seward's channel. Lincoln demonstrated over and over in his career an uncanny ability to woo an audience.

As Henry Ford once said, "If there is any secret of success, it lies in the ability to get the other person's point of view and see things from that person's angle as well as your own." Psychologists have actually developed complex measures for this ability (called "cognitive perspective taking") and studied it in historical figures, including many of history's most noted political as well as battlefield leaders.

For example, in one study of the careers of nineteen political leaders associated with five revolutions—ranging from the English civil war of the seventeenth century to the Russian and Cuban revolutions of the twentieth century—scholars found that the people displaying higher levels of perspective-taking ability (as shown in letters, speeches, and other writings) were more likely than those who lacked this ability to consolidate and stabilize their respective movements in the postrevolutionary period. Lenin had it, and he created the Communist government in Russia. His colleague Trotsky did not, and he was eventually shot by Stalin while living in exile in Mexico. Fidel Castro had it, and he has remained in power for nearly fifty years. His comrade-in-arms Che Guevara did not—and he was executed in Bolivia in 1967 while leading another South American revolutionary group.

The South's greatest general in the American Civil War, Robert E. Lee, had perspective-taking ability in abundance compared with all but one of the generals the North chose to lead its armies—the one who finally won the war for the North, Ulysses S. Grant. Both Lee and Grant had a gift for seeing the battlefield as an opponent might see it, thereby enabling them to better anticipate moves and plan their strategies. This skill involves both a measure of empathy ("General Lee is feeling stung from his last defeat, so I am guessing that will affect his decision today") and a degree of cognitive insight ("If I were Lee, I would see that high ground over there as the key to winning the battle"). In short, it means trying to feel what others feel and see what others see.

In persuasion, you are trying to win people over, not defeat them. But both war and interpersonal influence involve anticipating how other people will react to things you do and say. Your ability to see and feel things from their perspectives is thus crucially important.

In a professional relationship, this talent allows you to preserve "face" in delicate, politically charged situations, keeping communication channels open that might otherwise shut down. For example, the first female general in the Iraq War, General Rebecca Halstead, was having a hard time gaining respect from her superiors. After enduring several slights, she finally confronted her commanding officer.

"I know why you have a problem with my leadership," she said firmly. "It's because I went to West Point, I am younger than you and," here she paused. "And because I am shorter than you, right?" It was just what she needed to say to get her point across and clear the air.

Perspective-taking lapses, on the other hand, can be quite expensive. One such lapse by a colleague cost entrepreneur Wayne Huizenga—founder of Blockbuster Video and many other successful businesses—£100,000 as he was building the Blockbuster franchise system. He was hosting a dinner that included a Blockbuster video franchisee, the franchisee's biggest investor, and one of Huizenga's newly hired corporate lieutenants. The franchisee was enthusiastically pitching an idea he had for hiring "video consultants" to roam the aisles of Blockbuster stores advising customers on films they might like to rent, but Huizenga's newly hired colleague was not buying it. He shot down each of the franchisee's arguments for the concept, one by one, oblivious to the embarrassment this was causing the franchisee.

After the dinner, Huizenga took his executive aside. "You shot him down like a fighter pilot," Huizenga commented. "But you know who that was with him, don't you? That was his partner. . . . You won the battle, no question. But you lost the war." There would be a time for critiquing the video consultant idea, Huizenga said, but that dinner was not it. To regain the franchisee's goodwill, Huizenga called him the next day and invested £100,000 in the idea.

Where do you start on this journey toward others' perspectives? With self-awareness. Unless you are aware of your own needs, emotions, and communication impulses, you have little chance of seeing other people clearly—much less anticipating their feelings and crafting messages that will appeal to them.

Thus, Woo starts with you. You might be a quiet, low-key persuader who relies, as Abraham Lincoln frequently did, on credibility and a personal touch to make a point. Or you might be an aggressive and demanding person out there for everyone to see, hear, and respond to. Regardless, you need to understand your natural, preferred persuasion styles if you want to learn how to use those styles to meet different idea-selling challenges. Knowing your natural strengths and weaknesses can also reveal a learning agenda—the areas you need to study to improve your game.

In this chapter, we will help you gain those insights. We begin by explaining the six main channels of persuasion that provide the conduits for most idea-selling messages—and by giving you a personalized Six Channels Survey (see Appendix A) to determine which of these channels you tend to favour. Next, we introduce five persuasion styles: Driver, Commander, Promoter, Chess Player, and Advocate. The Persuasion Styles Assessment provided in Appendix B will help you understand your aptitudes for using each of these approaches. We provide examples of each of the five styles in action using stories from the lives of some very skilled persuaders: Andy Grove, J. P. Morgan, Andrew Carnegie, John D. Rockefeller, and Sam Walton.

As we suggested in the introduction, you can think of the six channels as six different notes on a piano, each of which can attract others' attention and influence their decisions. If you are considering how best to enlist a colleague's support for a new corporate initiative you favour, you might choose to emphasize rational arguments, the colleague's personal interests, and your relationship. But even after deciding to emphasize these factors, there remains the question of style—should you be direct or indirect? Should you gently hint at the relationship factor or come right out and bluntly tell the person, "Look, you owe me on this one"?

By locating your natural inclinations for using various channels and persuasion styles, you can identify your communication "baselines." These insights will help you in two ways. First, you will realize how you are likely to approach people when you do not have much time to prepare. Second, when you *do* prepare more carefully, you will understand better how you should adjust to be more effective.

## The Six Channels of Persuasion: An Introduction

Extensive research on how people influence one another in work settings has revealed that they return over and over to a relatively discrete number of persuasion moves. Although communication scholars have labeled as many as sixteen separate and identifiable strategies (including such things as issuing threats, giving simple orders, and making requests), we think six main persuasion channels dominate when people are selling ideas.

You can test our six-channels hypothesis in the laboratory of your own experience. Next time you step onto an airplane, notice the persuasion messages surrounding you as you board, buckle up, and take off. Here is what a typical plane ride might reveal.

### Channel Number 1: Interest-Based Persuasion

As you reach your seat, you may notice some deal making going on. We were on a plane recently and asked a young businesswoman who was about to take her aisle seat nearby to switch for one of our aisle seats. We explained that a switch would enable us to get some work done together. "Sure," she replied, "if one of you could help me get my bag into this overhead."

Interest-based persuasion takes place every time someone frames a sales pitch in terms of the other party's self-interest. A simple example might be: "Accepting my idea will help you on your next performance evaluation." But, as the airplane example shows, interests are also the bases for negotiations, both inside and outside the organization. In negotiation, each side has something the other side wants or could use—capabilities, resources, status, pieces of information, or authority to take some action—and they make a trade. The trade can be explicit, as it was in the airline example above, or it can be implicit, as happens when you ask someone to cover a client call for you and mentally note that you owe that person a reciprocal favour at some point in the future (more on this when we discuss relationships below).

Lincoln's appeal to Seward was based, in part, on mutual interests. Seward legitimized Lincoln's administration by joining it, and Lincoln provided Seward with status as the administration's most important cabinet officer, giving Seward the opportunity to make history. Lincoln's skill at diplomacy enabled them to make this trade.

Interestingly, many executives tell us that they do not think of themselves as negotiating at work even though they are appealing to people's interests and trading a variety of subtle psychological currencies day in and day out. That is fine with us. The essence of this persuasion channel is inducement, not trading. Thus, *you are engaged in interest-based persuasion whenever you pitch your idea as addressing the other party's underlying needs.*

### Channel Number 2: Authority

The airplane seat belt sign blinks on: authority-based persuasion. We recognize this signal and obey without giving the matter another thought. On a plane, most people are tuned to the "authority" channel because their safety depends on it.

As we noted in the last chapter, authority is the most commonly used influence tool in most work settings. The authority channel is usually used in "top-down" situations, when someone gives an order to someone lower in a hierarchy. But even a secretary can use this channel if he or she has jurisdiction over expense accounts or other procedures.

In the airplane example, we tend to defer to authority automatically because the seat belt sign is credible, routine, and inherently reasonable.

Social science research reveals that authority triggers a deep stimulus–response reaction when the right situational cues are in place. This accounts for the myriad occasions in everyone's working day when a superior makes a request, and a subordinate complies without questioning in any way the order's merits or wisdom.

In the early 1960s, in one of the most famous psychological experiments ever run, Yale University professor Stanley Milgram tested to see if he could figure out how otherwise peace-loving German citizens had succumbed to the Nazi regime under Hitler. His results were remarkable: he was able to persuade ordinary subjects from New Haven, Connecticut, to deliver what they honestly thought were a series of painful, high-voltage electric shocks (they were actually harmless) to other people. He did this by dressing his psychology lab assistants in white lab coats and styling his exercise in the language and rituals of science. His New Haven subjects had agreed to obey the orders of the assistants—the surrounding circumstances suggested a high level of legitimacy for the proceedings—and were constantly reassured that the responsibility for the outcomes of the experiment resided solely with the experimenters.

Just how far were these randomly selected citizens willing to go? Twenty-seven of the forty-one people who participated (over 67 percent) continued giving the shocks up to what they were told was the lethal level. *Psychology Today* reported in 2002 that a meta-analysis of all experiments of this type revealed a stable finding: roughly 60 percent of people presented with these authoritative—but not coercive—conditions can be counted on to obey authoritative orders rather than "rock the boat" and protest. This is admittedly an extreme example of unthinking, habitual deference to authority, but Milgram's experiment illustrates a basic truth. Most people are susceptible to assertive displays of positional authority—which explains why your formal position is such a vital part of your credibility in presenting ideas.

Nevertheless, Milgram's experiments did *not* reveal that people will do anything for others who are in authority. What they showed was that people will defer to authority when it is presented to them in a certain way, under extremely well-crafted conditions, and when the orders do not involve a direct violation of *their own* interests. Had Milgram asked his subjects to administer a series of painful shocks to themselves, he would have heard quite a bit more protest.

You are using authority-based persuasion *whenever you appeal to your formal position or authoritative rules or policies as a means of getting others to agree with your proposal.* But when selling important ideas in most organizations, you should not expect Milgram-like, automatic deference. Rather, effective appeals using authority are almost always accompanied by independent justifications and explanations to help persuade the audience that the exercise of authority is *legitimate and consistent with the audience's core interests* under the particular circumstances.

### Channel Number 3: Politics

Back on the plane, a nearby elderly passenger is hot and wants to complain about the lack of cool air circulating as the plane fills up. She fiddles with the air vent and nothing seems to happen. First move: build a coalition (a key skill in organizational politics). "Are you feeling a little stuffy?" she asks you. You politely nod. "Let's ask them to turn up the air conditioning." She pushes the attendant button. A stewardess appears. "We're feeling pretty warm here," she says on behalf of the newly formed "We Want Cooler Air" movement. "I'll see what I can do," replies the attendant, and then adds soothingly: "It will cool down quickly once we get into the air."

Social scientists define politics as processes by which individuals, usually working in groups, try to exert influence over the actions of a larger organization. As political theorist Hannah Arendt put it, "Political power corresponds to the human ability not just to act but to act in concert." We won't be discussing politics in the traditional sense in this book, i.e., the dynamics of elections and political parties. But the use of coalitions, pressure tactics, and power moves is not limited to government. People act in political ways inside many groups—from families to business firms.

A study of nearly five hundred organizations by two Swedish management scholars published in 2004 found that "some" political activity took place in nearly all (95 percent) of the surveyed organizations. A small number of firms (6 percent) had a "great deal" of politics and an equally small number (5 percent) had none at all. The balance of the sample was split roughly equally between those having politics to "a fair extent" and to "a fairly low extent." The kinds of activities reported most frequently included covert, informal decision-making processes (77 percent of organizations) and lobbying (75 percent). The activity reported least often was the use of passive resistance to frustrate change initiatives (60 percent). Other political behaviors included important people saying one thing and doing another (71 percent) and subgroups using bureaucratic procedures to frustrate change (64 percent).

If even the egalitarian Swedes have this much political activity at work, the authors note, it is a good bet that companies in other cultures face similar challenges. But many in both the academic and business communities refuse to acknowledge politics in organizational behavior because politics is seen as illegitimate. We consider ourselves realists in this regard. The issue is not whether there is politics in your organization; the issue is how skillfully you deal with it as part of your campaign to advance your ideas.

When most people use the words "organizational politics," they are thinking of its darker sides: egos, turf wars, and backstabbing. But politics has a light side, as well. When an organization faces up to politics and handles it well, different points of view and interest groups are acknowledged, forums exist to air these differences, and representatives of groups meet and argue openly for their interests— all in the service of the overall corporate good. In other words, healthy and productive political debate recognizes that many issues can be seen from multiple perspectives. And as Lincoln's story illustrates, political considerations such as injured pride and the need for status are simply part of the environment most people work in.

Thus, dark side or light, *you are using the political persuasion channel whenever you acknowledge that appearances may be as important as substance in your idea-selling strategy, work through coalitions and alliances, or make use of back channels and lobbying.* This channel naturally overlaps with, and cuts across, all the other channels. A given political move may incorporate interests, authority, relationships, values, and evidence-based persuasion.

### Channel Number 4: Rationality

As your plane taxis to takeoff, a video comes on telling you what to do in the "unlikely event of an emergency"—the seat cushion that can be used as a flotation device, and so forth. You know the video. The mode here is rational persuasion. You are not persuaded. First, you have heard the pitch so many times that you tune it out. Second, you have never heard of anyone actually surviving a plane crash by using the seat cushion as a flotation device. The video is full of detailed, specific information, but it lacks overall credibility.

We define rationality-based persuasion as *trying to influence someone's attitudes, beliefs, or actions by offering reasons and/or evidence to justify a proposal on its merits.* As the airplane example makes clear, the audience holds the keys to success in using this mode. If the audience is willing to listen to reason, you have a chance of influencing them. If not, no amount of data or logical persuasion will get them on your side.

Every organization gives at least lip service to the rationality mode and many are genuinely dedicated to making decisions based on the best arguments and evidence available. Thus, you almost always need to gather the best evidence and arguments you can as part of an idea-selling campaign.

IBM's legendary president, Tom Watson Sr., believed so thoroughly in a rational, thoughtful approach to business that he created one of the most famous corporate slogans of the twentieth century: THINK. The idea was born one day when Watson was working at the National Cash Register Company. Finding himself at a meeting where nobody was challenging anything being said, Watson burst out, "The trouble with everyone [here] is that we don't think enough." The following day he created a sign with five huge, all-capital letters on it and placed it at the podium where presentations were being made. The sign said "THINK."

At IBM, Watson's THINK sign could be found on every desk and in every conference room. But what, exactly, did Watson mean by it?

He once explained it this way: "By THINK, I mean *take everything into consideration* [emphasis added]. . . . [But] we're not interested in a logic course."

Watson's slogan sent a strong message to his employees about the culture he wanted to instill at IBM. It was a culture based on rational thought. But, as Watson insisted, logic alone seldom dictates a given result. In using the rationality channel to persuade, you must be prepared to engage in debate. Different people come to very different conclusions about the same evidence based on their respective needs and biases. In addition, you (or your evidence) may lack credibility in your audience's eyes and, like the passengers on the airplane listening to the flotation device lecture, the audience will tune you out. Thus, rationality in persuasion usually pivots on what philosophers call "practical reason." You need to get all the evidence on the table (or, as Watson said, "take everything into consideration"), and then you must encourage people to apply their professional judgment and experience.

### Channel Number 5:
### Inspiration and Emotion—The Vision Channel

You reach for the airline magazine to pass the time. It opens to a double-page advertisement for a luxury car that, if purchased, will transform you into someone who looks like James Bond (or dates him) and is vacationing at an expensive, well-known resort. This is what we call "visionary" persuasion: attempts to evoke emotions such as hope, desire, or team spirit to motivate you to adopt an attitude or to take a particular action. Once again, the attempt is unsuccessful. You are not the Bond (or Bond's) type. You like your dependable, five-year-old Honda.

At the deepest levels of human motivation lie people's feelings, beliefs, identities, spiritual roots, cultural ties, and life stories. Visionary devices such as stories and images help persuaders to access these levels, appealing directly to the audience's intuitions. As one persuasion expert has put it, "People make their decisions based on what the facts mean to them, not on the facts themselves."

You don't have to be a charismatic leader with a plan to rid the world of disease to become a skilled user of visionary persuasion tools. Beliefs and purposes come in many forms and cover all areas of life and work. An audience's everyday commitment to being a good citizen, a good professional, or a good parent is an excellent foundation for visionary persuasion.

When we speak of the visionary influence channel, therefore, we include *any appeal to an audience's overriding sense of purpose, values, or beliefs as the foundation for selling your idea.* Visionary persuasion thus often takes the form of a special type of reason-based argument in which your justifications relate to the higher aspirations and purposes embraced by your listeners. When you present an idea in such a way that it prompts an audience to say, "Supporting this proposal will help me become the type of person I want to be," or "Adopting this idea will help us feel that we belong to the type of organization people respect and admire," you are working in this channel.

### Channel Number 6: Relationships

Back on the plane, a young boy across the aisle is lobbying for a cookie from his father. "I told you the cookies were for later," says the dad. "Aw, Dad, I was really good in the airport. Can't I have half of one now?" Out comes a cookie and some deal making ensues over how to divide it.

As our book's title suggests, it is hard to overstate the importance of relationships in the Art of Woo. A positive relationship favorably predisposes an audience toward your message. In the words of psychologist Robert Cialdini, "We prefer to say 'yes' to people we know and like." A negative relationship, meanwhile, distorts almost everything an idea seller says. Lincoln's communication problem with Seward arose from the history of their relationship. Seward's wounded pride was sure to distort every message, transforming a straightforward job offer into an insult. Lincoln therefore had to design a sophisticated two-letter treatment to acknowledge Seward's wound and set the respectful tone for a future political partnership.

The research on how rapport and relationships work to facilitate (or block) communication is deep and wide. In an early study on selling insurance, researchers discovered that the best insurance salesmen were no different from the average in product knowledge, number of sales calls, or even number and type of questions asked. The only difference was in how quickly and authentically the best salesmen put their customers at ease by finding some common experience or affiliation the salesmen and customers shared—some similarity.

The world inside organizations is no different. As we will explore in chapter 4, research shows that the longer people at work know one another, the more their relationships tend to harden into positive and negative patterns. When people at work first meet, the basis for rapport or trust is very shallow, built mainly on demographic similarities such as age and gender. As the relationships lengthen, people rely on actual experiences with each other to form opinions about trust and credibility. Finally, for the longest running relationships, trust is based on similarity of perspective on a range of issues. Demographic similarity fades out as a factor and there is much less monitoring of actual behavior—because the other person has "passed the test."

Working relationships are also characterized by reciprocity, linking this channel to the interest-based persuasion channel discussed earlier. Within relationships, a host of subtle items can be exchanged. In the airplane example, the young boy appealed to his earlier good behavior in the airport as the basis for rewarding him now with the cookie. The currencies of exchange in relationships—both at home and at work—are endless: past or promised favours, information, gossip, access, temporary relief from company rules or policy, self-esteem stroking, opportunities for advancement, griping privileges, secrets, and on and on.

To sum up, you are accessing the relationship channel *whenever you use similarity, liking, rapport, and reciprocity, or rely on your existing network of contacts and friends, to open doors as part of an idea-selling strategy.*

## Six Channels Survey

The world of the airplane is not that different from your world at work. In fact, for pilots and flight attendants, it *is* a world of work. And people depend on these professionals to be effectively persuasive every time a plane takes off. Moreover, as the discussion of the six channels makes clear, selling ideas is not a matter of forcing or coercing people to do things, though this is all too often the default persuasion system in many organizations. Woo-based persuasion is about working hard to properly align interests, values, and relationships—and sending messages to others on channels they are tuned to.

With this background, you are now ready to take your first Woo self-assessment, the Six Channels Survey. Turn to Appendix A and follow the directions to discover the answers to two important questions. First, which of the six channels does your current job require you to use most often? This aspect of the survey will give you a snapshot of the way you are using influence tools to affect your professional environment. It can also provide insights into the corporate or organizational culture you work in.

Second, and just as important, the survey will reveal which of the six channels you would *prefer to be using* more often. In general, you are likely to be more effective (and less stressed) using tools you feel comfortable with. To the extent your job requires you to use the influence channels you prefer to use, there is a good "fit" between you and your professional role.

When you have completed your work in Appendix A, come back to this chapter and we will move on to the second Woo test: the Persuasion Styles Assessment.

## Personal Persuasion Styles:
## Self-Oriented Versus Other-Oriented

Looking back over the airplane examples described above, you may notice something that goes a bit deeper than the six channels we saw illustrated: some acts of persuasion are specially tailored to appeal to specific audiences while others are more akin to blunt announcements of the speaker's point of view to whoever happens to be listening. We call the former messages—ones specially tailored to an audience—"other-oriented" persuasion. The latter, unmodified announcements we call "self-oriented" persuasion.

For example, the magazine advertisement on the airplane was carefully crafted to appeal to a specific demographic—status-conscious, high-net-worth car buyers. Similarly, the little boy's method of begging a cookie from his father—the subtle "I've been good" appeal—was probably based on what had worked with this particular parent on earlier occasions. Both of these examples were instances of other-oriented persuasion. When you are working from the audience's point of view, you are initially focused more on social considerations—existing relationships, the political environment, the channel someone may be tuned to, or other people's interests. You then harness these insights to make your message especially appealing to a particular target audience.

By contrast, when you are working primarily from your own frame of reference, you tend to focus first on your internal perspective—the authority you want to assert, the need you want to express, or the evidence you want to demonstrate. Then you put your message out there with less attention to "spinning" it for the particular audience. The elderly passenger who wanted cooler air did not really care who the stewardess was and made no effort to individualize her appeal to this person. She just announced her preference. And the airline's authoritative seat belt sign and its informational pitch about using seat cushions as flotation devices were not specially tailored for particular people. They were blunt persuasion tools designed to convey generic messages required by law. All of these were examples of self-oriented persuasion.

Of course, persuasion events often consist of a seamless combination of moves that are both internally and externally focused. But if your preferences run strongly toward favoring one of these orientations over the other, that can define your overall communication style.

## Volume Control: Loud or Quiet

A second important variable that goes into the persuasion styles people display is the "volume" they give to their message. Back on the plane, you have probably noticed the difference between the "loud" people—the ones who want to strike up conversations with everyone around them—and quieter ones, who seem to prefer to sit and read a book or magazine. At work, you may also have noticed people who are more active at meetings—those who speak up right away and sometimes dominate the discussion—versus those who prefer to listen and then quietly give their views when asked.

One of the more important variables in how you come across to others in persuasion moments is the rapidity and ease with which you can escalate from a normal conversational tone to a tough (or enthusiastic) insistence on your point of view. Some people find this quite a natural transition. Others prefer to maintain a more even tone and are not as prone to wide swings in emphasis. Such people are no less passionate about their ideas, but they are quieter by disposition.

Most professionals know how to speak up if they need to and sit quietly when that is appropriate. But if you have a strong inclination toward communicating one way or the other, this will affect your choice of persuasion roles.

## What's Your Personal Style?

With this introduction, it is time to gain perspective on your own personal persuasion styles. Turn to Appendix B—the Persuasion Styles Assessment—and answer the questions provided there for a quick measurement of your "comfort levels" playing five persuasion roles: Driver, Commander, Promoter, Chess Player, and Advocate. We derived these roles by factoring in the two dimensions we discussed above: self-oriented versus other-oriented, and louder volume versus softer.

Figure 2.1 gives you a sense of how the five roles relate to one another. The two more other-oriented roles are the Promoter and the Chess Player. The two more self-oriented roles are the Driver and Commander. The Advocate role is placed squarely in the middle—a balance of both self- and other-oriented perspectives and a moderate tone or "volume."

Some people are comfortable using three or four of these styles; others prefer to play only one or two. We strongly suggest you turn to the Appendix B assessment now, before reading on. Then bring your scores from Appendix B back to this chapter so you can have them in hand as you read the stories and examples we provide below of each style in action.

---

Figure 2.1

Self-Oriented vs. Other-Oriented

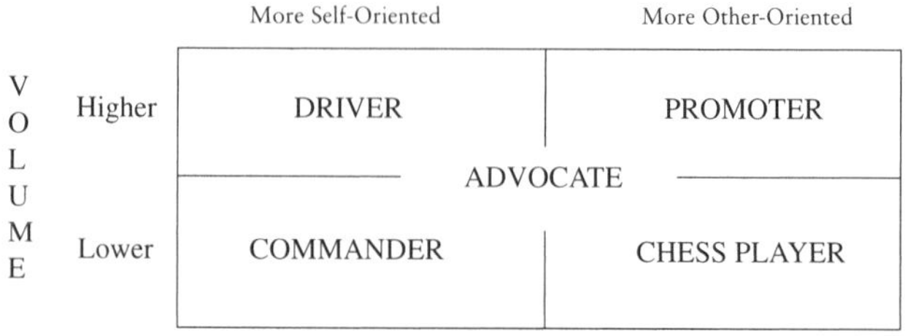

|  | | More Self-Oriented | More Other-Oriented |
|---|---|---|---|
| V O L U M E | Higher | DRIVER | PROMOTER |
| | | ADVOCATE | |
| | Lower | COMMANDER | CHESS PLAYER |

---

## Illustrating the Styles: Five Stories

To give you some idea of what these five styles look like when they are being enacted by skilled persuaders in the real world, we have collected examples from business history to illustrate them. In presenting these, we are not saying the individuals profiled below invariably used the styles we have assigned them. We are, rather, offering these stories as illustrations of what these styles look like in practice. As you read these accounts, note which of them are easiest for you to identify with. That sense of affinity may be a further sign (in addition to your Appendix B scores) of your preferred style.

### The Driver: Andy Grove
### (Higher Volume and Self-Oriented Perspective)

When individuals are high-volume and prefer to announce their own perspective without a lot of adjusts for their audience, other people are likely to experience them as demanding. Drivers are fond of saying things like "Do this my way—the *right* way—or you can hit the highway." In an ineffective persuader, this comes across as overbearing and one-dimensional. With enough authority, a Driver can literally terrorize an office. But by conveying a sense of self-awareness and showing true dedication to the organization's mission, even someone displaying this very strong style can be effectively persuasive.

Few business leaders have been stronger Drivers than Intel CEO Andy Grove. He once summed up his belief in his own point of view this way: "There is a right answer, the one that can give you the best delivery time and product quality at the lowest possible cost. To find the right answer, you must develop a clear understanding of the trade-offs between the various factors . . . and you must reduce the under-standing to a quantifiable set of relationships." As head of Intel, Andy Grove was also notorious for his blunt, sometimes bullying style of communication that sprang naturally from his high-intensity, quick-tempered personality. This mix of intensity, assertiveness, and strongly held opinions added up to one of the all-star Drivers in business history.

An Intel executive named Scott Gibson tells a story about how Grove chaired meetings that provides an extreme example of the "Driver" style in action. Grove kept a wooden bat near his chair. One day, just after a meeting had gotten started, several executives slipped into their seats a few minutes late. Grove fell silent at their arrival, then grabbed the bat, slammed it onto the table, and shouted, "I don't ever, ever want to be in a meeting with this group that doesn't start and end when it is scheduled!" Intel was subsequently famous for on-time meetings.

Were Grove less of a business genius—or if this were the only way Grove manifested his style—he would have gone down in history as a petty office tyrant who got his way solely because he was the boss. A deeper look at Grove's habits as a manager, however, reveals a more complex picture—one that shows a significant amount of self-aware-ness. True, he had a violent temper and could be a dictator when it came to office procedure and protocol. But he knew this about himself and compensated for it by making his blunt style of commu-nication the cultural norm within Intel. And it is just this sort of awareness that can transform an ineffective, over-the-top bully into an effective executive.

To assure that objective truth remained everyone's focus—even when Grove was shouting and screaming—he declared that the firm would embrace what he called a culture of "constructive confrontation." This corporate culture helped define whom Intel hired and who survived—especially after Grove's mentor and partner at Intel, the softer-styled Gordon Moore, passed the reins to Grove. When Grove lost control of his temper in the context of the search for the best, most scientifically valid ideas, everyone knew that his outburst was not personal. This was just Grove's way of being passionate about solving the problem at hand. And while the culture of constructive confrontation licensed Grove to be blunt, it also licensed others to be equally direct and required Grove to listen when they engaged him in battle.

An example of how this culture worked comes from an incident between Grove and his secretary, Sue McFarland. During her first performance review as Grove's assistant, McFarland was reduced to tears when Grove, in typical blunt style, told her she lacked ambition and deserved no raise whatever. But she remembered that Grove's constructive-confrontation culture was a two-way street. So she recovered herself, went home that night, and put together an airtight case refuting each and every one of Grove's charges. The next day she went in, confronted Grove, and walked out of his office with not only a raise but also permission to hire an assistant. As she later explained it, "He would tend to treat people like doormats, [but only] if they behaved like doormats."

### The Commander: J. P. Morgan
### (Lower Volume and a Self-Oriented Perspective)

You don't have to be an aggressive Driver when you want people to know exactly what you think. Indeed, a quiet, understated demeanor can often be much more effective. People listen when you speak your mind from a position of quiet confidence and credibility.

An excellent example of someone using the quieter Commander style in just the way we have in mind—and at just the right moment—comes from the life of a legendary Gilded Age financial tycoon, J. P. Morgan. In 1895, a financial panic in the markets set off a run on the gold reserves that served at that time as the basis of the U.S. currency.

With the markets in turmoil in New York and political chaos swirling around Washington, D.C., President Grover Cleveland called a meeting of his advisers, leading politicians, and Wall Street's top bankers, including the nation's most powerful financier, J. P. Morgan, to address the crisis.

Morgan sat silently as various leaders from Congress and Cleveland's cabinet offered a series of plans that Morgan knew would fail. Witnesses said it was all Morgan could do to keep himself under control at this meeting, where the incompetence and wishful thinking of the political elite were on full display. He was so agitated, people reported, that he ground an unlighted cigar into an ashtray. But he did not say a word.

Finally, a clerk arrived to report that the U.S. government had only £9 million in gold reserves remaining in its vaults. Morgan then spoke up for the first time, stating that he had personal knowledge of a check for £10 million that would be coming in later that day, which would exceed the government's ability to cover it. The government faced financial ruin.

"It will all be over by 3 P.M.," Morgan said quietly.

"OK," said President Cleveland, turning to him. "What is your suggestion?"

Certain that he had the president's full attention, Morgan laid out his plan to save the treasury. He offered to repatriate 3.5 million ounces of gold he controlled in Europe and agreed to take, in return, £65 million worth of thirty-year government bonds. Morgan then produced a legal memorandum showing that the government had authority to act as he proposed based on a little-known emergency law passed just after the Civil War.

The president was impressed, and Morgan's proposal was adopted.

Morgan addressed his audience in this case on both the Interest and the Rationality channels. His proposal was deftly designed to save the political careers of everyone in the room—thus addressing their interests—and it was complete in all its details in terms of reasoned argument.

In the hands of an ineffective persuader, the Commander becomes a "sphinx"—someone who gives few signals, keeps his or her own counsel, and puts a premium on maintaining as much decision control as possible. But J. P. Morgan played the role with skill: he was aware of his own quiet style and mindful of how he timed his demands and expressed his opinions. In the 1895 panic, Morgan employed his smoldering, restrained manner to make a momentous point using both his status as America's top financier and the elegance of his well-thought-through plan. His message gained power from the quiet way in which he communicated both his authority and expertise. Playing the Commander with finesse, he saved both America and his own financial empire from a fiscal catastrophe.

### The Promoter: Andrew Carnegie
### (Higher Volume and an Other-Oriented Perspective)

As we switch from the self-oriented perspective toward greater attention to the social environment, we shift toward people with more outgoing and gregarious personalities. When played ineffectively, the Promoter is all glad-handing and no substance—the classic back-slapping salesman. But when played well, this role features an out-front style and a gift for gaining and maintaining a wide circle of relationships.

Our example of this style in action comes from the life of a remarkable figure in U.S. business history, steel mogul Andrew Carnegie. Biographer David Nasaw writes that "one of Carnegie's many gifts as a businessman was his capacity to generate enthusiasm for his projects—in partners, potential customers, and the public at large." He was, in short, hardly the "dour Scotsman" of legend but was instead "a little man brimming with excitement for whatever business he was engaged in at the moment." He was a natural Promoter—optimistic, outgoing, and assertive. Remarkably, given the devastating labour disputes that were to mark his later career (especially the bloodshed that accompanied the Homestead Strike in 1892), Carnegie used his Promoter skills in the 1880s to help him sell the unions at his Pittsburgh steel plant on a hard-to-swallow idea: wage reductions.

In 1883, Carnegie faced one of his first serious labour crises. The prices for steel rails were falling rapidly and his plant managers were quoted in the press as saying that if prices did not stabilize soon,

Carnegie would be forced to shutter his business and ride out the downturn. Steel plants in Pittsburgh and elsewhere had already been pushed to this extreme.

Carnegie's philosophy regarding employees had been upbeat and respectful up to this time. He hired the best men, paid top wages, and ran his plants at peak capacity day and night to make his profits through high production volume. He had even installed reading rooms in his plants for the men (stocking, among other books, the ones he had written) and considered himself something of a socialist, at least in theory. In true Promoter style, Carnegie's success depended, in Nasaw's words, on "his ability to associate his own interests with those of his employees and the larger public."

But now it was clear that wages would have to be cut if the plant was to remain open. How could this be done without provoking a devastating strike?

Carnegie adopted a politically sophisticated negotiation strategy designed for delivery on the Rationality, Interest, and Relationship channels. First, he and his management team dissected, in exacting detail, the business problem they faced. They prepared a document that displayed the trade-offs between forcing layoffs on the one hand and reducing wages on the other. This analysis demonstrated that if wages were reduced 13 percent, the plant could remain in op-eration without layoffs—a key interest of the unions. Carnegie then sold this plan to the union leaders by offering to open his books so they could see for themselves the financial constraints the steel market was forcing on everyone in the business. He also made sure that his "open book" tactics were publicized to the entire Pittsburgh community—including the workers and their families—so everyone would be aware of the manner in which he was negotiating. He was, in short, mobilizing them as allies for his plan. He wanted people to trust him.

The results were exactly as Carnegie had hoped. The union leaders accepted the deal and sold it to their members. The local union news-paper, the *National Labour Tribune,* even ran editorials praising Carnegie's open management style. "Time was," the editors wrote, "when wage reductions were made arbitrarily. No reason was volun-teered, and none given if asked . . . Now this is all changed." It had been a masterful performance by someone skilled in the arts of the Promoter.

### The Chess Player: John D. Rockefeller
### (Lower Volume and an Other-Oriented Perspective)

If the Promoter is comfortable moving on the larger social stage of organizations and interest groups, the Chess Player prefers to operate the levers of interests, relationships, and politics in more intimate settings—quietly managing strategic encounters behind the scenes. A low-key personality combined with an overly developed concern for what other people are thinking can lead an inexperienced person to be too accommodating and passive. But the Chess Player is an effective strategist who is less extroverted than the Promoter but shares with the Promoter a keen interest in what makes other people tick.

A story from the early career of a third Gilded Age tycoon, oil baron John D. Rockefeller, illustrates the difference. In 1865, when he was just twenty-five years old and had not yet begun to build either his oil empire or his reputation, Rockefeller faced a delicate situation. He was, according to biographer Ron Chernow, a "quietly calculating" young man who had been appointed as a teenager to his church's board of trustees and was known for his accurate insights into the people around him. Moreover, he had "an unfailing knack for knowing who would help or hinder him in his career, an instinct that only sharpened with time."

At this pivotal point in his life, he found himself trapped in a business partnership with four older and wealthier men: Maurice Clark, Clark's two brothers (James and Richard), and a chemist named Samuel Andrews. Andrews was Rockefeller's ally in this group and the two of them favoured leveraging the partnership's assets to invest heavily in the oil business. But the Clarks repeatedly vetoed Rockefeller's ideas and bullied him, treating the young Rockefeller more as a clerk than a partner. When a dispute broke out over £100,000 Rockefeller borrowed to invest in a new oil refinery, it was the last straw: Rockefeller wanted out.

But there was a legal problem. Under the terms of the partnership agreement, the firm could be dissolved only if all the partners consented to it. The Clarks periodically threatened to dissolve the firm as a way to pressure their younger and more vulnerable member, but they were bluffing. They liked having him around to do their bidding.

Had he been more of a Driver, Rockefeller might have engaged his partners in a shouting match or threatened litigation, demanding they release him so he could follow his dreams. Had he been less ambitious, Rockefeller might have accommodated his partners and found a way for the relationship to work. As it was, he took the path of the Chess Player by carefully plotting a set of moves based on his partners' styles and personalities. It was a skilled play, with the message delivered mainly through the Politics channel.

First, Rockefeller quietly went to work behind the scenes, lining up support from some banks as well as his ally, Samuel Andrews. This gave him the alternative business platform he needed. Then he provoked another quarrel with his existing partners over an oil industry investment, something that required almost no effort because they objected to every decision he made. In the middle of the ensuing dispute, Maurice Clark barked the words that Rockefeller had hoped he would hear.

"If that's the way you want to do business," Maurice Clark said, "we'd better dissolve, and let you run your own affairs to suit yourself."

Rockefeller picked up on the comment immediately, suggesting that everyone meet at his home later that day for a discussion. The partners all gathered at the appointed time. Once there, Rockefeller asked each man to state his position on the idea of dissolution. Unaware of the trap Rockefeller was setting, the Clarks complied. "We'd better split up," James Clark declared. Maurice, Richard, and Rockefeller's coconspirator Sam Andrews all agreed.

The Clarks left the meeting certain that they had battered Rockefeller into submission once again. Rockefeller then hurried to the offices of the *Cleveland Leader* and placed a formal notice in the morning paper stating that he and his partners had unanimously agreed to part ways. The Clarks, caught in their own bluff, were stunned to read in the next day's paper that they were out of business.

"Do you really want to break it up?" asked an amazed Maurice Clark the next day.

"I really want to break it up," replied a satisfied Rockefeller, free at last to start building one of the largest fortunes amassed in American history.

You may feel a twinge of discomfort at Rockefeller's chessboard maneuverings. But he was a perceptive judge of human character and motives. And he was dealing with men who were much older and more experienced than he—men who had been repaying his business skills with high-handed arrogance. By communicating in a moderate tone and appearing to play to his partners' interests, the young Rockefeller arranged the situation so that his partners gave him exactly what he wanted.

Moreover, when the partnership assets were put up for sale as part of the dissolution a short time later, Rockefeller boldly outbid the Clarks, buying the right to keep the beginnings of his oil empire intact. When Rockefeller offered to write the Clarks a check on the spot, Maurice Clark, perhaps realizing for the first time the extraordinary ambition of the young man he was up against, replied, "I'm glad to trust you for it; settle at your convenience." Within three years—when he was only twenty-eight—Rockefeller was heading up the largest oil refiner in the world at the helm of a company that would become Standard Oil.

### The Advocate: Sam Walton
### (Moderate Volume and a Balance Between Self-Oriented and Other-Oriented Perspectives)

Our final example brings together a number of attributes—a moderate but persistent level of directness and enthusiasm, and a balance of both the self-oriented and other-oriented perspectives. We call this middle role the Advocate because, like a trial lawyer, this persuader uses a full range of tools to get his or her points across. Effectiveness at playing this role springs from experience and judgment. The Advocate strives for balance—persistence without shouting, mindful of the audience without losing perspective.

Our example of playing this role well comes from the career of Sam Walton, whom we met in the last chapter. As Wal-Mart's founder,

Sam could have simply ordered people to do what he wanted done. But he was seldom the Driver that Andy Grove could be. Instead, Walton relied on a more moderate combination of vision, persistence, relationships, and reason to get people to see things his way. His ideas carried substantial weight because of his position as the founder and chairman. But part of his genius was that he rarely, if ever, forced an idea through Wal-Mart's far-flung empire of stores that he could not first sell to his team. By protecting the self-esteem and autonomy of his executives, he was able to win their cooperation for various ideas he came up with to improve the company.

Take one of Wal-Mart's trademark practices: using "greeters" to meet customers as they enter the store. Walton got this idea one day in 1980 when visiting a Wal-Mart in Crowley, Louisiana. As he walked into the store on one of his many visits to Wal-Mart locations, he was surprised to be met by an elderly man who said, "Hi! How are ya? Glad you're here. If there is anything I can tell you about our store, just let me know." When Sam asked the store manager, Dan McAllister, about this, he discovered that McAllister's store had experienced a shoplifting problem. Rather than offend the 99 percent of his customers who were honest by posting an intimidating guard to check bags at the exit, McAllister had decided to place a friendly-looking older man out front to put shoplifters on notice that someone was going to be watching as they left the store. And to give this person something to do, McAllister had asked him to offer a friendly word of greeting to people as they entered the store. His customers loved it, and shoplifting went down.

One of Walton's associates, Tom Coughlin, who was with Sam when all this happened, tells the rest of the story this way:

> Sam thought that this was the greatest idea he'd ever heard of. He went right back to Bentonville and told everyone we ought to put greeters at the front of every single store. A lot of people thought he'd lost his mind. Our folks felt that putting someone at the door was a waste of money. They just couldn't see what Sam and Dan McAllister were seeing—that the greeter sent a warm, friendly message to the good customer, and a warning to the thief. They fought him all the way on it. Some people tried

hard to talk him out of it. They tried to ignore it. [But] Sam just kept pushing and pushing and pushing. Every week, every meeting, he'd talk about the greeters. . . . Sam was relentless.

Notice how Walton achieved credibility with this idea. First, it was not often that Sam Walton was enthusiastic about—much less obsessed by—an idea that *added to,* rather than reduced, expenses. This caught people's attention, helping them to see that Walton was genuinely motivated by the merits of the idea. Second, Walton immediately gave credit for the greeters program to the people in the field who had conceived it—conferring additional credibility on the plan as coming from the "bottom up." Third, Walton never let the issue become personalized even when people resisted it. There was no "don't you trust my judgment?" or "don't you think I know a thing or two about what is good for Wal-Mart?" Instead, he made it clear throughout this campaign that he thought the greeters program would be good for the company, and he was willing to let the debate go on as long as it took to fully explore the idea. He was "relentless," but he refused to dictate the decision.

After eighteen months of debate and experiment, Wal-Mart finally adopted the practice company-wide. Through his skilled advocacy, using messages delivered on the Rationality channel ("This idea is cost-effective"), the Interest channel ("This idea will address the shoplifting problem in the stores"), and the Vision channel ("This will help the image of our company"), the greeters program became an enduring, signature part of the Wal-Mart shopping experience.

## The Problem of Authenticity

The profiles above provide glimpses of what effective persuasion is all about. They may also help you gain insights into your most and least preferred persuasion styles. Reflect first on what you see as your persuasion strengths. Studying more about the modes of persuasion you most prefer will bring you from "good" to "great" as you gain additional knowledge and perspective.

Second, you should note the styles that feel the least natural. These are your disfavored roles, at least for now. The question is "why?" There are two possible reasons. First, you may simply not have had the opportunities to practice these styles and acquire confidence. A different job with different responsibilities, or changes in your personal life, may one day bring these roles into more focus.

Alternatively, you may simply lack the pushiness (on the one hand) or the ability to control your drive and enthusiasm (on the other) to sustain some of these roles credibly. Knowing such limitations is the beginning of wisdom in persuasion. If the situation calls for a hard-nosed Driver, and you are on the quiet side, you may need to bring along someone who can amplify your message. If you are a dyed-in-the-wool Driver and need to play a quieter role, you may want to bring someone into the process who can act as a buffer for your style.

For example, in 1859, when Andrew Carnegie was just twenty-four, he was promoted into his first managerial job as superintendent of the western division of the Pennsylvania Railroad. This position, which put him in charge of all railroad traffic between the Allegheny Mountains and Pittsburgh, Pennsylvania, was a big job for someone his age, especially given that his only prior work experience had been as the office boy and personal assistant to the previous superintendent, Tom Scott. The new position required Carnegie to work long hours, directly supervising the men who kept the railroad running and the tracks clear.

As we have already seen, Carnegie's boundless energy eventually helped him become an excellent Promoter. But in this early job, he played the Driver role and quickly proved himself to be completely ill-suited to directly managing low-level employees in their day-to-day work. As he would later write, "I was probably the most inconsiderate superintendent that ever was entrusted with the management of a great property, for, never knowing fatigue myself . . . I overworked the men and was not careful enough in considering the limits of human endurance." Biographer David Nasaw observes that Carnegie was simply "too impatient" to be an effective supervisor.

The lesson Carnegie took from this experience was notable. He recognized his lack of skill in managing line employees as more than just a temporary problem that he could fix by devoting himself to study. Instead, he decided then and there that he would avoid direct supervisory roles in the future. Nasaw writes that "though [Carnegie] would subsequently employ hundreds of thousands of workingmen, he would never again put himself in the position where he was responsible for supervising any of them." Instead, Carnegie succeeded by hiring extraordinarily talented individuals to run his enterprises, giving them goals and getting out of their way—freeing him to play his preferred Promoter role with enthusiasm.

The need in persuasion to manage appearances and adapt to audiences raises an important ethical issue: authenticity. Won't you lose credibility and self-respect if you become a shape-shifter, changing yourself for each new audience? As actress Judy Garland once said, "Always be a first-rate version of yourself instead of a second-rate version of somebody else."

The English philosopher and politician Francis Bacon, who rose to become one of the most powerful men in England in the late 1500s under Queen Elizabeth I, tried to manage virtually every impression he made with people at the royal court. He filled his journals with observations and advice to himself on how he should appear to others in pivotal encounters and drew lessons from each success and failure to take to his next meeting. For example, he once wrote that he needed to "suppress at once my speaking with panting and labour of breath and voice" in conversing with one of the queen's closest advisers. Bacon's goal was to create a separate and distinct "public self" as an instrument of persuasion.

Behavioral experts Rob Goffe and Gareth Jones have wrestled with the apparent paradox that impression management presents. Your personal credibility, which has its roots in perceived consistency and trustworthiness, provides the foundation for influence. Yet effective persuaders are, these authors say, "like chameleons, capable of adapting to the demands of the situations they face."

Is it really possible to be a "credible chameleon"?

Yes—but only within limits. You play many roles in your life such as spouse, parent, professional, employee, boss, sports fan, customer, community leader, student, and teacher. And in each of these roles you naturally display different aspects of yourself. Your child's third-grade teacher sees a different side of you than does your boss, and your brother or sister probably sees a different person than does your child. Nevertheless, it is always just "you." There is a core set of traits, commitments, standards, and impulses that connects you in these various roles.

Thus, the authenticity paradox diminishes when you see that you cannot help being a somewhat "different person" depending on who you are interacting with. And your awareness of these various roles gives you a range of "authentic selves" to display in persuasion. Goffe and Jones tell an illuminating story about Nestlé CEO Peter Brabeck-Letmathe. In one of Nestlé's annual reports, Brabeck-Letmathe is shown in the Swiss mountains wearing climbing clothes. In another publication, *The Nestlé Leadership and Management Principles,* he wears a dark suit and stands outside corporate headquarters. Is he an outdoorsman or an executive? As he explains: "I wanted to use the image of the mountaineer because water and the environment are emotional issues for many people. But the photo is not artificial. That's what I wear on weekends. I'm a climber. In the mountaineering picture, it's a human being talking. In the other picture, I am talking for the institution. The photographs are different, but they both capture something essential about me." Brabeck-Letmathe and his PR team know when to display certain essential qualities rather than others to make persuasive points. But they do not go outside Brabeck-Letmathe's actual life experience to construct these images, thus preserving his authenticity.

## Conclusion

In this chapter, we introduced the central player in the Art of Woo— you. To gain skill in persuasion you must first achieve self-awareness. All the great persuaders we met in this chapter—from the nineteenth century's Abraham Lincoln, J. P. Morgan, John D. Rockefeller, and Andrew Carnegie to the twentieth century's Andy Grove and Sam Walton—knew their strengths and weaknesses, learned from their mistakes, and honed their skills in the laboratory of personal experience.

Three questions are critical: (1) What is your comfort zone in terms of volume—loud or quiet? (2) Do you have a distinctly self-oriented or other-oriented perspective? and (3) What are your preferred channels— authority, rationality, vision, interests, relationships, or politics? The first two of these insights yield the five archetypal persuasion styles—the Driver, Commander, Promoter, Chess Player, and Advocate. A given persuasion problem may require you to display one or more of these styles, sequence through several of them, or combine some.

The third insight regarding your preferred channels reveals the messages you prefer to send. If you want your message to get across, it is up to you to know which channels you are normally tuned to, which the other side is likely to be listening on, and make any necessary adjustments.

We now move from our introductory chapters to the central portion of the book—our step-by-step planning process for selling ideas. We will start where all projects start, with ideas and goals. Then you will need to map out the decision-making process and find that all-important person—the decision maker. The next chapter provides the tools you need to get started on these important tasks.

chapter three

# Connect Your Ideas to People: Stepping-stones

A goal properly set is halfway reached.
—Abraham Lincoln

[Many people] assume that only senior executives make decisions or that only senior executives' decisions matter. This is a dangerous mistake.
—Peter Drucker

In the last chapter, you began the Woo process. You stepped back and assessed your own persuasion styles. In this chapter, we examine your ideas and the situation you face. Where do ideas come from? How can you use your experience to come up with new and better ones? And why is it important to polish them before starting the selling process? To answer these questions, we will tell the story of how an entrepreneur named Reed Hastings came up with an idea for a Web-based movie-rental business called "Netflix" and sold it to investors.

Next, with your idea in hand, you will be ready to map the situation ahead of you, charting the course that will lead to the people who can transform your idea into reality. Finally, as you plan your idea-selling strategy, you will need to set specific persuasion goals for each stage of the process. In some encounters, your goal will be to get introductions to key influencers; in other meetings, you will be looking for endorsements; eventually you will be asking for decisions. We conclude the chapter with a discussion of these goals and the importance of bringing sincere conviction, based on belief in your idea, to every interaction.

## It All Begins with Ideas

We will start with a story about an entrepreneur and the steps he followed to come up with an idea for a new business, polish that idea, and sell it to funding sources. At the most basic level, all idea sellers are entrepreneurs. In fact, scholars sometimes call people who spark new initiatives and programs inside organizations *intra*preneurs. Inside or outside of an organization, you need to bring lots of energy to the process of developing and promoting new concepts.

The entrepreneur's name in this case is Reed Hastings, and the business concept he came up with is called "Netflix." Netflix rents movies on DVDs using the Internet as its ordering platform and the postal service as the delivery system.

Hastings is a "serial entrepreneur." He specializes in coming up with new ideas for businesses, founding new firms, getting them off the ground, then selling them when they become successful. He had recently sold a software company prior to founding Netflix and was well off financially. But an entrepreneur without a current project is like a child without toys. Hastings was looking for his next big thing.

As he later told the story, the Netflix concept got its start one day when he discovered he had a huge late fee for a copy of the movie *Apollo 13* he had rented at his local video store. He had misplaced the cassette, forgotten about it, then discovered he owed the video store £40. His first reaction was embarrassment—he wanted to hide his stupidity from his wife. His next thought was "Am I really going to compromise the integrity of my marriage over a late fee?" He paid the money—and told his wife about his mistake.

Later, as he was driving to the gym, he began to think about the video store's business model. The store charged customers by the rental and penalized those who were late returning movies. The gym he was going to, by contrast, charged a flat fee and did not keep score on his usage. As someone who had just been burned by a big late fee, he liked the gym's business model better.

As he continued his drive, a question presented itself: would it be possible to run a movie rental business the way the gym worked—by charging a flat fee and not worrying about how many movies people rented or how long they kept them?

Being a serial entrepreneur, this was a familiar feeling for Hastings—the connection between an area of dissatisfaction in the marketplace (the movie rental late fee) and a way of reducing that dissatisfaction and making a profit. But could he come up with a compelling business model for a relatively expensive flat-fee video rental business when so much of the competition was charging for one rental at a time? And how could he get customers to return the movies they had watched without assessing a penalty?

Now it was time to do the hard work of turning his insight into a bona fide idea. With the help of friends, his spouse, his lawyer, and others, he worked on the idea until he had developed a full-fledged, formal profit model. The following elements eventually made it into his business plan: a vast library of tens of thousands of DVDs with multiple copies of the most watched films and television series, an online order-placing system accessible 24/7, a one- or two-day fulfillment-and-delivery system that used the postal service and included convenient envelopes for returning the DVDs at no additional cost, and a flat monthly fee that allowed unlimited rentals—but that limited customers to having only three or four DVDs at a time and required them to return one as a condition of getting the next one on their list. He capped the idea off by obtaining a business process patent on the whole system to discourage incumbent video rental companies from imitating his business model.

This, then, was the idea he sold to venture capitalists to get his funding. There were, of course, some long-term problems. First, his patent might not hold up and a larger competitor might drive him out of business. Second, online downloading of video content would eventually become easier than mailing DVDs in envelopes. But Netflix's online library of titles might become tomorrow's library of downloadable movies, positioning his company as a leader in that new market.

As Hastings' story shows, this final idea-polishing process is very important when it comes to actually selling an idea. One of Winston

Churchill's top advisers during World War II, General Sir Alan Brooke, once said that Churchill came up with an average of ten new ideas for winning the war every day—"one good, nine bad." Much of Brooke's job was making sure that the nine bad ones never saw the light of day. The entire military then set to the task of making the good one work.

## A Technique for Producing Ideas

You may think that Hastings' story is just a random example of idea generation, but it is much more than that. It tracks almost exactly a systematic, five-stage process for cultivating creativity described by James Webb Young in one of the best short business books we have ever encountered: a work called *A Technique for Producing Ideas.* Young was a successful advertising executive in the early 1900s who retired in 1928 and spent the 1930s teaching part-time at the University of Chicago's Graduate School of Business. He wrote this book in 1940.

Young explains that there is no such thing as a completely new idea—no matter how radical it may seem to an outsider. There are only new combinations of old elements. Thus, the key talent involved in generating new ideas is an ability to find relationships and patterns among things you already know. All of us have this ability. The trick is to harness it consciously, as Reed Hastings has done. You can do so by following the process Young describes.

## Stage 1: Define the Problem

The first stage in generating a new idea is to define the problem you are trying to solve. As we will see in chapter 7, problem definition is also critically important after you have an idea and are trying to convince other people to pay attention to it.

The more accurately you define the problem, the better. There is some art to this. If you define the problem too narrowly, you might unconsciously block out creative ideas and options that could prove quite valuable. If you define it too broadly, you will be flooded with irrelevant data and overwhelmed with the complexity of what you face—making it hard to separate the good ideas from the bad ones.

We observe mistakes in problem framing all the time in our negotiation courses. When people define the scope of a negotiation problem as being entirely about the price, they often miss nonmonetary, creative options that might elegantly solve their underlying problem. When they frame the negotiation problem too broadly—so that it encompasses the overall structure of their market or firm—they have trouble coming up with any strategy at all because no single negotiation can fix a problem of such wide scope.

Hastings framed his what-shall-I-do-next problem "just right"—not too narrowly and not too broadly. He was looking for a profitable new business model. That is broader than looking only for a new software business, which would have led him to ignore the connection between his video rental and gym experiences. But it is narrower than looking for just "something to do."

### Stage 2: Research Relentlessly

The next stage is to thoroughly research your problem. The more precisely you frame the question and research the relevant models, data, and options, the better. Hastings was spending most of his time on his business model hunt—but not by going to the library. He was reading trade and business publications, talking to other entrepreneurs, going on trips, and noticing trends. As the Netflix example shows, a lot of this research work is done for you by simply being fully committed to whatever activity you engage in. Your mind is picking up, retaining, and arranging both generalized and specific data all the time without your even realizing it. But concentrated, purposeful research with reference to a defined problem is extremely helpful when cooking up a new idea. As Young explains, "Gathering raw material . . . is such a terrible chore that we are constantly trying to dodge it." So this effort makes a difference.

Research prompts lots of different thoughts about how to solve the problem. Young calls this "mental digestion." Some people call this the "brainstorming" stage. Working alone or in groups, you are rewarded with little bursts of half-baked ideas and hit-or-miss notions. The point here is to keep at it, even if you become discouraged and are tempted to give up on the process.

### Stage 3: Let It Cook

Stage 3 is crucial: you must trust the unconscious part of your mind to do its part. This part of your mind is great at sifting through the data of your experience to find patterns, combinations, and possible solutions to the problem you have posed to yourself. Having the patience to let a problem "cook" like this is sometimes hard—especially if you need an idea on a deadline. As an experienced entrepreneur, Hastings knew this process well and trusted it to work.

### Stage 4: Catch the Idea as It Flies By

Stage 4 is to be alert, because the good ideas will start to come at odd moments—in the shower, as you are waking up, while you are gardening, or when you are taking a walk. The ideas will seem to come "out of nowhere," says Young. But we know better. They are the product of this relentless combination process. The job in Stage 4 is simple: catch the new ideas as they come. Don't let yourself forget them; write them down. As a serial entrepreneur, Hastings knows a new idea when he sees one. He is an expert at catching ideas as they fly by. And he alertly snapped up the seemingly random insight he had while driving to his gym and transformed it into a multimillion-dollar business.

### Stage 5: Shape and Polish

Stage 5, as we noted above, is the most important part: the shaping and polishing stage. You take the raw material of your new idea, turn it over in your head, adapt it, share it with others, and get feedback. The best ideas—those most genuinely suited to solving problems— will inspire enthusiasm, first in you and then, if you are skilled at the Art of Woo, in others. And as the polishing process continues, it will spur further ideas about how to make your solution more efficient, elegant, and enduring. The Netflix concept began as a way to eliminate annoying late fees from the video rental business. It ended with a sophisticated, patented—and profitable—business process.

A good way to see if your idea is really feasible is to have a group of smart, sympathetic friends you can rely on for constructive input.

History is replete with examples of so-called mastermind groups that have helped creative people shape their ideas, from Benjamin Franklin's famous eighteenth-century "Junto" that started many enduring social institutions in the city of Philadelphia to the Bloomsbury intellectual circle in England in the early 1900s that included novelist Virginia Woolf, economist John Maynard Keynes, and a variety of artists and thinkers. You don't need to be or know geniuses to exploit the power of collective thinking about an idea. You just need the humility to believe that two heads are better than one.

As you shape your idea, it helps to project it into the future—but to do this in a special way. Cognitive scientists have shown that people can uncover possible problems with new ideas most effectively if they use a technique called "taking a trip to the future." It works like this. Picture yourself in your home or office on the *day after* you have successfully sold your idea to an especially knowledgeable and critical audience. Then look back on your presentation and imagine the way you introduced your idea to the group. Next, think of the questions the audience asked, including the toughest and most challenging ones. If you were Reed Hastings, you might have been asked how you were going to deal with customer complaints that the best movies were unavailable, or what you planned to do when competitors offered their own, cheaper, by-mail movie rentals. As you reflect on what the audience wanted to know, write down all the issues and concerns that came up.

After subjecting your idea to both real and imaginary criticism, return to the polishing process. Your goal is to have a fully formed, well-thought-through idea that is ready to sell to decision makers. This polishing activity is never really completed—even fully implemented programs get better and better as people think of ways to improve them. But unless you do a good job of shaping the idea initially, it will never get past the first gatekeeper.

## From Ideas to Action: Deciding Who to Woo

Once you have a well-polished idea, you are ready to map the influence process you will use to sell it. Even the most unlikely ideas can be pushed through the most difficult environments if you act methodically—one idea, one ally, one e-mail, one conversation, one meeting, and one presentation at a time. And sometimes you can get to the decision maker and make a sale in one move—even with a very big initiative.

In his autobiography, *My Years with General Motors,* Alfred Sloan tells a story about how, soon after joining GM as a vice president in 1918, he sold an important idea to his CEO, William Durant, during a single conversation. At the time, public companies were not required by law to be audited, but Sloan thought both GM and its shareholders would benefit from engaging an independent auditor to go over its books on a regular basis. Audits present management with a clearer financial picture of the firm, but they can also pose risks if the auditors uncover irregularities. Mindful of these dangers, Sloan might have vetted his idea to his senior staff or formed a committee to study it before presenting it to Durant. But Sloan knew Durant was an "impulsive" decision maker who did not really understand or care about accounting. And Sloan did not want the idea to get bogged down in office politics—he was convinced it was the right thing to do. So he snuck it by Durant by downplaying it.

"My office was next door to his," Sloan wrote. "One day in 1919 I went in and told him that I thought that, in view of the large public interest in the corporation's shares, we should have an independent audit by a certified public accountant." Durant barely looked up from his work. He "said at once that he agreed with me, and told me to go and get one. That was the way he worked."

One-move idea sales can work even better with lower-level decision makers, provided you have taken the trouble to form good relationships with them. As Peter Drucker noted in one of the quotes that opened this chapter, it is a "dangerous mistake" to think that only those at higher levels make important decisions. The skilled idea seller does not go any higher in an organization for the green light than he or she needs to.

When Nelson Mandela was imprisoned on South Africa's notoriously brutal Robben Island, he survived for twenty-six years by focusing on specific goals for improving prison conditions and scouting exactly who would be the right people to sell his ideas to. One of his first important insights was that the lowest-level employees—the warders—had the most control over decisions related to prisoners' well-being. As Mandela learned, "The most important person in any prisoner's life is not the minister of justice, not the commissioner of prisons, not even the head of the prison, but the warder in one's section." If you needed an extra blanket and went to the minister of justice, "you would get no response." If you went to the commissioner of prisons, the commissioner would say, "It is against regulations." If you went to the head of the prison, he would respond, "If I give you an extra blanket, I must give one to everyone." But if you were on good terms with the warder, the warder would "simply go to the stockroom and fetch a blanket." In addition, and perhaps most important, when you had a good relationship with the warders, "it became difficult for the higher-ups to treat you roughly."

Thus, if you have access to the decision maker—whether that decision maker is at the top of the organization chart or somewhere near the bottom—and see no need to involve anyone else in the decision process (more on this when we discuss getting commitments in chapter 9), a simple meeting with a straightforward idea pitch is the way to go. But recall a research finding we mentioned in chapter 1: even uncomplicated decisions require contact with an average of eight people in most organizations and complex decisions usually involve as many as twenty people. The more typical decision process, therefore, will have multiple stages.

Consequently, you will need to plan what we call a "stepping-stone" influence process, which we describe next.

### Crossing the River One Stone at a Time

An example of how to map a stepping-stone process comes from the life of one of our students, a young man from India—we will call him Raj—who faced some sensitive family business issues in connection with an idea he was trying to sell.

As the oldest son of a wealthy Indian family, Raj was the heir to his family's large printing business. His father was eager for him to return home after graduation from college and take up his duties with the family firm. Raj, on the other hand, wanted to stay in America for a few more years and gain what he thought would be valuable business experience working for a global consulting company. How could Raj persuade his father to bless a decision to stay in America without trampling on this all-important relationship?

Raj had his idea and knew exactly what he wanted from his next persuasion encounter with his father. The problem was that he had not yet mapped the decision process within his family.

We asked him a simple question to get the ball rolling: how will this decision be made in your family?

"My mother, father, grandmother, and grandfather will all sit down together and discuss it," he replied.

"And of those four, who would be most sympathetic to your view?"

"My mother," he answered immediately.

"Does she have clout inside the family?"

"In Indian families, the wife is supreme inside the house. But this issue is both inside the house and outside the house. And she may be afraid that if I stay in America, I will meet an American girl and want to marry. She would be very opposed to that. There is also my grandfather. He founded the business and thinks some experience working on lots of projects for the consulting firm might be useful. But he cannot oppose my father."

"And your grandmother?"

"She will agree with my grandfather."

With this picture of the decision-making process in mind, we devised an idea-selling strategy. First, during his trip home over the Christmas holidays, he would have a heart-to-heart conversation with his mother and share his dream of gaining experience and having some freedom before coming home to help run the company. His goal would be to enlist her as his champion. He would, of course, have to convince her that he would commit to marrying an Indian woman.

The next step would be for his mother to approach the grandfather and grandmother in private to sell the idea of an alliance supporting Raj's plan. The three of them would then try to gain the father's approval. Above all: Raj should avoid speaking directly to his father on the issue, especially at any family gathering. Raj would not want his father to become committed in public to a "no" answer.

When Raj returned from Christmas vacation, he came to visit us. He was beaming. It had worked—but not exactly the way we had anticipated. Our questions had gotten Raj thinking about how decisions in his family were really made. So after he got home—but before he spoke with anyone—he asked his older sister for her advice. She approved the plan, but suggested speaking with the grandmother first. It turned out that the grandmother had more influence than Raj suspected. In fact, she was the real power in the family when it came to issues of this sort, though Raj had never been aware of it. Raj was her favorite grandchild—and under her gentle guidance and with some clear commitments from Raj about coming home within two years unmarried, the post-graduation sojourn was approved by the family council.

Raj's simple story illustrates a profound truth. To devise an idea-selling strategy, you must start with three key questions:

1. How do decisions like this get made in my organization?

2. Whom should I woo first to gain entry into that process?

3. What follow-up strategy should I use?

### Social Networks

To answer these questions, you need to know something about how your organization really works. In groups of all kinds, people get things done through informal social networks. The extent of your network constitutes your "social capital" and is one of your most important career assets. The "social intelligence" you have about how these networks actually operate is one of your most valuable knowledge assets. Indeed, researchers have confirmed that people who are knowledgable about the advice-giving and influence network within their organizations are seen by others as more powerful.

As Raj's story shows, social networks can operate in ways that are very different from the chain-of-command relationships identified on a standard organization chart. Raj's father was the nominal head of both his household and his business. Raj thought his mother was the

major influencer within this system, but it turned out that his grandmother was the real power behind the throne for the type of decision
he wanted made. Raj's sister turned out to be a key adviser on how
this system worked.

So the first move in a stepping-stone selling campaign is to determine what the actual decision process looks like. Nelson Mandela's
experience on Robben Island is again instructive.

By winning over the most sympathetic guards, one by one, Mandela advanced toward his overall goal of improving treatment for all
the inmates. He was, in effect, using the Chess Player role we studied
in the last chapter for a decades-long campaign to influence the
prison hierarchy. The secret to influencing his jailers lay neither in
challenging their authority, which increased their anger, nor in un-
conditionally submitting to them, which decreased their respect. Instead, he wooed them by understanding their mind-set: their
language, values, and history. He learned to speak Afrikaans, think in
Afrikaner terms, and appreciate the best and most popular Afrikaans
books. This made it much easier for him to strike up casual conversations with the warders and learn even more about their culture.

The hardened antiapartheid prisoners at the island quickly learned
from observing the success of Mandela's efforts. One of them commented: "I realized the importance of learning Afrikaans history, of
reading Afrikaans literature, of trying to understand these ordinary
men . . . how they are indoctrinated, how they react." Mandela knew
precisely why this was important: "You must understand the mind of
the opposing commander . . . you can't understand him unless you
understand his literature and his language."

When it came to influencing the most senior officials, by contrast,
Mandela relied more on his political skills and his knowledge of how
power tends to corrupt the people who have it. The Robben Island
commander for many years, Colonel Piet Badenhorst, was particularly brutal and made a game of trying to provoke Mandela, shouting
in Afrikaans when he saw him in the yard: "Mandela, you must pull
your finger out of your arse." But Mandela said nothing in response
to these taunts, knowing that reacting would make it harder to get
what he wanted. He realized that with Badenhorst there would be no
relationship-based persuasion. It was all about power.

Mandela eventually won this battle by orchestrating Badenhorst's departure from Robben Island. It was the culmination of a carefully plotted stepping-stone process. First, Mandela and his allies got word of Badenhorst's prisoner abuse to friends on the outside, who published their stories in the press. Mandela was an international figure by this time, and the South African government knew the world was watching what happened on Robben Island. The government responded by sending three investigative judges to the island to make a report. They requested a face-to-face conversation with Mandela. But Mandela, to everyone's surprise, took step two of his plan and insisted that Badenhorst be present. In true Chess Player fashion, Mandela was setting Badenhorst up for his own fall.

The final move came at the hearing itself. As Mandela described a recent beating to the judges, Badenhorst could not restrain himself, just as Mandela had anticipated. "If you talk about things you haven't seen," Badenhorst interrupted angrily, "you will get yourself in trouble." Mandela declined to address his foe directly. Instead, he addressed the judges, pointing to the horrors that occurred when visitors departed.

"If he can threaten me here, in your presence," Mandela said quietly, "you can imagine what he does when you are not here."

Mandela's well-timed comment hit home. The judges left the island and reported that abuses were, in fact, taking place. And three months after the meeting, Badenhorst was transferred—along with a gang of the most violent warders. Over time, as the force of Mandela's personal character pervaded the entire prison, he became, in the words of his biographer, a "star attraction" among the more enlightened warders. They would share meals and even play tennis with him.

By the time Mandela was released from Robben Island, he had so thoroughly transformed the situation that it was the South African government that was trying to sell *him* an idea—the idea that he should leave the prison. Mandela resisted this offer, realizing that his own incarceration had become an important bargaining chip in the fight for equality. It was only when his antiapartheid principles had been completely agreed to that he consented to be set free.

Mandela's story illustrates just how important it is to accurately map the decision process you face so that you can execute the appropriate strategies. Books such as Duncan J. Watts's *Six Degrees: The Science of a Connected Age* (and other social network texts in the bibliography at the end of the book) provide additional resources on exactly how you can do this within your own organization. In the meantime, we will give you a visual illustration of how it works.

Social network expert Rob Cross once conducted an analysis of a large oil company and created a map of the differences between the formal organization and the informal one that existed below the surface (see Figure 3.1).

Look at the formal organization chart at the top of Figure 3.1. Imagine yourself in Cohen's position, at the top of Group A of the production division. Suppose you wanted to sell an idea to the senior vice president of manufacturing, Jones. The obvious path based on the formal reporting relationships (the diagram at the top) would be to sell your boss, Williams, and then get Williams to help you sell it to his boss, Jones. And that might work—but mapping that pathway for your idea would not be a wise use of either your social capital or social intelligence.

The social network diagram at the bottom of Figure 3.1, which shows people's informal relationships with one another rather than the formal hierarchy, reveals that an employee named Cole, who is near the bottom of Group A, has stronger social network relationships to both Williams and Jones than you do. In fact, Cole knows someone in every unit in the division. Because Cole is so well connected, you would do well to enlist him as an ally in explaining your idea to others across the group.

That raises another strategy question. Should you follow the shortest social network route and ask Cole to take your idea directly to the overall boss, Jones? Probably not. Formal reporting relationships are very important in terms of status within most groups. You report to Williams and Williams may resent your attempt to go "over his head" to Jones without first consulting him.

Balancing the considerations raised by both the formal and the informal diagrams, you might map your strategy for this idea as follows: (1) enlist Cole as an ally, (2) have Cole approach Andrews to be part of your alliance, (3) ask for a meeting with your boss, Williams, at which both Cole and especially Andrews support your

Figure 3.1

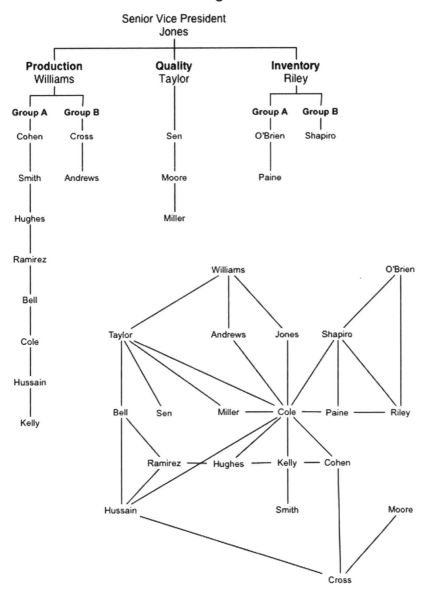

Adapted from Rob Cross and Andrew Parker. *The Hidden Power of Social Networks* (Harvard Business School Press, 2004), 5.

idea, (4) then have Williams represent your collective views to Jones in whatever way Williams deems best. As an investment in the future, you would also want to use this occasion to strengthen your social ties with both Williams and Jones. And if you were advising Jones as a leadership coach, you would probably tell him to spend more time getting to know the people who work for him on a personal level.

### Four Key Roles: Boundary Spanners, Connectors, Peripheral Players, and Subgroups

Take another look at the social network diagram on the right of Figure 3.1. Social network experts have discovered that there are four distinct types of actors within the "informal" organization: *boundary spanners, connectors, peripheral players,* and *subgroups.*

**Boundary Spanners.** Boundary Spanners are people (such as Cole in our example) who have relationships with members of different Subgroups within an organization or who bridge your organization with outside groups. If you look closely at the diagram on the bottom of Figure 3.1, you will notice that Cole has informal relationships with at least one person in every Subgroup. Boundary Spanners can help you understand the perspective of specific functions outside your specialty ("What do the lawyers generally think?"), assist with gaining access to people in other parts of your organization ("Can you introduce me to someone in marketing?"), and advise you on your idea-selling strategy by helping you map the informal systems they know about.

Sociologists have found that, in communities as well as companies, certain well-connected people play the "bridging" role between groups. This accounts for the well-known "six degrees of separation" phenomenon. Pick any famous person at random, and you will often find that you are no more than six relationships away from them (i.e., you know someone, who knows someone, etc., who knows the person in question). Do this experiment repeatedly, and you will begin to find that one or two people's names frequently come up in the chain of relationships that connect you to others. These people are the central switching points within your social network. When you view your organization through a social network lens, you will see how such Boundary Spanners can help you to communicate and to gather important political intelligence across organizational boundaries.

Professional politicians are, of course, the ultimate Spanners. Their success in politics depends on their relationships within two distinct networks. First, to get elected, they must know people from as many groups as possible who may vote for them. Second, once elected, they need to build personal bridges with as many other elected officials as possible to get things done. A famous Louisiana politician named Earl Long once summed up his talent as a politician as follows: "The kind of thing I'm good at is knowing every politician in the state and remembering where he itches."

But you don't have to be a politician to exploit the benefits that come with spanning social networks. Studies of such communities as the high-tech world of California's Silicon Valley, celebrity-studded Hollywood, and the political infrastructures of major cities show that a handful of people—sometimes no more than 100 to 200—control a disproportionate amount of the actual decision-making power in these areas. These "super" Boundary Spanners serve on multiple boards for both private companies and important local charities, are regulars at high-profile social events, and, when they are not holding important jobs themselves, are advising those who do. They may have no actual decision-making power of their own, but their position in their networks gives them enormous influence over a wide range of decisions.

Rock star Bono, lead singer of the group U2 and a social entrepreneur whom we will meet later in the book, has an interesting strategy for locating the key Boundary Spanners when he is raising money for his causes. When he first approaches a new government group, industry association, or nonprofit network, he asks everyone he speaks with a key question: "Who is the Elvis here?" He wants to find his way as quickly as possible to the pivotal person who controls the actual influence in the network.

Interestingly, this same insight into the importance of centrality within an informal network forms the foundation for the ranking system used by one of the best and most widely used Internet search engines—Google. When you conduct a Google search, the sites that appear at the top of the list are not the ones that pay the most money to Google or that some expert has determined is the best site for your query. They are simply the sites with the most network centrality—the ones with the most links between them and the rest of the Internet.

**Connectors.** In addition to being a Boundary Spanner, Cole is also a Connector, someone who has a wide set of relationships *within his own group* (he is tied in with Cohen, Kelly, Hughes, and Hussain within his own "C&G" business unit). While Spanners are people who help bridge the gaps between groups, Connectors are the people who have wide sets of ties within their own units and can use those ties to help you navigate inside them. Raj's sister was a Connector within her family. In business, it is not uncommon for a Connector to also be a Boundary Spanner who bridges to at least one outside group.

**Peripheral Players.** People at the edges of a network (like Jones in our Figure 3.1 illustration) are less connected than either Boundary Spanners or Connectors. Indeed, sometimes these Peripheral Players are self-consciously isolated. People at the edges of the informal organization may be specialists who can give you a quick course on a technical aspect of your idea when you need it ("Can you explain in a few words how this machine really works?") but who have no interest in organizational politics. They may be people who are trying to achieve a better work–life balance and have checked out of the social networking system within an organization. Alternatively, their role in the organization may call on them to be isolated so they can maintain a certain distance or perspective on the rest of the organization. Sometimes an organization's lawyers or accountants are asked to stay on the periphery for just this reason.

An example of how astute use of a Peripheral Player can help in an idea-selling campaign comes from American politics in the 1930s. When Franklin D. Roosevelt was elected president, he took a big step toward gender equality in his administration by appointing the first woman in American history to occupy a major cabinet position—a social activist named Frances Perkins, whom he named secretary of labour. As part of the drive to create the Social Security system (we will tell the story about how Perkins sold this idea to Roosevelt in the next section), Roosevelt asked Perkins to chair the committee he charged with formulating this program. The group had six months to come up with a working proposal for a national social insurance program.

One of the biggest problems the committee faced was a legal question: would a social insurance system of any kind pass muster under the Constitution? Lawyers differed in their opinions, and Perkins was worried that the entire system might ultimately be struck down by the courts unless they built it on the right legal foundation.

Perkins used her social network to get some help on this issue by arranging to consult with a Peripheral Player in the political process—Justice Harlan Stone of the U.S. Supreme Court. Within the U.S. government, the Supreme Court is formally set apart to act as a referee for the other two, more political branches, Congress and the Office of the President. The Court also constitutes a distinct Subgroup (more on this below), and it is highly improper for members of the Court to comment informally on cases or other matters that might come before them. But Justices are people, too, and they play roles in the elaborate social system of Washington, D.C. This makes them part of Washington's informal social network, albeit at the periphery.

Perkins exploited this social reality to get help with her Social Security initiative. Her first step was to get invited to tea with the wife of Justice Harlan Stone, a woman she knew from other social occasions in Washington. She knew that the tea would be scheduled for late in the afternoon, when Justice Stone was likely to be home. She arrived at the Stones' house at 5:45 P.M., and Mrs. Stone took Perkins upstairs where a large group of people had gathered. The Justice was just getting his cup of tea as she approached the tea table.

"How are you getting on?" he inquired.

"All right," Perkins replied. Then, realizing that she might not have another opportunity to pop her question, given the social obligations that came with being a guest at this event, she got right to her point.

"Well, you know we are having big trouble, Mr. Justice," she said.

Justice Stone looked at her with new interest.

Perkins went on to describe the legal debate the commission was having. "We are not quite sure, you know, what will be a wise method of establishing this law. It is a very difficult constitutional problem, you know."

Stone leaned toward her and looked around to see if anybody was listening. Then he signaled her to come a little closer.

"The taxing power, my dear, the taxing power," he said quietly. "You can do anything under the taxing power." At the time of this conversation, there was an important debate going on within the Court over the proper reach of congressional power to regulate business under such Constitutional provisions as the Commerce Clause and the Due Process Clause. But the Court had steadfastly held that Congress had broad powers to levy taxes, even when such taxes fell unfairly on one economic group at the expense of another. Justice Stone was giving Perkins a hint: pitch the Social Security system as a tax program and it was sure to avoid this legal debate.

At the next meeting of her committee, the legal question came up for discussion and Perkins advocated firmly for basing the Social Security legislation on "the taxing power." The committee endorsed her idea, though Perkins never told anyone where her new-found conviction on this issue had come from. When, years later, a legal challenge to the Social Security system finally made its way to the Supreme Court, the law passed with flying colors as a valid exercise of Congress's power to tax. Reflecting years later about the founding of the Social Security system, she said, "The taxing power of the United States—you can do anything under it. And so it proved . . ."

**Subgroups.** The fourth and final type of social network player is the Subgroup (like the inventory group of Riley, O'Brian, Shapiro, and Paine in Figure 3.1 or the U.S. Supreme Court in the Perkins story). Subgroups may form on the basis of function, role, hierarchy, gender, or any number of factors. These groups can represent important political constituencies for you if your idea impacts them in some way. They tend to support or oppose new ideas or initiatives as a block. We will explore this dynamic later in chapter 9, when we discuss organizational politics and the problem of gaining commitment to new ideas.

## Setting Specific Persuasion Goals for Each Encounter

The stepping-stone process for selling ideas requires you to persuade different people to do different things at different stages. Thus, you will need to set specific, somewhat different goals as you move from one encounter to the next. Research shows that people with specific, high aspirations tend to accomplish more than people who have vague, do-my-best goals. And people who commit themselves to their goals by writing them down and discussing them with others tend to achieve more than people who keep their goals to themselves. You will want to bring these habits to the process of setting goals in an idea-selling campaign.

Early on, you may simply be trying to introduce your idea and get key people thinking about it by floating "trial balloons." Later, you may be seeking input to help shape your idea into a final product. Finally, you may be asking for specific forms of cooperation as you work through your social network toward the ultimate decision makers. Each of the four social network players, for example, presents opportunities to advance distinctive goals: information goals with Boundary Spanners and Peripheral Players, endorsement goals with Connectors, and coalition formation goals with Subgroups. Eventually you will ask for approval and action from decision makers.

To help you think more strategically about what you might want from each encounter, here is a list of seven specific goals to think about as you map the decision process that lies ahead:

- *Brainstorming or Idea-Polishing Goals:* You want someone to help you think about your idea. This does not require them to endorse it or even like it.

- *Facilitative Goals:* Again, without asking for someone to endorse your idea, you need him or her to help you map the process or gain access to someone who is a stepping-stone on your map. Successfully achieving this sort of goal might involve permission to use someone's name to approach someone else whom you do not know.

- *Attitude Goals:* Now you are trying to actively persuade—to alter people's minds in a positive way about your idea. An attitude is a point of view or predisposition toward some idea, issue, or action. You want your persuasion partner to say—and believe—that "this is a good idea." The more tightly you can hitch your idea to an existing, positive attitude held by your partner, the better.

- *Authorization Goals:* You want approval for resources needed to advance your idea to the next stage. This is more difficult and normally requires a person who controls resources to have a favorable attitude about your idea. We will see in the next chapter that your personal credibility is vitally important to achieve this and the remaining three goal types.

- *Endorsement Goals:* You are looking for allies who will sign on to actively support your idea—either privately, in public, or both.

- *Decision Goals:* You want approval for your idea from a person or committee charged with making a decision. This generally requires both positive attitudes and endorsements.

- *Implementation and Action Goals:* You want to transform an approval into specific forms of action involving concrete steps on a timetable. This requires commitment of resources. Note that, at implementation, you may be required to sell your idea all over again to the people who will implement it.

Of course, you can have more than one goal for any given encounter. For example, you should always be trying to create favorable attitudes toward your idea even if you do not absolutely need such an attitude to get brainstorming or facilitative help. In addition, the earlier you are in an idea-selling campaign, the more strategic and politically sensitive you need to be in approaching people. For example, when developing an idea that will require time and resources, you may need to talk to the ultimate decision maker early on to get permission to explore an idea further. When you do this, you should be careful to assure the decision maker that his or her preliminary endorsement to invest resources in no way implies approval for the final product. A second story about Frances Perkins' effort to establish the Social Security system in the United States illustrates the limited scope of idea-selling goals early in an idea-selling process.

Perkins had compiled an impressive record by the time she was named secretary of labour, emerging first as a leader of social causes in New York City and then serving as industrial commissioner under FDR when he was governor of New York State. As her career developed, she dreamed of creating an extensive plan for national labour and economic security. This had crystallized into the idea for the Social Security system by the time Roosevelt asked her to join his cabinet.

It was early 1933, just after the election, when Roosevelt called Perkins to a meeting at his Manhattan town house. Because she had not yet agreed to serve, Perkins knew that this was her moment of maximum leverage with the president-elect. On the other hand, she did not want to overplay her hand by demanding a full commitment from Roosevelt on something as daring and untested as Social Security. Her specific goal for the meeting was therefore to get something important but modest—authorization to explore the idea.

As they sat together, Perkins laid out her ambitious vision and asked, "Are you sure you want these things done? Because you don't want me for secretary of labour if you don't."

Roosevelt was understandably startled when he understood the scope of her goals.

"Well, do you think it can be done?" asked Roosevelt.

"I don't know," Perkins replied frankly. But then she observed: "Lots of other problems have been solved by the people of the United States, and there is no reason why this one shouldn't be solved."

"Well," Roosevelt pressed, "do you think you can do it?"

"I want to know I have your authorization," Perkins said. "I won't ask you to promise anything."

"All right," said the president, "I will authorize you to try, and if you succeed, that's fine." Roosevelt said nothing about what would happen if she failed, but it was clear enough in the code of politics: Perkins would take the blame.

At this early stage of Perkins' idea-selling campaign, she did not seek her boss's commitment to her program—simply his "authorization." She avoided asking for resources, an agreement that Roosevelt would serve as an idea champion, or even a preliminary commitment. She knew that powerful people and groups passionately opposed social insurance of any kind, calling it wishful thinking, anti-American, and even communistic. As the story about Perkins' whispered conversation with Supreme Justice Harlan Stone (recounted above) indicated, some supporters worried that it might be unconstitutional. It was too soon for Roosevelt to approve an idea that had so many details yet to be specified. The time for formal endorsements and decisions would come later.

When the Social Security system finally came up for a vote in Congress in 1935, Perkins had done such a fine job selling the idea to the country that Roosevelt was happy to throw the full weight of his presidency behind it. The law, which passed by overwhelming majorities in both the House of Representatives and the Senate, went down in history as one of Roosevelt's signature accomplishments.

## A Word About Commitment and Conviction

As we conclude this chapter, we want to emphasize an important point that has been implicit throughout all the examples we have shared with you above—from Reed Hastings' discovery of the Netflix business model and Frances Perkins' campaign for her Social Security idea, to Nelson Mandela's strategy for easing the suffering of prisoners on Robben Island and Raj's lobbying to delay returning to his family's business. In all these examples, the persuaders brought an optimistic, energetic attitude to each influence encounter—even when, as in Mandela's case, the situation was unimaginably difficult and the odds of winning remote.

This is not a coincidence. President Lyndon B. Johnson once said, "What convinces is conviction." And Abraham Lincoln, in a eulogy to the great American orator, Henry Clay, stated that the secret of Clay's eloquence "did not consist, as many fine specimens of eloquence" do, in the "elegant arrangement of words and sentences; but rather of that deeply earnest and impassioned tone and manner, which can proceed only from great sincerity and a thorough conviction in the speaker of the justice and importance of his cause."

One of the reasons that we spent time at the beginning of this chapter showing you where ideas come from was to lay the foundation for what we will say here: people tend to believe you more when you yourself believe in what you are selling. By engaging in a thorough job of searching for, discovering, and shaping your idea, you will have a much better story to tell about it as you present it to others. It will be a story you can believe in and that very belief will help make you more persuasive.

We will be discussing credibility in more detail in the next chapter, but for now we will leave you with this important thought. The Art of Woo, as the name suggests, contains an important element of passion. As you develop your ideas, map your strategy, and set goals for each encounter, remember to bring your sense of purpose and persistence with you. These are qualities that will animate everything you say and do. And your audience's sixth sense will pick that up without even being aware of it and attend to your ideas more carefully.

## Conclusion

This chapter completes our look at Step 1 of the Woo process—*Survey Your Situation*. This stage requires you to:

- Develop your idea into a polished concept,

- Map the decision-making system, and

- Devise a stepping-stone strategy for your idea-selling campaign, determining whom to call on and in what order.

Finally, prior to each meeting or contact, you need to set specific persuasion goals related to getting input, gaining access, changing attitudes, obtaining authorizations, winning endorsements, making decisions, or achieving implementation. You also should think carefully about your own persuasion style to see if some adjustments might help you communicate more effectively as you move up the chain of command to the decision maker.

With all this effort, you might think your job is almost done. And many unskilled persuaders do, in fact, stop here. That is why so many good ideas fail to attract the attention they deserve and end up in the "reject" file.

When you see your idea from your own point of view, *you* get excited. But to sell an idea, you need to get other people just as excited as you are, and that requires you to see it from their perspectives. If you want to get your young kids enthused about the new car you are planning to buy, don't talk to them about the heated front seats. Talk about the DVD player in the back—where they will spend all their time.

The next three chapters will help you see the world as your counterpart sees it by introducing Step 2 of the process: *Confront the Five Barriers*. We start in chapter 4 with two personal factors that can be either showstoppers or turbochargers for any idea campaign: relationships and credibility. Subsequent chapters treat communication problems, contrary beliefs, and conflicting interests.

As you sit down to sell your idea, will other people be predisposed to listen to you or will they have doubts about you as they look across the table?

## chapter four

# Build Relationships and Credibility: Trust

I don't consider I have power. I have relationships.
—Lew Wasserman, CEO of MCA and Universal Studios

One can stand as the greatest orator the world has known,
possess the quickest mind, employ the cleverest psychology,
and have mastered all the technical devices of argument,
but if one is not credible, one might as well preach to the
pelicans.
—Gerry Spence, American super-lawyer

With your idea-selling strategy in hand, you are ready to move to the other side of the table. How will you and your initative look to other people? Step 2 of the Woo process helps you examine five potential barriers that may stand in your way—barriers that can become assets if you prepare well. They are: a lack of relationships, poor credibility, miscommunication, contrary beliefs, and conflicting interests. This chapter deals with the first two of these issues.

Let's get started by looking at the idea-selling strategies behind one of the greatest adventure stories of the early twentieth century: the race to make the first nonstop flight across the Atlantic. We recount this story in some detail because it illustrates both the importance of relationships and credibility in idea selling and provides an excellent review of the stepping-stone strategy we described in the last chapter.

## Lucky Lindy's Big Idea

In 1926, while flying the mail between St. Louis and Chicago, a twenty-four-year-old pilot named Charles Lindbergh decided to enter the race to be the first person to fly nonstop from New York to Paris and lay claim to the £25,000 Orteig Prize. Some of the world's greatest aviators were already in this race, including the famed Arctic explorer Admiral Richard E. Byrd and several World War I French flying aces. But Lindbergh figured his years as a stunt pilot and his experience navigating at night gave him a shot. He had just three problems: he had no plane, no money, and no supporters. To accomplish his goal, he laid out a meticulous idea-selling strategy that he describes in detail in his prize-winning book, *The Spirit of St. Louis.*

His first step was to locate a plane that could make the trip. Research led him to a prototype aircraft called the "Bellanca," a single-engine plane designed by an Italian named Giuseppe Bellanca and owned by New Jersey–based Wright Aeronautical Corporation. He liked the idea of a single-engine plane—it was simpler, lighter, and cheaper than the three-engine aircraft most people were considering for the flight. It also gave him a good reason to make the flight alone, which was the way he wanted to do it.

Lindbergh knew no one at Wright and no had contacts to provide an introduction. He had, in short, no relationships or credibility on which to build an approach. "I probably won't be very successful if I simply go to the Wright Corporation and say I want to use a Bellanca airplane for a flight to Paris," he mused. "Aviation is full of promoters and people looking for a job." He therefore resolved to recruit a group of "men with both influence and money" to back him. That way he could approach Wright as the leader of a group that "intends to purchase an airplane" rather than as an unknown pilot trying to persuade Wright to hire him and enter the New York-to-Paris race.

The first person he called was Earl Thompson, a St. Louis insurance executive whom he had taught to fly. Figuring he would have trouble trying to "sell [Thompson] a flight across the ocean [while he was sitting] at an office desk," Lindbergh arranged to meet him at his home after dinner one evening. The cautious Thompson was encouraging, but he was nervous about "the idea of a single engine out over the ocean."

Lindbergh found his first true supporter at his next meeting—with a man who owned St. Louis's airport, Major Charles Lambert. Lambert was a pioneer himself, having first flown with Orville Wright. Unlike Thompson, Lambert appreciated the elegance of Lindbergh's one-engine, one-pilot solution and offered to back him with one thousand dollars, provided he could attract other supporters.

Lindbergh then called on his airmail boss, Bill Robertson. The first thing he did was tell Robertson that Major Lambert had pledged a thousand dollars to the effort. His boss was properly impressed. "Say, you're lucky to get Major Lambert interested," Robertson said. He agreed that Lindbergh could say Robertson Aircraft Corporation was a backer, giving Lindbergh his first corporate sponsor.

With the beginnings of a group in place, he was ready to approach Wright Aeronautical. His choice of contact medium was interesting: a long-distance telephone call. "A long-distance call would carry a prestige which no letter or telegram, signed by an unknown pilot, could possibly have," he concluded. The strategy worked—he was put through to a senior Wright executive and given an immediate appointment as the "representative" of a St. Louis group interested in buying the Bellanca for this historic flight.

A few weeks later, dressed in a tailor-made suit that had cost him a month's wages, he showed up at Wright's headquarters in Paterson, New Jersey. And once there, he was introduced to Giuseppe Bellanca, who became increasingly excited by the idea of using his plane to cross the Atlantic. No commitments were made, but Lindbergh was finding new stepping-stones at each stage of his journey.

Back in St. Louis with a fresh story to tell about his contacts with Mr. Bellanca, he got Harry Knight, the president of the St. Louis Flying Club, on his team. And Knight put him in touch with the most well-connected businessman in town: Harold Bixby, the head of the St. Louis Chamber of Commerce. Bixby was the key backer Lindbergh had been looking for. As someone who was always on the lookout for ways to promote the city, Bixby immediately saw the potential for this flight to put St. Louis on the map as a leader in aviation and innovation. It was Bixby who came up with the rah-rah name for Lindbergh's plane—*The Spirit of St. Louis*—even before Lindbergh had acquired an aircraft, and it was Bixby who took care of raising the money needed for the project. By the time Lindbergh started negotiating in earnest to buy the Bellanca, he was the head of a well-heeled and enthusiastic St. Louis syndicate. He now had resources and supporters. All he needed was the plane.

## A Look at Lindbergh's Strategy

Let's stop the story here for a moment to examine what has gotten Lindbergh this far. He started with nothing but an idea. Now he has the most important men in St. Louis behind him and he is about to open negotiations with a top aircraft designer to buy a high-performance plane.

Lindbergh's success began with his awareness that he had a credibility problem. He could fly as well as anyone alive—but few people would take him seriously as a candidate for winning the Orteig Prize. He was just an unknown mail pilot from the Midwest.

Lindbergh's dilemma illustrates a fundamental characteristic of credibility: It is not something you *have*, like flying skill or courage. Rather, credibility is something other people *bestow*, like friendship. It is a perception in your audience's mind regarding your decision-making authority, competence, expertise, trustworthiness, or character. You don't have to know people firsthand for them to endow you with credibility. As Lindbergh's story shows, your reputation or the reputations of people with whom you associate can be enough to trigger the necessary perceptions of credibility. We will delve into the foundations for credibility later in this chapter.

Lindbergh's need for credibility thrust the issue of relationships front and center. He started building his team of backers by approaching people he knew from his job as a mail pilot—a man he had taught to fly, the owner of his company's airport, and his boss. These were all Peripheral Players (see chapter 3) within the greater St. Louis community, but they led him to Harry Knight, a Boundary Spanner between the people who liked to fly and the local business community. And Knight put him in touch with the keystone for the entire project, Chamber of Commerce president Harold Bixby. With Bixby on his team, Lindbergh acquired both credibility and relationships. His project was launched.

## Back to St. Louis

Lindbergh had done a great job of setting up his syndicate, but he never closed on his purchase of the Bellanca. After an exchange of telegrams with the Bellanca's new owners—a company called Columbia Aircraft Company—Columbia offered to sell the plane for £15,000. As Lindbergh put his check for that amount on a conference table in the Woolworth Building in New York, Columbia's CEO, Charlie Levine, put a last-minute demand next to it.

Levine insisted on picking his own pilot for the flight.

"You understand we cannot let just anybody pilot our airplane across the ocean," Levine said. "We would select a good crew. Your organization in St. Louis would have all the credit for the flight, all the publicity."

It was his credibility problem again. Lindbergh picked up his check and walked away. When he returned to St. Louis, he was so discouraged he tried to talk Bixby and Knight into switching the team's focus to a record-breaking distance flight over the Pacific. But his St. Louis backers had seen firsthand just how good a pilot and how determined a person Lindbergh was. "Let's stay with the Paris flight," Bixby said. "We're not whipped yet." Within a few weeks, a California company named Ryan Air, as unknown to the world as Lindbergh was, agreed to build a custom-made plane for Lindbergh for £10,000, and it was this plane that Lindbergh eventually flew.

And what became of Columbia's Charlie Levine? He decided to enter the race to cross the Atlantic using the Bellanca aircraft refitted with two seats and renamed the *Columbia*. Levine's plane and crew were at Roosevelt Field in New York on May 16, 1927, the day Lindbergh took off for Paris. But as *The Spirit of St. Louis* disappeared into the morning mist that day, Levine and his group were in their hangar bickering over who should fly their plane. Levine had hired two pilots and then refused to name his choice between them so "both boys would have their heart in their work right up to the last moment." Giuseppe Bellanca, weary of Levine's self-promotion and egotism, was ready to quit—and Levine's navigator, Bert Acosta, had defected to a third crew led by polar explorer Admiral Byrd. As one press account put it, "tension and uncertainty" reigned.

The *Columbia* finally got off the ground on June 4 with Clarence Chamberlin as the pilot and Levine himself as a passenger, and it became the second plane to make the nonstop flight. Ironically, as it made its way across the Atlantic, the *Columbia* passed directly over the U.S. cruiser *Memphis,* which was carrying Lindbergh back to New York for his ticker-tape parade.

## Summing Up

Looking back on this story, it is easy to see how relationships and credibility fit together in an idea-selling process. Lindbergh's need for credibility drove him to recruit his backers; his skills at forming relationships allowed him to put his group together; and those same relationships sustained him through the tough days when he had to build his own plane from scratch.

Levine, by contrast, ignored the relationship factor entirely, setting his crew members against one another and making himself and his ego the primary objects of everyone's attention. As a man of means and power, he did not need to worry much about his credibility—but no idea as complex as organizing the first flight across the Atlantic can be done alone. Levine's egotism and erratic behavior cost him a date with history.

## Above All, Honor Your Relationships

Managing relationships is a fundamental skill in business, so it is no surprise this skill plays a crucial role in selling ideas. Relationships give people a level of trust and confidence in each other, facilitating communication and making it easier to cooperate. Each time you sit down to talk with people in a working context—even with people you know well—it helps to take a few moments to establish—or reestablish—rapport, find out how your counterpart is doing, and reinforce the common interests or experiences that make your relationship work. People respond well to—and remember—others who take an interest in them, especially when there is no obvious strategic benefit that flows from that interaction.

Andrew Carnegie once described Abraham Lincoln's gift for creating relationships with virtually everyone he met. Carnegie was in charge of the railroads during the Civil War and Lincoln "would occasionally come to [my] office and sit at a desk awaiting replies to telegrams, or perhaps merely anxious for information." Carnegie went on to note that "[Lincoln's] manners were perfect because natural; and he had a kind word for everybody, even the youngest boy in the office. His attentions were not graduated. They were the same to all, as deferential in talking to a messenger boy as to Secretary [of State] Seward. His charm lay in the total absence of manner. It was not so much perhaps what he said as the way in which he said it that never failed to win one. . . . I never met a man who so thoroughly made himself one with all men as Mr. Lincoln."

Carnegie himself learned the importance of developing relationships through day-to-day interactions at a very early age. When he was a teenager, Carnegie worked as a messenger for a telegraph company in Pittsburgh, and he delivered telegrams to many of the city's leading businessmen. To advance his career, he made a conscious effort to memorize all their names so that he could acknowledge them when he saw them on the street. In his autobiography, Carnegie elevated this activity to the level of a principle: "Slight attentions . . . often bring back reward as great as it is unlooked for. No kind action is ever lost. Even to this day I occasionally meet men whom I had forgotten, who recall some trifling attention I have been able to pay them." A business epigram sums up this idea quite simply: "No salesman ever went broke who knew the names of his customers' kids."

Three well-researched social psychological foundations form the basis for the relationships both Lincoln and Carnegie were so skilled at building: similarity, liking, and reciprocity. Add these three ingredients to a history of positive interactions between two people and you get a crucial idea-selling asset: trust.

### Similarity and Liking

Selling ideas to colleagues is seldom the same as conventional salesmanship. But in the area of relationships, there are common features.

First, face time matters. The more you work with people, the more familiar they become with you, laying the groundwork for functioning relationships. In a 1987 experiment, R. F. Bornstein and two other psychologists demonstrated the connection between recognizing faces and feeling positive emotions. They flashed the faces of several people on a screen so quickly that subjects were not even aware of seeing them. Later, when the subjects were given time to examine photographs of the faces they had seen, no one could recall any of them. Yet in subsequent face-to-face encounters with the subjects, those people whose images had been flashed most often were rated as the most likable. Moreover, the subjects sided with these "likable people" more often when the experimenter staged disagreements between them and other people the subjects had never seen.

In addition to familiarity, a second trigger for the liking response is a perception of similarity between two people. As we noted in chapter 2, a University of Chicago study on life insurance sales found that the most reliable predictor of success in making a sale—trumping product knowledge, the need for insurance, and even the agent's speaking ability—was the level of personal rapport the agent established with the prospect based on the discovery of shared opinions, background facts, tastes, affiliations, and lifestyle choices. A couple of examples will illustrate how this works.

Steve Ross, founder of the Time Warner media empire, once sold the president of Atlantic Records, Ahmet Ertegun, on a deal using a similarity-based gambit. Ross knew very little about rock-and-roll, but one day his son mentioned a new group that Atlantic Records had put together called Blind Faith, featuring Stevie Winwood and some former members of a group called Cream. A colleague later remarked that Blind Faith had recently sold out Madison Square Garden without even releasing a record.

The day after Ross heard these stories, he was having dinner with Ertegun and getting nowhere with his deal. Ertegun thought Time Warner would be a poor choice as a partner because so few people there knew anything about pop music and culture. As the story goes, Ertegun started to say, "I have this new group, Blind Faith . . ."

Ross jumped in: "You mean the guys from the old Cream and Stevie Winwood, and they just sold out Madison Square Garden without cutting a record?"

"Yeah, man, you got it!" Ertegun said excitedly.

That broke the ice, and the two men went on to form an alliance.

Even something as elusive as personal style can be enough to strike a chord of similarity. Early in his battle to get a casino license in Atlantic City, real estate mogul Donald Trump decided he needed to hire a local lawyer to help him drive through his application. A young man named Nick Ribis was recommended to him by several well-placed media people in New York. Ribis won Trump over in their opening conversation by showing he could match Trump, ego for ego.

"Look," said Trump after being introduced to Ribis, "I'm not sure a lawyer as young as you are can handle a big project like this."

Nick did not miss a beat. "To tell you the truth, Mr. Trump, I've never had a client as young as you who could afford my bill."

The two men immediately hit it off and worked closely on a successful legal strategy to get the casino license.

Familiarity, similarity, and liking should not be overrated: few people will buy a high-risk idea from you just because you have the office next door or you both went to the same college. Indeed, if the only thing you bring to the table is a smooth ability to establish social rapport, you will probably be seen as a lightweight in terms of your ideas. A down-home American phrase from the Old West—"all hat, no cattle"—sums up the problem with people who excel at social interactions but have no real substance.

Nevertheless, a lack of attention to rapport creates needless barriers to persuasion. Playboy founder Hugh Hefner was once denied a liquor license for one of his clubs in New Jersey because state officials believed he had offered bribes to obtain one in Manhattan. Hefner made the trip to the state capital at Trenton to plead his case that the allegations were false. He failed to make a sale because he showed up at the hearing as a caricature of himself—smoking a pipe, wearing a silk suit and shirt, and escorting one of his famous Playboy bunnies. No one in the state government wanted to be seen anywhere near him.

Lessons? Develop the habit of using similarity and liking to build goodwill with people—especially when you do not need to do it. And avoid creating needless barriers to persuasion by indulging your ego and alienating your audience.

### Reciprocity

This brings us to a third, independent basis for working relationships: reciprocity. Relationships in the working world come in many forms, some closer than others. As networking guru, popular author, and entrepreneur Harvey Mackay has stated, "A network [relationship] is not a love-in; it is a relationship formed to meet the needs of both parties on an ongoing basis." Thus, assuming you can establish and maintain a degree of civility and rapport, you can create perfectly functional, working relationships based on mutual exchanges without a great deal of personal liking. Indeed, exchange-based relationships probably play a more consistently important role in the process of selling ideas than do relationships based on genuine forms of personal liking. One of the most famous studies in modern sociology, titled "The Strength of Weak Ties," by Professor Mark Granovetter of Stanford, showed that people looking for jobs found them more often through loose networks of relatively weak, reciprocity-based relationships than through either advertisements or close friends and family. In China, one's reciprocity network has a special name: *guanxi*. It is considered one of the most important assets a person has.

The norm of reciprocity is one of the most robust social psychological norms in human society. Put in its simplest terms, reciprocity means that we tend to do things for other people who do things for us. Reciprocity can be observed at the bargaining table when people take turns making concessions and exchanging information. In selling ideas, the most common form of reciprocity consists of relationships based on reciprocal obligations. Students of office politics even speak of "favour banks"—obligations you can store up within a social network by doing things for others and then calling in these favours at opportune times. Reciprocity can also take the form of mutual exchanges of resources, services, emotional support, status, and information.

In banking and professional services markets, for example, Professor Brian Uzzi of Northwestern University's Kellogg School has shown that business customers with personal connections to bankers pay lower interest rates on loans than do customers who lack these contacts. And similar studies of French banks have reached identical results. The same pattern holds for corporate leaders who have continuing ties to senior members of law firms and receive billing discounts more often than do people without such ties.

A study of Silicon Valley in California concluded that "social embeddedness" between entrepreneurs and venture capitalists—that is, extensive participation in social and business events by people in these two worlds—was the key to being successful in that area's high-tech economy. One venture capitalist observed: "When analyzing an investment project, I give great importance to the quality of entrepreneurs. I mobilize my networks to obtain, informally, information on their personality, their past, their experiences. . . ." And if such information is not forthcoming, he continued, "I prefer to back off from investing . . . [because it] constitutes too big a risk."

Reciprocal relationships even dominate in the seemingly impersonal options and commodities markets. A student of ours did a study while working as an intern at a commodities trading firm. As one of his contacts told him: "This is a people business. If you make a couple of good trades but totally piss everyone off, it's hard for you to last, because no one wants to deal with guys who just sit there and wait to pick them off." In exchange for giving the other side price breaks, traders receive access to deals and other favours.

Finally, as the Lindbergh story shows, you can benefit from the reciprocity system even when nobody owes you any personal favours. All you need are allies and champions who are willing to use their networks and associated reciprocity systems to advance your cause.

### Relationship Levels

Selling ideas almost always involves continuous, ongoing relationships. There are few "one shot" deals within organizations; every move you make leaves a trace—for better or for worse. And your actions will affect not only the perceptions of the people you deal with directly but also everyone they communicate with inside their own networks.

A recent study of supervisory relationships in different work settings identified three distinctive relationship modes: Rapport-Level, Reciprocity-Level, and Trust-Level. The most casual relationships at work depend on the "surface similarity" between people—such things as gender, common experience, shared background, or group memberships that people use to break the ice and establish rapport. Relationships can stay at this amiable, rapport-based level for a long time if job requirements make no further demands on them.

Success at Rapport-Level relationships often depends on minute attention to social cues such as acknowledging people, holding doors, and so on. A little rudeness directed at someone you do not know well can be very costly whereas a little kindness can, as Andrew Carnegie noted above, be remembered for years.

Abraham Lincoln's habit of treating everyone he met as an equal meant that almost all his Rapport-Level encounters created goodwill. And Charles Lindbergh's elaborate preparations for his first approach to the Wright Aeronautical company—his expensive new suit and telephone call—illustrate the kinds of things idea sellers do when they are trying to woo someone by creating a good impression.

Reciprocity-Level relationships push past initial impressions and stereotypes to actual, observed behavior. When people work together on something, they have a chance to measure reliability, conscientiousness, and competence. The surface characteristics that drew their attention in the early stages of the relationship fade into the background and people's conduct pushes into the foreground to form the basis for judgments and perceptions. When the Silicon Valley venture capitalist quoted above uses his social network to acquire information about an entrepreneur, part of what he is seeking is reciprocity data: is the person a reliable partner in his or her business dealings?

The third and final level for working relationships—Trust-Level—is the most committed of the three. This arises when people have gathered enough information about, and personal experience with, someone to form solid beliefs about that person's character, motives, and traits as a person. For example, by the time Charles Lindbergh became discouraged and wanted to drop out of the transatlantic race, his backers,

Knight and Bixby, had seen enough of him in action to trust that he would find a way to win, whatever the obstacle. They had formed fixed, positive impressions of Lindbergh's character and perseverance.

People in Trust-Level relationships no longer have to prove themselves to each other. In fact, they tend to give each other the benefit of the doubt. Trust is thus harder to break even when someone does not perform as expected. A failure to deliver on a promise, which would tip over a Reciprocity-Level relationship, is more likely to be excused by people who genuinely trust each other.

The differences between Trust-Level working relationships and genuine personal friendships are difficult to define—and the research does not explore these differences. Suffice it to say that we think you can have a Trust-Level working relationship with someone without necessarily including them on your short list of close friends. Different people probably have different capacities for folding Trust-Level working relationships into their personal lives.

To summarize: successful idea selling begins and ends with your ability to establish, maintain, and deepen your connections with people. When meeting people for the first time, Rapport-Level skills are critical. In activating a network to gain information and access, Reciprocity-Level relationships will play a big part. And in the toughest situations— when a conflict develops over the idea or implementation problems loom—Trust-Level relationships will be needed to get you over the hump.

As you survey your idea-selling strategy, therefore, make a note of the relationship levels you enjoy with each of the people you need to influence. And take whatever steps you can to improve those relationships before setting your strategy in motion. Your Reciprocity- and Trust-Level relationships will usually provide the best platforms for opening the doors to new relationship opportunities. And as the process unfolds, some of those new Rapport-Level connections will deepen into relationships characterized by reciprocity and trust.

### *Relationship Builders: E-mail, Phone, or Face-to-Face?*

In the world of electronic communication, you have a dizzying number of choices for building relationships. When should you use e-mail or instant messaging? Is the phone "high-touch" enough? We are often asked to suggest rules of thumb for deciding on the appropriate mediums for persuasion. We have a simple answer: when practicing the Art of Woo, there is no substitute for meeting face-to-face. Lindbergh used his telephone call to make a good first impression on the executives at Wright Aeronautical Corporation. But his goal was to arrange a meeting. Technology may have changed since then, but the need to sit down with people has not.

Let's look at a brief story about Time Warner CEO Richard Parsons for another example of the difference meetings can make.

In 2005, legendary corporate raider Carl Icahn, a major Time Warner stockholder, set his sights on Parsons, holding him personally responsible for the firm's sagging stock price. At the time of the media giant's merger with AOL, four years earlier, the market value of the combined companies was two hundred billion dollars. It had plummeted to less than half that amount when Icahn started making his moves. He hatched a scheme to overhaul the board and break up what the *New York Times* had described as the "worst merger in business history." His first goal was to get rid of Parsons.

Parsons, of course, had other ideas. When he got wind of Icahn's intentions, he set to work researching everything he could find out about the man. Then he did something that most corporate leaders under such a threat would never dream of doing: he walked the three blocks between Time Warner's New York headquarters and Icahn's office and asked Icahn to explain his position in person.

"We parted amicably," said Parsons about this conversation. Icahn, known for an aggressive, take-no-prisoners style, had a different take on the meeting. As Parsons was getting ready to leave, Icahn told him: "I can't be responsible if this gets ugly."

But the meeting with Parsons gave Icahn some things to think about. He got a firsthand look at why Parsons is considered one of the most politically savvy, relationship-oriented CEOs in America. And he began to see that Parsons and he shared a common goal— enhancing shareholder value. This did not stop him from waging a public war to get Parsons removed, but it gave him a hint as to why Parsons's board and Time Warner's other major investors were very likely to stand solidly behind their chief.

After several subsequent face-to-face meetings, Icahn had to admit that Parsons had his charms. "I got to like the guy after meeting him a few times. He legitimately and honestly is trying to enhance value," he commented—almost in spite of himself. And Icahn eventually concluded that Parsons had too much credibility with investors for Icahn to dislodge him. Icahn dropped his takeover attempt.

As the Parsons-Icahn story suggests, face-to-face, informal meetings provide the widest bandwidth for interpersonal communication. Such settings enable people to catch nonverbal cues such as voice tone, body language, and emotional emphasis and get immediate feedback from their listeners. And when, like Parsons, you are looking to truly understand another person's point of view in a tense situation or, like Lindbergh, trying to build important relationships with key people in a stepping-stone strategy, there is simply no substitute for sitting down with them.

This is bad news because in today's multitasking world, where communication has accelerated to a blinding pace, convenience usually trumps judgment when it comes to developing relationships. E-mail is particularly tempting—and dangerous—in this regard.

For example, recall the example we gave in chapter 1 of the employee who sent an e-mail requesting a raise and ended up getting fired after his request was circulated much more widely than he had anticipated. Consider also the sad tale of Canadian economist Pierre Lemieux. Lemieux once e-mailed a noted colleague, inviting him to join a research group. When Lemieux received an unenthusiastic reply, he forwarded it to another colleague with the comment, "Look at what this S.O.B. thinks." In his haste, Lemieux hit the wrong "send" button, and his S.O.B. comment went directly back to his noted colleague. Lemieux apologized, but he acknowledged that the "professional friendship took a hit." A careless "click" had cost him influence with a key person in his network.

When you want to build a relationship with an important person in an idea-selling campaign, take the time to meet face-to-face. If conflicting schedules or distances make this impossible, spend some time composing a careful message. Research shows that e-mail messages are more likely to be successful if you personalize your note and build some rapport, forecast the agenda, and then get to the heart of your communication. Finally, don't send until you reread your message and edit it with an eye to how it will be seen when received. All this may take a few more minutes to do, but it will pay large dividends over time in terms of your working relationships.

And be careful about the "reply" button.

We will return to the question of communication mediums in chapter 7, when we discuss the best way to pitch an idea.

## Credibility: Now You Have It, Now You Don't

As Lindbergh's story shows, relationships can do more for you than simply ease communication and access. They can also be sources of credibility. By associating yourself with people and institutions known and respected by your audience, the audience will be inclined to listen to what you have to say.

But credibility by association can take you only so far. In the end, credibility derives mainly from what an audience thinks about *your own* actions and reputation. In this section, therefore, we will take a deeper look at this critical variable.

Most experts agree that credibility comes down to audience perceptions of three key things: competence, expertise, and trustworthiness. Thus, your credibility resides *in your audience's mind* rather than in your objective credentials or skills. This means it is especially fragile. You can lose it in a single moment of poor judgment, miscalculation, or misconduct.

Near the end of World War II, there were few people with more credibility in the world than British Prime Minister Winston Churchill. Yet he lost an election before the war with Japan was over. How did this happen?

With members of his Conservative Party banking on Churchill's overwhelming popularity, an election was called just after the Allies defeated Germany. But in the heat of the campaign, Churchill gave a speech in which he warned that his Socialist opponents would use "Gestapo" tactics to carry out their nationalization programs. The reference to the Gestapo instantly cost Churchill his credibility. People who had revered him as a wartime leader now saw him as out of sync with the new peacetime situation. It would be years before Churchill would once again regain his leading place in British politics.

Below, we will look at each of the three platforms on which you can build credibility in an idea-selling campaign.

### Credibility Platform Number 1: Demonstrated Competence

One of the most common ways to build credibility in work settings is to demonstrate a proven track record for competence and reliability in the domain of your idea. If your audience knows you are a top performer, all kinds of obstacles dissolve.

When Sony Corporation founder Akio Morita first broached the idea of setting up a stand-alone company in the United States—to be called Sony Corporation of America—his board back in Tokyo was skeptical. But his proven track record, Morita later wrote, put the burden on his board to "come up with very good reasons why we shouldn't do it." When they could not, "My colleagues in Tokyo decided that since I knew the American scene best, they would leave it up to me."

The high-tech giant Intel was formed one day in 1968 in a suburban front yard near Palo Alto, California. One of Intel's founders, Bob Noyce, was mowing his lawn and talking in animated tones with his friend Gordon Moore. Something clicked between the two men—both of whom were senior executives at nearby Fairchild Semiconductor—and they decided to actually do something they had long dreamed and talked about: start their own company. Moore, who was the top man in Fairchild's research and development department, agreed to handle the product side of the new business. And Noyce, a veteran negotiator who had spearheaded the deal that put Fairchild on the map, would go get the money.

As Tim Jackson, author of *Inside Intel,* tells the story, Noyce got his half of the job done with just one phone call. He contacted a venture financing guru named Arthur Rock, a man he knew well from past deals and with whom he hiked and camped. In relationship terms, these two men enjoyed a Trust-Level connection.

As Rock would later recall, "Bob [Noyce] just called me on the phone. We'd been friends for a long time . . . Documents? There was practically nothing. Noyce's reputation was good enough. We put out a page-and-a-half little circular, but I'd raised the money even before people saw it." That day, Rock called fifteen people and got fifteen backers for Intel, including Noyce's alma mater, Grinnell College in Iowa (whose investment adviser was Warren Buffett of Omaha, Nebraska). The combination of Noyce's and Moore's track records and Rock's contact list was unbeatable. Just like that, Intel had the roughly £4.5 million in seed capital it needed—and was on its way to earning its shareholders many billions in return.

### Credibility Platform Number 2: Expertise

Expertise is a credibility cousin to competence. When you are asking someone to believe your facts on a technical matter, your credibility depends on being seen as an expert, someone who has thoroughly done his or her homework. Whereas people will give you competence-based credibility when they think you have accomplished something worthy, they will give you expertise-based credibility when they think you have a specialized area of knowledge.

If you are respected enough, your expertise can overcome even the most socially awkward presentation styles. One of the greatest thinkers of the modern era, the Scottish philosopher Adam Smith—author of *The Wealth of Nations*—was seen by his contemporaries as one of the most boring presenters of his age. Samuel Johnson is reported to have called him "as dull a dog as he ever met with." He was, according to accounts, a "scrawny and bucktoothed" hypochondriac who could become so distracted by his own arguments that he once fell into a tanners' pit while lecturing on economics during a tour of a Glasgow factory. But Smith never lacked for credibility. His ideas circulated widely in his own day and continue to form the foundation for modern capitalism.

On the other hand, no matter how slick your presentation slides, you will lose your audience if you show a lack of expertise. When John Scully moved from a top position at Pepsi, where he was a marketing expert, to help Steve Jobs lead Apple Computer in the 1980s, he created immediate credibility problems for himself by failing to study up on Apple's technology before engaging with the staff. In one of the first meetings Scully attended after joining the firm, a business manager named Peter Kavanaugh asked Scully what he planned to do about the "connectivity" problem—the issue of how desktop computers could be linked to one another. As Kavanaugh later told the story, Scully leaned over to an aide and asked, "What is connectivity?" From that moment, Scully had problems being taken seriously within Apple's high-tech culture.

When it comes to data, your credibility will depend on the reliability of the sources you cite for evidence as well as your own expertise. Thus, each time you present an idea, you should find an appropriate opportunity to refer to well-established authorities in your domain and demonstrate that you have done your research. And you should try to find out what sources *your audience* considers reliable. You may consider the statistics from the World Bank to be the last word on your topic, but if the audience does not agree, you had better find other sources.

Attachments showing your complete data set and analysis can also send the message that you have thoroughly prepared your case. Even if people never look at your data, such attachments send the message that you did the required background work, allowing you to get to the more interesting and original parts of your idea.

### Credibility Platform Number 3: Trustworthiness

Success guru Stephen Covey says that trust is "the one thing that changes everything." With it, almost any business difficulty can be overcome. Without it, you have a hard time getting anything significant done. We agree. But we think a couple of points are worth making about this, one of your most vital personal assets.

First, trust comes in small, medium, and large amounts. A little trust is a lot better than no trust at all. By showing reliability and integrity in everything you do—not just the obvious things when everyone is watching—you build the foundations for people who do not know you well to trust you a little bit. And that forms the basis on which you can build more trust as they get to know you better.

Second, perceptions of trustworthiness come in many forms. For example, when you are selling an idea from a position of authority, it helps if those under you perceive that you are wielding your authority *legitimately*—that is, that you are working in the best interests of the organization, not to aggrandize yourself. In a recent study of fifteen legendary business leaders of the past twenty years—people from GE's Jack Welsh and IBM's Lou Gerstner to Microsoft's Bill Gates—researchers discovered that the top skill shared by them was an ability, despite their strong wills and outsize egos, to convince others that corporate interests always came ahead of everyone's personal agendas, including their own.

Aristotle once said that "a just ruler seems to make nothing out of his office . . . [but rather] he labours for others." This means that your credibility goes up when you keep the focus on the problem rather than on such things as who will get credit for solving it. This attitude encourages others to participate and helps them get behind your idea.

An interesting example of gaining and using this type of credibility comes from the aircraft industry. It is a story of how a program manager took an aircraft-building program from being near cancellation to winning one of the nation's top prizes for quality—the Baldrige Award.

In 1993, a McDonnell Douglas plant in California that produced the Air Force's giant C-17 cargo plane was in disarray. Production was behind schedule, quality was poor, and costs were up. The Air Force gave the company an ultimatum: fix the program or close the plant.

There were ten thousand people involved in this program, and a man named Don Kozlowski (called "Koz" by his team) stepped up to take on the challenge of fixing the problem. As the program leader, he had the positional authority to implement just about any idea he could come up with. But in an organization this size with a product this complicated, it takes more than orders to get people moving in the same direction. Moreover, it was not at all clear what kind of intervention would solve a problem that had this many moving parts.

The more Koz studied the problem, the more he came to the conclusion that the issue lay in the production process itself. Inside the giant hangars where the planes were constructed, each one moved through a series of "positions"—similar to the assembly line of an automobile plant but on a much grander scale. The schedule was key. To keep the production process working, with its thousands of parts arriving and its thousands of workers putting these parts into each plane, the aircraft frames had to keep moving from one position to another—on time—or the entire system would go into gridlock.

But the system had been gradually falling apart until it had stopped working. When parts arrived late, as they did increasingly, they had to be put into place at the very end of the assembly line—a process that sometimes involved taking whole sections of the plane apart and putting it back together again. When sloppy work was discovered down the line, that work had to be fixed at the end of the entire process, too.

Koz's idea was to fix the planes by fixing the process for producing them. He stood up one day at a meeting of top managers in the plant and announced that, from that day forward, the workers would "hold the aircraft" in position until all the work for that position was done and done right. In the past, the plant priorities had been "schedule first and quality second," but from now on they would be "quality first and schedule second." According to plant quality manager Debbie Collard, whom we interviewed for this book, "some people thought he was crazy." They feared that a plane this complex simply could not be built this way.

But the plan worked. Why? As Collard told us, Koz "was the leader of the program and had been in that position for a while. He had worked closely not only with his leadership team, but also with people at all levels in the organization, and was especially known for listening to input and advice from people on the shop floor. So he had total credibility at all levels at the time he made the decision that no out-of-position work would be done. Had he *not* had that credibility, it wouldn't have worked."

In other words, Koz had taken the time to develop relationships and establish credibility *before* he had to give this order. When he did give it, therefore, the order was not seen as arbitrary or officious. Instead, everyone at the plant believed that Koz was doing this for one and only one reason: to save their jobs. They pulled together behind him to make it work.

In addition, Koz's intimate knowledge of how the people below him did their work gave him an insight into the most effective way to communicate his idea. He chose to issue a plain, easy-to-grasp command—backed with complete conviction—and then did not budge from his position. Koz's new reference point—the stationary plane—galvanized a whole series of changes. The procurement department jumped to the phones and started bargaining hard with suppliers to get the parts to the plant floor on time. The workers, knowing that each bolt, no matter how small, could hold up the whole line if it was not screwed in right, started paying much closer attention to what they were doing. Inspectors looked over their work with relentless attention.

By the time Koz moved on to his next job in 1997, the C-17s produced at his plant were defect-free, under budget, and delivered to the Air Force on time. In 1998, the program—now a part of Boeing—won the Malcolm Baldrige National Quality Award from the National Institute of Standards and Technology.

Koz's story illustrates a key element of credibility when you sell an idea from a leadership position: you need to bend over backward to protect people's "feeling of importance" as you exercise authority. As Dale Carnegie pointed out in his classic *How to Win Friends and Influence People*, the need to feel important is one of the most powerful desires people have. When you use your authority to give an order or command in a way that ignores these feelings, people will respond with resentment, if not anger. Super-lawyer Gerry Spence puts it this way: "Power is like a pistol with barrels that point in both directions. When one with power pulls the trigger against someone with lesser power, one barrel fires in the direction of the intended victim while the other fires into the person who has pulled the trigger."

The secret of using authority to push new initiatives through a complex organization, therefore, often resides in combining tact, self-conscious relationship building, and firm commitment so that those lower in the organization buy the idea without feeling disenfranchised. Credibility comes from combining your formal position with perceptions of trustworthiness and legitimacy.

Initial impressions count for a great deal when it comes to trustworthiness, which helps explain why leaders pay such close attention to their first substantive moves in new positions and entire books are written to advise them on successfully managing their "first hundred days" in a new job. Research on how reputations spread within organizations has shown that people are much quicker to spread negative stories about breaches of trust than they are negative stories about someone's job skills. And research on the Internet auction site eBay shows that the first handful of ratings a new seller receives from buyers establishes the seller's reputation for trustworthiness. If those initial ratings are good, the seller gets business; if bad, the seller has a permanent problem.

Outside of leadership contexts, perceptions of trustworthiness often arise from the *consistency between what you say and what you do*. If you are implementing a cost-cutting initiative, you had better stop staying in four-star hotels and flying first class yourself before you start enforcing the rules on others. If you are trying to persuade your child to stop smoking, start by throwing away your own cigarettes. When you give advice, in short, you need to "walk the talk." The slightest hint of hypocrisy creates a distinctive "reject the message because of the messenger" effect.

Who has success on the motivational speaker circuit? Sports coaches who have won championships, blind people, accident survivors, war veterans, victims of personal tragedies, and mountain climbers who suffered near-death experiences. What do people like these have in common? They have personal stories that closely match the message they deliver. They are living examples of the "never say die" and "every day's a new day" mental attitudes they preach. And there is a reason these speakers often get paid outsize fees: a personalized message can carry a big motivational punch because the speaker has credibility.

Gerry Spence once wrote: "How often have we seen a child win an argument with simple language that innocently reveals the truth? We see everyday people win great encounters because they were believed. They offered no pretensions, no phony veneers of style. They made no attempt to charm or manipulate. We had the sense that what we saw was what we got, the real person with all of the blemishes— but real."

We will look at the power of first-person narratives and emotional honesty in more detail in chapter 8 when we discuss how to make your idea pitch memorable. But for now, let's just say that if you bring the power of trustworthiness to your encounters, you are sure to make many idea sales.

## Conclusion

In this chapter we introduced the first two of the five potential barriers that you must confront and overcome in the idea-selling process: relationships and credibility. With these obstacles in mind, we can see exactly what challenges Charles Lindbergh faced in his idea-selling campaign.

He started with a big idea—flying solo in a single-engine plane across the Atlantic Ocean. It was something so outrageous in terms of the conventional wisdom that he was sure to encounter a credibility problem.

He also began with only a few working relationships, mainly people he knew through his job as a mail pilot. His ability to inspire people and get them to like and trust him, however, served him well. His stepping-stone strategy and the deepening of his existing relationships into firmly committed, Trust-Level connections helped him put together a loyal and efficient team.

Lindbergh's credibility was built on all three platforms. His backers saw him as trustworthy, competent, and an expert in his domain. He did not enjoy this same level of credibility with Charles Levine and the New York crowd, so he had to go his own way, by designing and building *The Spirit of St. Louis* with an unknown aircraft company.

In the end, Lindbergh won the race across the Atlantic not because he had the best plane or because he was the best pilot. The fact that Levine crossed the same ocean a few weeks after Lindbergh showed that the actual flying part of the adventure was not its most difficult aspect. Lindbergh won because he and his team were able, through the strength of their relationships, to execute their plan better than his rivals could execute theirs. They had more Woo.

In the next chapter, we turn to the next two barriers that can block even the best of ideas: communication mismatches and entrenched, hostile beliefs. As you try to get inside the hearts and minds of the people across the table, you must speak their language and, if at all possible, avoid violating their core values. Get ready to meet a modern master of the Art of Woo: Bono—U2 lead singer, activist, and social entrepreneur. He will show us how to avoid both pitfalls.

## chapter five

# Respect Their Beliefs:
# A Common Language

The secret of effective persuasion comes in knowing the
heart of the person you wish to persuade and ordering your
words to fit.
—Han Fei Tzu, Chinese philosopher (third century B.C.)

The human understanding, when it has once adopted an opinion . . . draws all things else to support and agree
with it.
—Sir Francis Bacon (1620)

We now shift focus from the factors that define how other people will see you as an *individual*—your relationships and credibility—to two of the three barriers that may stand in the way of their seeing your *ideas* clearly: the language you use and your audience's values and beliefs. As is the case with all five of the barriers we confront in Step 2 of the Woo process, these two can either sink your idea or be transformed into persuasion opportunities.

We begin with a story from the life of one of our era's true Woo Masters—U2 lead singer Bono. Bono is more than a well-known singer: he is an authentic social activist with a bold agenda for helping the world's poorest people. And he has a gift for turning would-be enemies into fervent allies by selecting just the right language and saluting just the right values.

## Bono Makes a Sale

On September 20, 2000, Bono walked into the office of a seventy-eight-year-old, arch-conservative U.S. senator named Jesse Helms. Bono was making the rounds in Washington, D.C., to recruit allies for Jubilee 2000—a program for getting governments to forgive the crushing debts faced by African countries so more local resources could be directed at the AIDS epidemic. Bono was hoping to enlist Helms as a champion for Jubilee 2000 in the U.S. Congress.

"I had never heard of him," Helms later told a reporter. "But the ladies in my office told me all about him . . ."

Bono walked into Helms's office in the Dirksen Senate Office Building around 5:30 P.M., accompanied by John Kasich, an Ohio Republican Congressman who was head of the House Budget Committee. Kasich, an avid U2 fan, had already signed up as a Jubilee 2000 supporter.

As Helms and Bono sat down together—with Kasich watching silently from a nearby couch—the straitlaced Helms found himself looking at a scruffy, middle-aged Irish rocker who had been born into a working-class family in Dublin, played competitive chess at the age of twelve, lost his mother at fourteen, and, in angry rebellion against his father, started his first band when he was sixteen. Bono was wearing his usual pair of wraparound, tinted glasses, and his shirt hung out over the pants of his dark green suit.

Bono's standard pitch for aid to Africa led with a detailed profile of the AIDS problem there. He had gathered his information during months of research, including interviews with experts such as World Bank president James Wolfensohn, former Federal Reserve Board chairman Paul Volcker, and Harvard development economist Jeffrey Sachs. He liked to hurl metrics at his audience as fast as it could keep up. Indeed, after one such meeting at the Bill and Melinda Gates Foundation, the Foundation's chief, Patty Stonesifer, was completely won over. "He was every bit the geek that we are," she commented. "He just happens to be a geek who is a fantastic musician." Bill Gates, who had predicted that the meeting with Bono "wouldn't be all that valuable," became a big supporter.

But as Bono launched into his litany of statistics in Helms's office, he saw that he was losing his audience. Helms did not speak "geek," and the elderly man's eyes began to wander. The meeting was coming to a rapid end.

So Bono adjusted, switching to a completely different language. Bono, himself a born-again Christian and close student of the Bible, had heard that Helms was a religious man. So he started speaking of Jesus's concern for the poor and the afflicted.

"I started talking about Scripture," Bono later recounted. "I talked about AIDS as the leprosy of our age." As Bono warmed to his subject, he pointed out that there were more than twenty-one hundred verses of Scripture in the Bible pertaining to poverty, a number second only to the number of verses dealing with redemption. Helms was listening now. As the *New York Times Magazine* later reported, Bono told of the married women and their children dying of AIDS and of governments burdened with debt that could do nothing about it. "Helms listened," reported James Taub in the *Times,* "and his eyes began to well up. Finally the flinty old Southerner rose to his feet, grabbed for his cane, and said, 'I want to give you a blessing!' He embraced the singer, saying, 'I want to do anything I can to help you.' "

And help he did. With Helms's support, Congress appropriated £435 million just weeks after this meeting to bring down the debt owed by African nations to the United States. Soon after that, Bono invited Helms and his grandchildren to be his guests at a sold-out Washington, D.C., concert by U2—Helms's first rock experience. In April 2006, as part of a special issue of *Time* magazine devoted to the hundred most influential people of the generation, Helms wrote a short tribute to Bono, one of the winners. "After so many years in Washington," Helms wrote, "I had met enough people to quickly figure out who was genuine and who is there for show. I knew as soon as I met Bono that he was genuine. . . . There is no pretense about him. . . . Bono enjoys telling people that . . . [I told him] . . . the audience [at the U2 concert] reminded me of a cornfield rustling in the wind. It was also a reminder of the millions he manages to touch every day with his music and his heart."

## Bono's Strategy

Let's take a moment to review where we are—because Bono's encounter with Jesse Helms captures much of what we have covered in the book so far. Bono once summed up his persuasion skills with a simple statement: "I'm a salesman," he said. He is, indeed. What was his strategy?

First, Bono brought a very well-prepared, polished idea to the table with him when he went into Helms's office. He had done his homework and had a clear, focused goal for this encounter: he wanted Helms to be his U.S. Senate champion for the Jubilee 2000 agenda.

Second, he had done a great job of understanding the decision-making process for U.S. cancellation of African debt. He had mapped a careful stepping-stone strategy. Bono's first stop had been Congressman John Kasich, a U2 fan who already favoured eliminating African debt. Bono then used his relationship with Kasich to obtain his appointment to see Helms—an "Elvis" in the Senate's decision process (see chapter 3) who would make the perfect champion for Bono's agenda.

Next came credibility. Bono's celebrity status could have easily worked against him here. Movie stars and rock idols frequently adopt pet social causes to burnish their images, and people in power, as Helms later remarked, are usually not impressed. Celebrities have credibility with fans, but not always with policy makers.

It was at just this point that Bono's genius as a persuader took over. He had done his homework on the Africa problem and hoped to rely on his expertise to establish credibility. But when he sensed Helms's lack of interest in his data-filled pitch, he shifted to another credibility platform—the values he shared with Helms as a born-again Christian. Using the metaphorical language of their personal beliefs, he intensified his message, adding passion to his purpose and expertise. Chapter 8 will explore why emotion-filled metaphors such as "AIDS is the leprosy of our age" can resonate so powerfully with an audience. For now, it is enough to note that Bono had these metaphors at his disposal and the good judgment to use them.

Perhaps most important, Bono's overall presentation rang true and thus won him Helms's personal trust. Within the span of this short meeting, in other words, Bono had created the foundation for a Trust-Level relationship, which then blossomed in follow-up meetings and events. Helms's staff, of course, checked all of Bono's data and claims after the meeting was over. But the idea stood up—and so did the relationship.

## Tune to the Other Person's Channel

Bono succeeded because he was able to find a language that Jesse Helms understood, tune into Helms's persuasion channel, and make a sale.

You may not be as charismatic as Bono, but you can follow his system for selling ideas. Bono did not pull Jesse Helms's religion out of the air like a magician. He had done his research and knew that Helms was a fundamentalist Christian. In the back of his mind, Bono had a visionary, religious pitch as "Plan B" for selling Jubilee 2000 if his usual "geek speak" did not work. And he could use this pitch with credibility because he was a born-again Christian himself.

The basic persuasion languages people speak parallel the six channels of persuasion we explored earlier in chapter 2. These are the languages of authority, rationality, vision, interests, politics, and relationships. Your success as a persuader depends on your ability to find the channel—or channels—your audience is tuned to and then communicate using appropriate language.

As the Bono story suggests, channel shifting is a skill common to all great persuaders. Napoleon's "Battery of the Men Without Fear," discussed in chapter 1, worked because Napoleon was smart enough to shift from the language of authority to the language of inspiration. Napoleon's men competed for the honor of being known as the members of a courageous band.

Corporate leaders use Napoleon's technique whenever they label special innovation efforts as "skunk works" or give out names such as the "Dream Team" to groups working on high-priority projects. They are bypassing the language of authority to help people identify with their work, making it more meaningful—and sometimes fun. Steven Jobs, for example, once had an assistant at Apple raise a Jolly Roger flag over the building where his team of top programmers and engineers were working night and day on designing the new Macintosh computer. They loved being labeled the "pirates" who were out to sink mighty IBM.

As surely as finding the right language helps persuasion, failing to do so can doom an idea-selling effort. Woodrow Wilson was one of America's smartest and best-educated presidents—he was the head of Princeton University before occupying the White House. But his equally bright advisers soon learned that persuading Wilson required more than having good, rational arguments. He was once engaged in a heated debate with his advisers over pension legislation. Wilson, who was tuned to the political channel, wanted to get the legislation passed to take credit for doing something on an issue the public cared about. His advisers, however, were focused on economic policy considerations. As his advisers' economic arguments mounted up against his plan, Wilson finally exclaimed, "Logic! Logic! I don't care a damn for logic. I am going to include [the] pensions!" The rational arguments his advisers were advancing—which might have worked fine in a Princeton seminar—were unpersuasive. By failing to come up with some serious *political* objections to the plan, the advisers lost the debate.

## Listen to Your Audience

What was the critical turning point in Bono's meeting with Jesse Helms? The moment Bono realized he was losing his audience and switched to the visionary mode. And the personal quality that allowed Bono to make this switch was his keen self-awareness as a persuader—a factor we introduced in chapter 2.

Self-awareness is an internal thermometer that tells you whether you are happy, sad, insecure, or confident. In a persuasion encounter, the more self-awareness you bring to the table, the more you can monitor your own feelings and measure the reactions your audience is feeding back to you. Persuaders with a lack of confidence, a bout of nerves, or a fear of failure often tend to focus almost exclusively on the content of their message. They are listening to what they are saying and thinking about what they will say next.

By contrast, people who know their message cold can deliver it while simultaneously monitoring the moment-to-moment reactions of listeners as *they* experience the persuasion process. "I am feeling frustrated," a self-aware persuader might say to herself. "Is that because my audience is not listening? I may need to throw away my prepared pitch and try something new."

By monitoring your audience and adjusting your pitch, you can keep everyone's attention and stay in the game. When you fail to adjust, you end up speaking in what amounts to a "foreign" language. The audience is then left to wonder whether you failed to prepare or just lack basic social awareness. Neither is helpful to your credibility.

The following examples show the damage such lapses can cause.

A young man named Rich Melmon joined Intel in the early 1970s as a bright, freshly minted MBA. A marketing manager, he came up with a number of innovative ideas, and as an enthusiastic Promoter (see chapter 2), he never tired of sharing his ideas with his coworkers. Intel was (and remains) an organization with a reputation for encouraging innovation, but it has an engineering culture. Numbers rule. Melmon never quite figured this out. As a visionary persuader, he thought in terms of images and excitement.

This proved costly because one of Melmon's brightest ideas was a radically new use for computers. He was convinced that there was a huge market for small, desktop computers that people would buy for their homes. His boss, Bill Davidson, got so tired of hearing about Melmon's "personal computer" idea that he made Melmon promise not to mention it at any more lunches. Two years later, when Intel CEO Gordon Moore finally asked for a report on the concept of the PC, Rich Melmon had moved on. Intel's engineers, meanwhile, saw the device in purely functional rather than marketing terms. When Moore asked his engineers what a PC might be good for, one replied, "Maybe housewives could store their recipes in it." The idea died.

Because he could not curb his enthusiasm long enough to learn how to speak to Intel's engineers, Melmon lost his sale.

An even more extreme example of death-by-using-the-wrong-language comes from a story that surfaced on the Web site YouTube before circling the globe. It involved a miscued job application.

As a senior at Yale University, Aleksey Vayner set his sights on landing a Wall Street job at a staid investment firm, UBS. His recruiting materials included a cover letter, his résumé to the company, and, to help differentiate himself from the thousands of other college students applying for a position, a link to a personal video. Had Vayner made a video featuring his expertise in finance or his experience leading a student organization, this method of communication might have worked, even for Wall Street. It was an innovative, outside-the-box communication idea.

But Vayner produced a personal motivational video based on the clichéd maxims of success gurus. Titled "Impossible Is Nothing," the video explained in vivid detail Vayner's success philosophy. As he intoned rules such as "Failure cannot be considered an option" and "Ignore the losers," the video clips showed him bench-pressing free weights, playing various solo sports, dancing, and breaking a column of bricks with his bare hands. Through the magic of electronic communication, Vayner's over-the-top promotional tape soon spread around the world, and his story was featured in European and American newspapers, *The New Yorker* magazine, and hundreds of Internet blogs. The video itself was posted, where it enjoyed a short run as one of the most-watched items in America for several days.

Needless to say, Vayner did not get an interview at UBS. As one executive recruiter commented, "If you are applying for a reality television show, I can see this." Vayner's one bright spot was interest shown in him by some New York public relations and advertising firms, which considered his video as evidence that he might have a natural, if quirky, talent for visionary persuasion. "I'd hire him in a heartbeat," noted one PR executive.

## Speaking Your Organization's Language

Human minds and organizational cultures are too idiosyncratic to make a complete list of all the languages people use to sell ideas. The visionary persuasion channel, for example, includes everything from the vocabulary of the Bible and Aleksey Vayner's success bromides to Rich Melmon's marketing imagery. And you would probably cite the Bible quite differently in a pitch to born-again Christians than to conservative Catholic theologians. So tuning to your audience's basic channel—be it visionary, rational, interest-based, political, relational, or authority-based—is only the beginning of your preparation, not the end.

Once you have identified your audience's channel, therefore, your next step is to research the specific words, frameworks, or metaphors your audience is most likely to respond to. You will usually find hints and clues about these all around you in most organizations—if you will only take the time to notice. Almost every corporate culture has favoured buzzwords to help you frame your ideas.

Compare Rich Melmon's story above to another, more successful one from the tech sector—this one about an aggressive advertising executive who persuaded Microsoft to shift its strategy for selling online advertising. The story demonstrates both the importance of adjusting to your audience's channel and the need to decode the culture to find the right presentation methods.

A woman named Joanne Bradford joined Microsoft in 2001 as head of online advertising for MSN—Microsoft's online network—after spending thirteen years selling print ads for a major magazine company. She was an outstanding saleswoman who excelled at developing and managing relationships, an executive who had, according to news reports about her, "the gift of gab and a memory for names and faces."

As the head of online advertising sales at Microsoft, however, she found herself a stranger in a strange land. Soon after joining the company, for example, she flew to California with CEO Steve Ballmer to visit large corporate advertisers. On the plane, she shared a twenty-six-page study of online advertising, hoping to convince him that Microsoft should invest major resources in her area—doubling or tripling the sales force. She was caught off guard by Ballmer's response: he spent ten minutes speed-reading the report and the rest of the trip pummeling her with data-oriented questions she couldn't answer.

She fared just as poorly in conversations with her immediate superior, a Microsoft veteran more interested in how competitors like AOL were delivering e-mail and instant messaging than in what MSN could do to sell ads. At one meeting, he pounded on the table and called her advertising ideas "stupid." As she kept running into brick walls, Bradford began to question her role at the company. At one point she called her husband from an Atlanta hotel room with a sad conclusion. "These people don't like me," she said.

At last, weary of trying to sell her ideas on her own terms, she finally looked around her and noticed how new ideas were actually developed and promoted at Microsoft. Then she changed strategy. Using computer-generated data, she began translating her enthusiasm into terms that Microsoft's engineers could understand. Her surveys started to include data on how much time her ad staff was spending meeting with customers versus doing administrative tasks. She used the numbers to create charts showing the relationship between revenue projections and staffing. She showed in concrete terms how increases in staff support would translate into increases in ad revenue. At last her bosses began to take notice and she began building her credibility in meetings across the company.

She also used advertisers to generate leverage with her internal constituencies. Before a meeting with her boss, she coached a group from General Motors, which was looking to increase online advertising, to give him an earful about the insufficient resources Microsoft was devoting to online ads. It was much harder for him to dismiss the ideas of paying customers.

Once she had created positive buzz for her ideas both inside and outside the company, she was ready to make her annual pitch for more staff and resources at a division-wide event where in previous years she had flamed out. There, backed by her data-rich presentation, she made a case for bringing on additional sales people. This time, she got a positive response: her boss signed off on a proposal to hire 150 new recruits.

What did Bradford do that Melmon failed to do? In a technical, engineering culture, she learned to translate advertising and marketing ideas into metrics her audience could understand. And once she started speaking the right language, she made her sale.

## Taking It to the Personal Level

Of course, even within a given corporate culture, the people you are selling your idea to will have their own individual, sometimes quirky way of processing information and concepts. It will therefore help to gather as much information as you can on the thought processes, values, and preferences of each person in your stepping-stone strategy.

Does the CEO manage to work the words *global* and *teamwork* into every speech? If you are selling him an idea, you should work these words in, too.

Sometimes you can gain insights into people's preferred language by finding out how they speak or communicate when *they* are selling ideas. What are the metaphors they use to explain or discuss issues of interest? If they are people-oriented, do they speak in terms of a "corporate family"? If they are data-driven, do they like their numbers in visual form? With more information, you may be able to refine your pitch even further to fit their mind-set.

For example, if you were preparing to sell an idea to Intel's former CEO Andy Grove, your "channel search" would immediately reveal his strong bias toward rationality—a preference shared by the entire company, as we saw above. But by digging a little deeper into his writings, you could uncover even more specific ideas on how to frame and present your proposal.

In his best-selling book, *Only the Paranoid Survive,* Grove developed an idea he called the "strategic inflection point." Industries are subject to severe, disruptive changes, Grove argued, that fundamentally change the rules of the business they are in. The "inflection point" metaphor comes from the visual display of a graph—it is the point on a graph where the slope makes a sudden dip or rise due to an underlying change in one of the variables defining the curve.

After he retired from Intel, Grove got involved in analyzing the woes of the American health care system. His advice to cure its ills? "Shift left," said Grove. He was using another graph as a metaphor—this one illustrating the tendency of products and services to grow more complex (on the bottom, horizontal axis) over time (on the vertical axis). The farther to the right you go on the graph, the more complex a product or service gets. Grove was suggesting that by shifting information systems back toward more simplicity (that is, back toward the left of the bottom axis), health care providers would be able to regain control of the system and deliver better treatments. He favoured plain-vanilla medical records stored on easily accessible word-processing files rather than complex records stored in highly technical databases, and he wanted to see more walk-in clinics at places like Wal-Mart rather than construction of expensive, specialized health care facilities.

Based on Grove's preference for explaining his own ideas in terms of graph-based metaphors, how would you advise someone to sell him an idea? We would bet that Grove likes presentations that feature precision and visual displays of data showing underlying relationships. He would want to know what hypotheses could be tested, the relationships that might exist between dynamic forces, and which solutions could withstand significant stresses.

If there is one lesson to be gleaned from all of our examples of tuning to your audience's channel and speaking in its language, however, it is this: *do your homework—come prepared with a Plan B.* For the most important encounters, follow Bono's model. Spend time investigating how you should approach each specific person you will meet. Search for the special words that your audience will find familiar and that can convey your idea in the most user-friendly way. Then be flexible. Be ready to shift strategies based on your audience's real-time reactions and feedback.

## Beliefs and Values: The Language of Purpose

As we have seen, people's beliefs and values often provide a language you can use to frame your ideas in especially persuasive ways. It therefore pays to discover and, if appropriate, salute your audience's core values whenever possible.

In organizational life, the language of "purpose" enters the vocabulary through corporate mission statements and credos. Examples include such famous corporate value statements as Johnson & Johnson's "Credo," Hewlett-Packard's "HP Way," and Google's "Don't Be Evil" motto. It seldom harms an idea pitch to link it to an organization's core purposes.

But make sure your audience actually believes in the values statement you reference. At a seminar we were teaching for a major oil company recently, we accidentally set off a roar of laughter when we read part of its mission statement aloud. As our all-day workshop was coming to a conclusion, the corporate director of the program had taken us aside and asked us to link our day's lessons back to the company's credo. So when class resumed, we started to read one of these principles to the group. The executives in the room immediately began to howl with laughter. To these participants—all of whom were senior leaders of various business units and most of whom were crusty, experienced field engineers—these fluffy ideas about "nurturing employees" and "empowering teams" had been repeated so often they had become a joke. Another participant told us later that she had formerly worked at Johnson & Johnson, where the famous Credo really meant something important. She said she genuinely missed the sense of purpose and meaning that the J&J Credo had provided her on a daily basis.

So when, as is true at Johnson & Johnson, organizational mission statements are living parts of the way a group works—that is, the people in charge actually believe in the standards they or the company founders have endorsed—then these idealistic statements of beliefs and values can serve as powerful premises for arguments in support of important initiatives. But far more important than the "sacred text" of a mission statement are the living core values and aspirations of the people you are trying to persuade.

Thus, if your organization's values do not provide a reference point for your idea, see if you can discover personal, professional, and social values that can serve as an anchor. In 1960, for example, when the fast-food chain McDonald's opened its two hundredth restaurant in Knoxville, Tennessee, a nearby competitor dropped its prices so low that the McDonald's owner, a former Marine Corps officer named Litton Cochran, faced ruin. The other restaurant was selling a complete meal of a hamburger, milk shake, and fries for a price that was below the cost of the meal's components. Litton took a flight to Chicago to plead with McDonald's CEO Ray Kroc for the resources to file a lawsuit for unfair competition.

But Kroc pushed back, relying on the value of self-reliance—something he knew this ex-Marine would salute. "If we have to resort to this—bringing in the government to beat our competition," Kroc said, "then we deserve to go broke." He urged Litton to go back to Knoxville and win the battle in the marketplace with better service. Litton took the words to heart and ended up not only staying in business but also opening ten additional restaurants in the city. And he became, according to Kroc, a passionate speaker at local colleges on the subject of self-reliance and the free enterprise system.

A similar one-on-one appeal to values also saved the day in one of the most spectacular business failures in American history—the multibillion-dollar, 1998 collapse of the hedge fund Long-Term Capital Management (LTCM). The firm was founded by star trader John Meriwether with the help of two Nobel Prize–winning economists, Myron Scholes and Robert Merton. When it collapsed, it threatened to take a big part of Wall Street with it. Negotiations to protect the overall financial markets from a liquidity crisis came down to a single conversation in the corner of a conference room in New York. Fourteen banks had been lined up to provide a bailout, and the partners of LTCM were all gathered with their lawyers to sign the final papers. But one of the LTCM partners, Larry Hildebrand, balked. Worth close to half a billion dollars before the crisis, Hildebrand faced personal ruin with this deal—plus he would be forced to stay with LTCM for years to help with the workout. If he didn't sign, on the other hand, he could simply file for bankruptcy, put the entire matter behind him, and move on.

With the seconds ticking down to the deadline, everyone in the room was focused on Hildebrand, but their arguments were having no effect. Finally, the lead lawyer for the bailout, Herb Allison, took Hildebrand aside and reminded him that his actions would affect the very foundations of the capital markets. The goal here was not to destroy anybody, Allison said. It was to restore the public's faith in the financial system. Meriwether then joined the hushed conversation. "Larry, you'd better listen to Herb," he said. For the first time that afternoon Hildebrand listened—and he signed.

## Beliefs as Barriers to Persuasion

Psychologists have a variety of explanations for why appeals to core beliefs work: belief bias (the tendency of people to accept any and all conclusions that fit within their systems of belief), the consistency principle (the need for people to behave in ways that are consistent with previously declared values or norms), and the pull of "power" or "God" terms (the tendency of people to respond to appeals invoking ultimate values such as safety, connection, community, or truth). These explanations all point to the same conclusion: if an idea promises to reinforce one of your audience's core beliefs or the values related to them, the idea gains tremendous traction.

But the very power of your audience's beliefs also creates hidden barriers to persuasion. Psychologists call this the "worldview defense" phenomenon, and it has been demonstrated in more than three hundred lab experiments with subjects from many different cultures. Well-known examples of this are easy to find. Some people—many of them radical anti-Semites—refuse to believe the Holocaust happened and no amount of historical evidence, testimony by witnesses and participants, or even photographs, can shake them from this conviction. A group of radical tax protesters in the United States refuse to pay their taxes every year because they believe that the income tax is unconstitutional. The fact that the U.S. Supreme Court has expressly upheld the income tax under the Constitution does not sway them. Nor do the legal opinions of thousands of lawyers and the behavior of millions of citizens. The harder the government pushes, the more deeply committed they become to their beliefs, discounting all the evidence that runs contrary to their views and suffering imprisonment and financial ruin as a result.

Surprisingly, this phenomenon afflicts scientists as well as dogmatic ideologues. For example, in the historic effort to map the human genome, virtually everyone in the scientific community believed that a painstaking, gene-by-gene mapping process, destined to take decades, was the only way to assure a complete, accurate map. When geneticist James Weber and computational biologist Eugene Myers made a landmark presentation at a 1996 conference in Bermuda outlining a "shotgun sequencing" method for speeding up the process, leading scientists refused to take it seriously. "Flawed and unworkable," said the experts. But one man—a little-known researcher and former surfer named Craig Venter—was not so sure. He called Myers and together they made history, turning the human genome–mapping effort into a high-profile race, which they won four years later in 2000.

The inventor of the theory of evolution, Charles Darwin, once remarked that it was so difficult for him to overcome his own beliefs when he was gathering data that he made a conscious effort to seek out contrary examples. And the temptation to skip over evidence that contradicted his beliefs was so strong that he made a habit of immediately writing all such evidence down. Otherwise, he reported, he was sure to forget it.

If even committed scientists have trouble overcoming the biases caused by their own beliefs, imagine the problems such beliefs cause in ordinary organizational life. Under such circumstances, it will not matter how much authority an idea seller may have. Ideas that violate basic beliefs will simply be rejected.

A good illustration of this problem comes from the life of James E. Webb, a man who helped put the first man on the moon in the late 1960s as the leader of the National Aeronautics and Space Administration. An ex–fighter pilot and trained lawyer, Webb first made a name for himself in the 1940s as President Harry Truman's director of the White House Bureau of the Budget. In this position, Webb came up with a great idea that is still around today—the periodic reporting of leading "economic indicators" for the nation that are used to project future growth. These monthly compilations of huge amounts of economic data were a radical innovation at the time and allowed the president to see exactly what the economy was doing in an easy-to-understand summary.

Webb's success in his budget post prompted Truman to name him in 1949 as under secretary of state, the number two person under a new secretary of state, Dean Acheson. Truman's idea was for Webb to be the "Mr. Inside" at the State Department—the COO running the day-to-day operations of the bureaucracy—while Dean Acheson covered the globe as the diplomatic "Mr. Outside."

Shortly after moving into his new office, Webb realized that the decentralized nature of diplomacy made it hard for him to know exactly what was going on within the State Department's far-flung, complex bureaucracy. And this lack of information hindered policy making. To solve the problem, he decided to implement a version of his successful "economic indicators" idea. He gathered the State Department leaders together and announced that he was centralizing the flow of information and instituting a new report on "foreign policy indicators." All departments and embassies across the world would henceforth produce a set of findings and analyses in statistical form, which Webb would summarize in periodic reports to the secretary of state and the president.

His State Department audience was stunned. This new system invaded every diplomat's autonomy and ran against deeply entrenched beliefs about how foreign policy was conducted. How could political assessments on the leadership qualities of a country's opposition party or the relationships within a dictator's inner circle reduce themselves to statistics? The diplomats protested, argued, and objected. But Webb was steadfast.

Then came open rebellion. A senior diplomat was quoted as saying, "He won't get these things. We'll see to it that he doesn't . . . Preposterous. It can't be allowed to happen."

And it didn't. The data did not come in, and no amount of ordering or commanding could force it out of the field offices. Webb lost credibility within the State Department and eventually left for a job in the early 1950s to lead a division of an oil company in Oklahoma. He did not return to Washington until 1961, when President Kennedy tapped him to lead the moon mission. By then, Webb was older, wiser, and more realistic about "ordering" people to change their beliefs. His political skills, forged from his failures at the State Department, are widely credited for keeping an unstable alliance of military, scientific, political, and bureaucratic constituencies together to put the Apollo astronauts on the moon.

Webb's story yields several lessons. Not only did he fail to salute the basic values and beliefs of his organization, but he also used the wrong language—trying to sell a data-based idea to a group of conceptually minded diplomats. What's more, he had a credibility problem with the bureaucracy because he lacked foreign policy experience, and he displayed no appreciation for the State Department's decentralized culture, trying to force too much change too fast. Finally, he lacked personal relationships with people in the field who might have served as champions and change agents for such a program. With so many factors working against him, it is no surprise he failed to make the sale.

## Cures for Belief Bias

When your research and preparation reveal that your idea may collide with a core belief of your audience, what can you do? Here are some possible cures for the blindness that beliefs can cause.

## Be Persistent

One option is persistence. If you have the time and are sure enough of your idea, you can simply keep at it until you begin to win people over. Webb tried this tack and failed—but, as we noted above, he had many factors working against him, the most important of which was a lack of credibility. Rich Melmon experienced a similar failure by being overly persistent at Intel—but his youth and inexperience, coupled with his refusal to translate his idea into technical language, are probably what doomed his campaign for the PC.

A better model for using persistence to overcome entrenched beliefs is Sam Walton's campaign to hire "greeters" at Wal-Mart—discussed in chapter 2. The greeters idea violated the company's core belief in minimizing overhead expenses, but Walton had credibility and was eventually able to show how the idea would pay for itself by reducing shoplifting and helping to maintain a positive, folksy atmosphere in the stores.

## Shift Audiences

A second option is to stop hammering at the people who reject your idea and seek a new audience. This was Charles Lindbergh's strategy. He kept talking to people until he found the ones who were willing to accept his one-engine plan and then he built his organization around them. Given the overwhelming amount of psychological research on people's stubbornness when it comes to defending their beliefs, there is a lot of wisdom in this option. In an organizational context, this usually means going outside your unit or division to find people who think differently from those whose beliefs are blinding them to the opportunities presented in your idea.

## Fly Under the Radar Screen

A third option is to position your idea as something so small and unimportant that it poses no serious challenge to the accepted belief system. In the early 1980s, for example, it was hard for anyone at IBM to get a hearing for ideas that took personal computers seriously. According to Paul Carroll's authoritative study *Big Blues,* low-level internal task forces had forecast that the industry was about to change, but the people at the top, blinded by their belief that no new markets were left to conquer, refused to take these warnings seriously.

Nevertheless, an IBM senior manager named Bill Lowe succeeded in obtaining development funds for an experimental PC project that set the stage for IBM's entry into that market. He did it by keeping the project so small nobody could be bothered to oppose it. When it became clear that Lowe's little program would take no resources away from the focus on the company's corporate customers, the IBM Management Committee let it pass as one of the dozen or so things it approved in a given week. The PC initiative, in short, flew in under the radar screen of IBM's core beliefs.

### Ask Them to Take Just One Small Step

Another option is to break your idea into small bites that demand less commitment from your audience. Psychologists have discovered that people have "anchor positions" on various beliefs and opinions, and their willingness to be flexible on these positions can depend on how much they are asked to change. The less you ask of the audience, the more willing they are to move in your direction. When you run into a wall of resistance, therefore, don't ask people to adopt your idea in its entirety—as James Webb did at the State Department. Instead, try asking for permission to run a small-scale "test" or "pilot project" that does not commit anyone to a final decision. Get them to take one small step.

A fascinating example of this approach comes from the American Revolution and a speech General George Washington used to keep his army together near the beginning of the war. It occurred on New Year's Eve in 1776, and is retold in David McCullough's prize-winning book about that pivotal year in U.S. history.

George Washington and his ragtag Continental Army had just won a battle in nearby Trenton, New Jersey, in late December 1776, but he was about to lose the war because his soldiers' enlistment contracts terminated on January 1, 1777. The troops were tired, cold, hungry, and ready to go home. They believed that they had done their part and nothing could convince them otherwise.

To sell the troops on staying with the army, Washington's staff came up with an incentive program (we will deal more with this form of persuasion in chapter 6): anyone who agreed to stay in the army for an additional six more months would receive a ten-dollar bonus.

The army was mustered on the freezing afternoon of December 31, and the plan was announced. Drums rolled and the soldiers were told to take one step forward if they were willing to sign up for the plan. But nobody moved.

Seeing that he was about to lose everything he and his men had fought for, Washington switched persuasion channels. He rode to the front of the columns and, according to witnesses, made the following appeal, his voice ringing out in the cold air:

> My brave fellows. You have done all I asked you to do, and more than could be reasonably expected. But your country is at stake. Your wives, your houses, all that you hold dear. You have worn yourselves out with fatigues and hardships, but we know not how to spare you. If you will consent to stay one month longer, you will render that service to the cause of liberty and to your country which you can probably never do under any other circumstances.

The drums rolled again, again there was a pause, but this time a few scattered men took the one small step forward, then more, and finally the entire army stepped up to fight for another round. The "one month longer" that Washington asked for came and went, turning into long years of service. But the men stuck with Washington and eventually achieved their country's independence.

Washington's impromptu speech is a classic in the persuasion literature. It represented an astute decision to change from the language of interests and incentives to the language of values and beliefs. His army was not in this war for the money, so additional funds, while welcome, were not going to keep them there.

He began by praising his men, bolstering their pride. They had exceeded everyone's expectations. Next he acknowledged their exhaustion and suffering. They were listening now because this was their true experience. He then appealed directly to the purposes that had brought them all to the situation they were in—their families, their country, and the cause. Finally—and this was the reason the speech worked—Washington did not ask his soldiers to come off their "anchor position" by much. He needed just "one month longer"—a period that would be especially precious. Add Washington's reputation for personal character and trustworthiness—the credibility he had gained as someone who shared his men's hardships—and you can see why this speech was effective.

### Position Your Idea Around a Deeper Core Value

The final cure to belief bias is to reposition your idea so people see it as *consistent* with an underlying value that runs deeper than the belief you have collided with. For example, suppose you are trying to sell your organization on changing to a new software system and your audience believes that the platform it now uses works just fine. Attacking the existing platform will simply trigger belief bias and people will stop listening. However, if you can refocus your audience on the underlying *purposes* the existing platform serves—such as efficiency or reliability—you open the door to pitching your new solution as addressing those purposes in a better way.

Another successful idea sale will show how this solution works. It made the cover of *BusinessWeek* magazine and illustrates how you can combine all the belief bias "cures" we have reviewed into a single idea-selling strategy.

Jody Thompson and Cali Ressler are two human resources executives at the multibillion-dollar retailer Best Buy who have started a revolution in the way businesses think about work. As of this writing, nobody is sure whether their approach is going to take the American workplace by storm or fade as a fad, but one thing is sure: they have done a masterful job of selling their idea to a very skeptical, in some cases even hostile, audience.

Best Buy's corporate headquarters in Minneapolis, Minnesota, used to be the kind of place where employees raced into the office at daybreak and trudged home long after sundown. Some people were required to sign out for lunch, list their destination, and commit to returning at a particular time. One manager even demanded that his team track every fifteen minutes of work. The reigning philosophy was strictly traditional: if the boss can't see you, you're not working.

But Thompson and Ressler saw developments outside the company that were transforming how work actually got done: virtual meetings, wireless connectivity, offices without walls, and the freedom to be productive in new ways. Inspired by a vision of an electronic office and worried about the signs of stress and burnout they saw all around them in Best Buy's workaholic culture, they cooked up an idea called ROWE, short for "results-only work environment."

But they had no illusions: it was going to be a tough sell in a company run on conventional, punch-clock norms. They were especially wary of taking their idea straight to CEO Brad Anderson, a by-the-numbers executive who had worked his way up from being a Best Buy sales clerk over several decades at the company. So they kept working out the ROWE concept and bided their time.

Their first break came when they heard that top performers in two key units—real estate and communications—were complaining about crushing levels of stress and threatening to quit just as Best Buy was getting ready to launch a new, company-wide initiative. Armed with survey data that showed employees in other parts of the company were sagging under the weight of endless days filled with pressure, Thompson and Ressler approached the units' managers and proposed an HR experiment: why not try measuring employee performance based entirely on output? No obligatory face time. No logging hours for hours' sake. Fewer meetings. The unit managers agreed and the experiment got under way without the need for official sign-off by senior-level administrators.

Needless to say, the employees loved it and morale soared. Moreover, the experiment quickly created a "buzz" around the firm as workers chained to their desks saw colleagues from these two departments working in new ways at their own pace—and wherever they wanted to work. This was not just "flextime"—a system that allowed employees to move an hour of office time from the early morning to the late afternoon or a workday from Tuesday to Saturday. This was freedom to design jobs in the best way to actually accomplish specific goals.

The ROWE virus began to spread and, as it did, Thompson and Ressler began building their case for their presentation to the CEO. There was plenty of opposition from traditional managers, who believed that "working" meant "working at the office," so Thompson and Ressler decided to go one level deeper within the corporate culture to find the banner for ROWE. The reason why the office culture was important at Best Buy was its fierce dedication to execution and productivity. So they began gathering data and testimonials that showed how ROWE served these key corporate values better than did the punch clock.

By the time word of the program reached the upper echelons, Thompson and Ressler had built a powerful countercultural movement among middle managers. Politically, they had a grassroots effort going. And, by operating below the radar, Thompson and Ressler had time to build a database of hard numbers to show that the program was making a difference where it counted. Productivity was up. And so was job satisfaction and retention—two measures that were critical to CEO Anderson's latest initiative, a "customer centricity" campaign.

A senior manager who was initially skeptical about the program became a convert when he saw the numerical results: "For years I had been focused on the wrong currency. I was always looking to see if people were here. I should have been looking at what they were getting done."

A full two years after their initial stealth experiment, Thompson and Ressler finally asked for a make-or-break meeting with Brad Anderson to sell their idea. "We purposely waited until [after] the tipping point before we took it to him," Thompson later told *BusinessWeek*.

Anderson loved it—in part because he liked the numbers he saw and in part because he liked the bottom-up way Thompson and Ressler had developed it, which perfectly mirrored the way Anderson himself had grown up in the company. This was an idea "born and nurtured by a handful of passionate employees," Anderson later described it. He even put his muscle behind starting a new subsidiary to sell the ROWE concept, processes, and metrics to other companies coping with productivity and burnout problems.

How did Thompson and Ressler make this sale?

- They began by shifting to the right initial audience: sympathetic middle managers rather than hostile senior leadership.

- Then they piloted the program, asking a few people at Best Buy to take "one small step" that did not require them to throw out all their existing beliefs about office work.

- All this took place under the radar screen of the top leaders.

- They were persistent in building support for ROWE over the course of a few years—not weeks or months.

- They positioned their idea to resonate with Best Buy's productivity culture and the CEO's "customer centricity" initiative.

- Finally, they waited until they had enough hard data to make their case in a language Best Buy's leaders would understand—metrics.

Thompson and Ressler have continued to build support for their vision of a flexible, results-focused Best Buy. Recently they launched a new pilot, called Cube-Free, which encourages employees to redesign their office spaces to promote collaboration and teamwork as they see fit. With the success of ROWE to build on, their credibility in promoting this new initiative is high.

## Conclusion

In this chapter, we shifted our focus from two potential barriers that may affect how people will see you as the messenger for your idea—relationships and credibility—to two considerations that may drive their reactions to your message: your audience's preferred language and the beliefs that your idea may advance or contradict. Our advice has been straightforward: speak to people in a language they will understand and, if possible, salute the flags of their beliefs and values.

The chapter featured both perils and possibilities. As James Webb's failure to sell his "foreign policy indicator" idea at the State Department and Rich Melmon's experience at Intel showed, nothing can sink a proposal faster than belief bias or a refusal to adopt the favoured language of communication in an organization. On the other hand, if you can communicate on the right persuasion channel and show how your idea furthers your audience's core purposes—as Bono did with Jesse Helms, and as Thompson and Ressler did at Best Buy—you are well on the way to successfully wooing any group.

From here, we move to an exploration of the final barrier you must confront in Step 2 of the Woo process: how people's underlying interests may affect their reactions to your idea. Some persuasion scholars insist that such interests are all that matter in interpersonal influence. They hold that no one will agree to anything unless it advances his or her self-interest and that most of the reasons, evidence, and values offered as justifications in persuasion are really just rationalizations for actions people want to take for much more selfish purposes. We are not sure we would go that far, but there is no doubt that one of the most important questions your audience will ask is "What's in it for *me?*" So you had better have your answer ready.

chapter six

# Give Them Incentives to Say Yes:
# Interests and Needs

No appeal to reason that is not also an appeal to a want
can ever be effective.
—H. A. Overstreet, *Influencing Human Behavior* (1925)

The shortest and best way to make your fortune is to let people
see clearly that it is in their interests to promote yours.
—Jean de la Bruyère (1645–1696)

A story goes that Andrew Carnegie had two nephews who could not find the time to write home from college. The boys' parents had tried everything to encourage their sons to write, but to no avail. Finally, Carnegie bet a hundred dollars he could get the young men to contact home immediately without spending a nickel and without making a threat. The boys' parents told him to go ahead and try, but they doubted he could do it. Carnegie then wrote his nephews a short letter wishing them well and saying that he had enclosed some money for each of them.

But he did not enclose any money.

The nephews wrote home immediately, asking if their uncle had forgotten something when mailing the letter.

Carnegie won his bet because he understood the power of self-interest when it comes to persuasion. Another man named Carnegie—success guru Dale—once summed up the importance of interests as follows: "The only way on earth to influence other people is to talk about what they want and show them how to get it." We agree—up to a point. Self-interest is a powerful motivator, but it is not the *only* explanation for human action. In the previous chapter, for example, we saw how George Washington's offer of additional pay to his army failed to persuade his men to re-enlist. They responded instead to Washington's call for them to do their duty for "one month more."

Moreover, Dale Carnegie's implicit assumption that people always know what they want may not be true. In practicing the Art of Woo, you can often educate people about their own interests and needs.

Despite these reservations, we respect self-interest as a motive when you are trying to win someone over. So in this chapter we show you how to appeal to people's natural desires to advance their own goals. First, we explore how effective idea sellers frame their proposals in terms of other people's interests. Second, we look at how you can effectively negotiate solutions when you confront a mix of shared and conflicting interests. We will be returning to some of these themes in chapter 9, when we look at how to overcome politics and sustain organizational commitment to your idea after you make a sale.

## Everybody's Favorite Topic: Their Own Needs

At the very center of human influence, like the bull's-eye in the middle of a target, are the self-interests, problems, and needs of the people you are trying to woo. If you can show people that your idea furthers their interests, you will usually have a much easier time gaining their support.

A popular book on conventional selling, *Soft Selling in a Hard World*, goes so far as to advise salespeople to eliminate the word *I* from their selling presentations. The customer is mainly interested in his or her own needs, author Jerry Vass argues, and could care less who the salesperson is. The best salespeople therefore focus on asking questions, listening closely to the customer's underlying needs, and showing how what they sell solves a problem related to these needs.

The same advice applies when you are selling ideas. When you approach people in your stepping-stone strategy, you must not only use their language and honor their beliefs—you must also find ways to frame your idea in terms of their needs and problems.

Academic studies in psychology confirm two important findings about the role of self-interest in persuasion. First, as the story about

Andrew Carnegie's nephews suggests, people pay much closer attention to messages they see as having important personal consequences than ones that do not. A glance at nonfiction bestseller lists in publishing confirms this basic truth. These lists are filled with titles such as *You: On a Diet*, *Why We Want You to Be Rich*, and *Younger You.*

Second, people's self-interest strongly affects the way they think about proposals. Naturally enough, people tend to favour ideas that benefit them and oppose those that will force them to shoulder significant costs. But research has also shown that audiences see arguments as *more persuasive* when they stand to gain from an idea and less persuasive when they stand to lose. In short, people's interests serve as windows through which they see your ideas. When you can find and address their interests, they open the windows to let your ideas in; if they see your idea as running against their needs, the windows close.

Here are three important questions to help you think about your audience's interests in a systematic way: (1) Why might it already be in the other party's interests to support my idea? (2) What do other parties want that I can give them to gain their support? and (3) Why might they say no? Your answers to these questions will help you frame your idea so that it has maximum appeal. Let's look closely at each question.

### Why Might It Already Be in the Other Party's Interests to Support My Idea?

This question helps you think of the interests—personal as well as professional—your counterpart might share with you. What problems, hopes, needs, fears, desires, and goals do they face that your idea might help them with? Framing your idea in terms of these goals will get their attention.

When Donald Trump was just starting off as a New York City real estate developer, for example, one of his first projects was to take an old, boarded-up hotel near Grand Central Station called the Commodore and turn it into the Grand Hyatt. At the time, this area was an urban eyesore and getting worse by the month. Many people thought Trump was crazy to take on this project because lenders would charge extra-high interest rates for loans on such a risky property.

But Trump did not see the project as a private development; he saw it as a private–public partnership. His target audiences for the idea, therefore, were not banks or other lenders. His targets were public officials whom he could address in terms of their interests in rejuvenating the city and their cravings for positive personal publicity. As Richard Kaplan, head of the New York City Urban Development Corporation said, Trump "saw that lenders . . . would throw away the usual rules [if public officials got behind the idea]." This meant that banks might actually *lower* their rates so they could jump on board for the public relations value. He succeeded in selling the entire project as a "rescue mission" for the "heart of Manhattan"— something all the relevant players wanted a piece of. And when he got it approved, Trump made sure that everyone involved—himself first of all—were seen as the people who had "saved" New York.

Similarly, when Steve Jobs was trying to persuade Steve Wozniak to start what would become Apple Computer, he showed his persuasion skills by shifting the discussion away from an issue they disagreed about to an interest they shared. Jobs' idea was to build printed circuit boards that local hobbyists could use as the base for building their own PCs. He intended to build each board for twenty dollars and sell it for forty dollars. If he and Wozniak each put in a thousand dollars, Jobs argued, they could build one hundred such boards and double their money.

Wozniak objected that there were only about five hundred local hobbyists to whom they could sell these boards and most of them were already using Altair machines that did not need one. Wozniak did not think there were even fifty people who would buy the product Jobs wanted to sell, much less a hundred. They would lose their shirts.

Jobs then shifted his pitch to shared interests that went beyond finances: their relationship and their independence. As Wozniak describes the conversation in his autobiography, *Woz*, "We were in his car and he said—and I can remember him saying this like it was yesterday: 'Well, even if we lose our money, we'll have a company. For once in our lives, we'll have a company.' " That appeal was just what Wozniak needed to hear. "That convinced me," he wrote. "And I was excited to think about us like that. To be two best friends starting a company. Wow. I knew right then that I'd do it. How could I not?"

Within a matter of weeks, the pair had scraped together the needed money, come up with the name "Apple" based on the name of an Oregon commune Jobs had visited called the "Apple Orchard," and launched what would rapidly become a successful enterprise doing something neither of them had anticipated: building entire PCs.

### What Do Other Parties Want That I Can Give Them to Gain Their Support?

Even if your idea does not directly further someone's interests, there may be other things you can do at relatively low cost in return for their support. In the course of selling your idea, therefore, it always pays to think about the problems and issues the other party faces and then create a package deal that advances your respective interests. A key point to remember inside most organizations is that people's self-esteem and pride can be rich sources of low-cost trade-offs in such packages.

For example, a medical center we know faced a serious crisis when a change in government regulations forced the hospital CEO to take away a major insurance benefit enjoyed by a low-paid but important group of workers: hospital residents (doctors in training). As the CEO prepared his formal announcement to make this change, rumors spread that the residents were organizing a job action to demand compensation to make up for the loss. The hospital, meanwhile, was in no position to give this group a raise without also raising the pay of many other workers, something it could not afford to do.

Finding himself between a rock and hard place, the CEO asked the residents' leaders to join a committee to explore their overall situation at the hospital. His charge to the administrator leading this committee was simple: find out as much as possible about what the residents' real interests were. His hope was that something would turn up that he could take action on. After a week of meetings, his administrator reported back that the residents would be willing to accept their reduced insurance benefit if the hospital would agree to one very important demand: they wanted to wear the same, somewhat longer white coats that full-fledged physicians wore so patients would treat them with the same respect. The CEO ordered the new coats without delay.

Good old-fashioned human vanity helps to close sales surprisingly often. For example, when Andrew Carnegie was a young boy, his mother let him keep a number of pet rabbits in the backyard. He persuaded the children in his neighborhood to gather the food for these pets by promising them he would name the new baby rabbits after the kids who brought the food. In today's world, fund-raisers for churches, schools, and universities follow the young Carnegie's example every day, selling ideas for new pews, classrooms, and physics labs by promising to place donors' names on them.

To summarize: Look for items the other side values that you can provide cheaply in return for their support. And remember that the human need for self-esteem and a feeling of importance is one of the dominant motives in human life. Never underestimate its power to help you find supporters when you are selling an idea.

### Why Might They Say No?

If your audience thinks your idea might make it worse off, count on stiff resistance. We have a working assumption about this: *people seldom do anything that is directly against their interests, at least as they understand those interests.* In the worst case—when you determine that there really is a strict conflict of interest that cannot be overcome by any amount of persuasion, framing, or creativity—you will have to accept that no sale is possible.

But you will be amazed at the number of times an objection that looks on the surface to be an idea stopper turns out on closer examination to be something you can handle relatively easily. As part of your preparation, therefore, ask yourself why *you* might say no if you were sitting across the table. Then use your answers to refine your proposal. And when you hear unanticipated objections during the idea-selling process, probe to see if there is any way you can work around them. Don't give up until you are sure that your interests cannot be reconciled.

When James Webb, whom we met in chapter 5 struggling to sell his idea of "foreign policy indicators" to the U.S. State Department, returned to Washington, D.C., in the 1960s to run the Apollo lunar-landing program, he faced enormous obstacles. One serious dispute arose over control of the space program and pitted him against the Air Force and Defense Secretary Robert McNamara. President Kennedy had announced that America would put a man on the moon, but he had not specified exactly how the government would allocate power to direct its space efforts. The Air Force wanted to extend its franchise from air to space, while Webb wanted to control everything about the space mission through his own agency, the National Aeronautics and Space Administration (NASA).

Both Webb and McNamara had, as one commentator noted at the time, "imperialistic tendencies." And both were tough, tested administrators. Webb later wrote that McNamara's bureaucratic style was to "knock you down on the floor with a sledgehammer, and then, while you [were] down, ask you to sign off on a particular decision."

The battle took shape when McNamara formally proposed in late 1962 that the Air Force "take over all manned flight in earth orbit," leaving NASA with "all flights beyond earth orbit." That meant that NASA would have the moon mission but would be stripped of all the activities that would lead up to that mission. In other words, the Defense Department would be the lead agency for space. This was a direct attack on NASA's mission as an agency, and Webb fired back a memo noting that the proposed change would "place in doubt" the space program's image as an effort "dedicated to the peaceful exploration of space."

Webb did not like McNamara's brusque style and had been careful to insulate himself from McNamara using study groups and task forces staffed by lower-level officials at the two agencies. But in this case it was obvious that a showdown between the two men was the only way to resolve the matter. Webb went to McNamara's office ready for a winner-take-all battle.

Once at the meeting, however, Webb was astonished at the way McNamara proceeded. After Webb stated his strong opening position that NASA had no intention of ceding control over orbital space flights, McNamara immediately backed down. It turned out that space was the *Air Force's* issue more than it was McNamara's. McNamara, in other words, was making a public fuss over who controlled space mainly to demonstrate loyalty to his Air Force generals, not because he believed they were right. To Webb, he acknowledged that manned space flight, which was NASA's main reason for existence, was only a secondary concern for the Department of Defense. The two men then agreed on language for a memo that was sent to all concerned parties in the weeks that followed. The memo stated that NASA was in full charge of the space program but noted that orbital flights would carry certain military experiments—at military expense. Any further joint programs would be developed, the memo concluded, "only by mutual agreement."

As Webb's story shows, conflicting interests are not always the end of idea sales. If the interests you share with the other party outweigh the areas of disagreement, you can still move forward. And, as the Webb-McNamara dispute illustrates, two sides can have different priorities on an issue, making compromises possible. Finally, if the number of people who will win with your new idea outnumber or outrank the people who will lose, then you might still succeed.

But in all these cases, you will need to resort to one or both of two specialized processes that supplement the Art of Woo: bargaining (treated below) and politics (handled in chapter 9). Bargaining helps people find resolutions for conflicting interests in one-on-one or group encounters, while political strategies provide the mechanisms for determining the winners and losers in larger organizational settings.

## Using Negotiation to Sell Ideas

Whenever there is not enough of something to go around, you face the possibility of negotiating to decide who will get how much of it. Inside organizations, such things as budgets, hiring authority, control over programs, and project assignments are often subject to some form of bargaining.

As we noted in the introduction, this book is a sequel to Richard's work on the art of negotiation, *Bargaining for Advantage*. We refer you to that book for an in-depth treatment of this subject. Here we will summarize the most important aspects of bargaining when it comes to selling ideas in relationship-sensitive situations. As you explore this section, note the subtle yet important differences between bargaining inside organizations—where ongoing relationships are always an important factor—and negotiating in other, more market-based contexts.

To begin, let's look at a simple example of an organization-based negotiation. It comes from the history of the famous Manhattan Project during World War II, which led to the development of the first atomic bomb. The job of coordinating the efforts of the world's most brilliant—and quirky—geniuses to beat Nazi Germany in the race to create the world's first atomic bomb fell to a man named Robert Oppenheimer, one of the top physicists in the 1930s and 1940s. As a colleague later observed, leading the Los Alamos lab in New Mexico, where the Manhattan Project was housed, transformed Oppenheimer from a "hesitant, diffident" academic into a "decisive executive." Oppenheimer's success in this effort depended on his being able to discover and address various individual needs and interests of the scientists working below him and then use his negotiation and management skills to keep the project moving forward.

One situation he faced involved Edward Teller, the man who later invented the hydrogen bomb. Teller grew frustrated because Oppenheimer insisted he concentrate on fission development, which Teller considered "too routine." In a display of diva-like anger, Teller withdrew from the fission-development team and threatened to leave the Manhattan Project entirely unless his demands for more interesting work were met. Oppenheimer's job was to sell Teller on the idea of staying.

Oppenheimer called Teller into his office and let Teller vent his frustrations about his work assignment. Then he started asking questions, quickly uncovering two things Teller wanted. First, Teller was eager to spend time investigating the possibility of a hydrogen device, a much longer-range prospect than the atomic bomb but one that had a great deal more theoretical interest in terms of physics. Second, Teller wanted more face time directly with Oppenheimer—an interaction he missed because of the Manhattan Project's bureaucratic structure.

Oppenheimer then offered a deal. First, he agreed to let Teller dabble in his hydrogen project—but only during limited times. Second, he agreed to schedule Teller for weekly, one-hour brainstorming sessions—a concession Oppenheimer positioned as a major sacrifice because his hectic schedule as director of the overall project did not leave much free time. In return, Teller had to agree to stay on the all-important fission development project and follow orders.

Teller agreed. The beauty of this arrangement from Oppenheimer's point of view was its low cost to the overall effort. True, he had to compromise a bit on the hydrogen research project. But he welcomed the excuse to schedule some dedicated time to theorize with his brilliant colleague. He would get just as much stimulation from the meetings as Teller would. By uncovering Teller's interests instead of going to war with him over "who was in charge," Oppenheimer kept both Teller and the Manhattan Project on task.

## The Stages of Negotiation

The Oppenheimer–Teller story illustrates a number of patterns that characterize the negotiation process. First, unlike persuasion, which can have a fluid, hard-to-predict structure to it, negotiations follow almost ritualized steps: preparing, probing, proposing, and closing. Second, because of the presence of conflicting interests, certain psychological factors play predictable roles in the way negotiations unfold. We review these factors within the context of the four negotiation stages outlined below.

### Stage 1: Preparing

Preparing to negotiate involves checking off six key elements—what *Bargaining for Advantage* calls the "Six Foundations" of effective negotiation. These include how each person's bargaining style may affect the process, your goals and bottom lines, the standards and norms that the parties will bring to the table, the background relationship you have with your counterpart, whether shared or conflicting interests dominate the situation, and which party enjoys the advantage in terms of leverage.

**Bargaining Styles.** Research has shown that people have distinct styles for handling negotiations. Unlike the five persuasion styles we discussed in chapter 2—Driver, Commander, Promoter, Chess Player, and Advocate—bargaining style preferences relate to resolving conflicts.

The styles include competing (looking for ways to win the negotiation game), collaborating (seeking and exploiting mutual interests), compromising (splitting the difference between respective positions), accommodating (conceding to the other party's demands), or avoiding (trying to dodge or defer the conflict of interest altogether). *Bargaining for Advantage* includes a specific Bargaining Styles Assessment Tool as an appendix, and we encourage you to consult both that assessment and the associated analysis to dig deeper into your bargaining styles when your idea-selling campaign requires you to negotiate.

One shorthand way to assess your preferred styles is to take what we call the "table test"—a test Richard gives at the beginning of his earlier book. Imagine you are at a big round table with nine strangers. You can look across the table and see the person sitting opposite you. Someone enters the room and proposes an offer: "I'll give a thousand dollars to each of the first two people who can convince the person sitting opposite to get up, come around the table, and stand behind his or her chair." Think about this situation for a moment and note the immediate responses that come to mind.

If your inclination was not to play this strange game, that is the "avoider" response. Why risk looking like a fool for a mere chance to win this race? Underneath this response is a lack of confidence in, or familiarity with, the negotiation tools that might be needed to win.

If you offered the person sitting opposite a fifty-fifty split of the thousand-dollar prize, that is the "compromiser" response. This is a perfectly fair solution but leaves an important question unanswered: which of you will run around the table? And while you are sorting this out, some people at the table will already be in motion.

One of those people will be the accommodator. This type of person does not waste time haggling. He or she just solves the problem for the other party by immediately getting up and racing to stand behind the opposite chair. There is just one problem with this response: the other side gets all the money. Perhaps that person will share; perhaps not. No one knows each other, so who can tell?

The fourth response is the competitive one. The competitor will devise a strategy that *forces* the other person to do the running, perhaps by claiming to have a broken leg. This means the competitor gets the thousand dollars, but he may have a hard time selling this proposal unless the other person is accommodating.

The final and most creative response is collaborative. You shout, "Let's both get moving! We can both make a thousand dollars!" And off you go. Instead of trying to divide a thousand dollars, you find a way for both sides to win.

**Goals and Bottom Lines.** Goal setting in negotiation is much more targeted than goal setting in persuasion—and is aimed squarely at the issues in conflict. Each side is likely to have walk-away positions—or "bottom lines"—on the toughest issues (a level that would prompt them to terminate the negotiation rather than say "yes") and an aspiration level (what they optimistically hope to achieve). By contrast, as we discussed in chapter 3, goal setting in persuasion can be much more general—ranging from gaining access to a decision maker to changing attitudes and securing endorsements.

Specific bargaining goals help to focus and energize the negotiation process. Research has shown that people with specific, ambitious goals tend to outperform people with do-your-best or modest aspirations. If you are negotiating for a reassignment of work, for example, it is wise to go to the meeting with a specific new job in mind that would satisfy your interests—as Teller did when he met with Oppenheimer to change his assignment from the fission to the hydrogen bomb research effort.

The specificity of negotiation goals can sometimes become a trap inside organizations because they make shared interests between the parties—such as Jobs' and Wozniak's common desire to own a company of their own—harder to locate and exploit. Both sides get so wrapped up in jockeying for advantage vis-à-vis their bargaining targets that they lose sight of larger interests they may hold in common. Skilled negotiators such as Oppenheimer, however, recognize this trap and spend the early part of the negotiation process asking questions that can help them identify any shared interests that might be used to help build bridges over the issue in conflict.

**Standards and Norms.** Authoritative standards and norms, such as company policies, operating procedures, or budgetary practices, usually form the background for idea-selling negotiations within organizations. Your preparation should therefore include a survey of the standards-based arguments you will use to advance and defend your position, and you should expect the other side to come prepared with their own arguments and their own preferred readings of relevant policies.

If you are negotiating a budget for your idea, for example, try to find budgets for similar programs or initiatives that you can cite as precedents. And be ready to defend your numbers against arguments that your program is more like another initiative that got *fewer* resources than the program or precedent you have cited. Note well: standards derived from sources outside an organization are often less persuasive than standards that come from the practices and procedures inside it.

Regardless, the most powerful standards at the bargaining table are not the ones you like the best or even the ones most people would agree with. They are the ones that *the other side genuinely believes are fair and legitimate.* Thus, in the negotiation process, skilled negotiators listen carefully to how the other party justifies its demands, searching for clues that will lead them to the standards and norms the other party will find hard to reject. Two psychological phenomena form the basis for why standards are so important in negotiation: the human need to behave in ways that are consistent with past behavior and the human tendency to defer to authority, noted in chapter 2.

Within organizations, authoritative standards resolve many potential disputes because a decision maker's credibility depends on his or her being even-handed and consistent in applying company rules and policies. Thus, when a standard favours your preferred solution, be sure to put that argument front and center. And when you are asking for an exception, make it as limited and principled as possible.

Relationships. The relationship factor plays much the same role in negotiation as it does in ordinary persuasion. Our discussion of relationships in chapter 4 therefore carries over to the negotiation context. The psychology of similarity and liking helps you build rapport at the beginning of a negotiation, and the norm of reciprocity helps set the rhythm of both information exchange and concession making as the bargaining process proceeds. Finally, as the example of Apple's two founders shows, you will negotiate in a more mutually accommodating and beneficial way when you enjoy a Trust-Level relationship with the other party.

**Interests.** As we have noted in this chapter, successful persuasion often depends on showing how your idea furthers other people's interests. When you find your audience pushing back hard on your idea, that is often a sign that you have touched a conflicting interest. The three questions we introduced at the beginning of this chapter— (1) Why might it already be in the other party's interests to support my idea? (2) What do other parties want that I can give them to gain their support? and (3) Why might they say no?—are all important in preparing to negotiate. And, as the examples in this chapter have demonstrated, the more shared interests you find, the easier it is to resolve the conflicting ones.

**Leverage.** When it comes to negotiation, the final decision as to who will compromise often comes down to a question of something called "leverage"—the balance of hopes and fears at the table. Whichever side thinks it has the least to lose from saying "no deal" generally has the most leverage and whichever party thinks it has the most to lose has the least leverage.

In market transactions, one of the most important measures of leverage is something negotiation scholars call your "BATNA"—or Best Alternative to a Negotiated Agreement. This is what each party will do if it walks away from the deal. Everything else being equal, the better your walk-away alternative, the more leverage you have.

But when you are selling ideas within the flow of ongoing relationships, the concept of BATNA does not apply quite as neatly. People do not—and often cannot—"walk away" from a relationship just because a boss, colleague, or controller is being stubborn. Indeed, a threat to walk away in such circumstances is, eight times out of ten, made in anger—as was the case with Teller's threatened resignation from the Manhattan Project—or delivered as a high-stakes bluff. For example, the founder of Phillips Petroleum—Frank Phillips— once resolved a major dispute with his board of directors by submitting a formal, detailed letter of resignation. He knew that the board could not accept it because the company was too closely associated in the financial community's mind with him and his family. But by refusing to accept it, the board was in effect conceding to Phillips on the issue they were debating. His bluff worked and he won his point.

So if people do not walk away from organizational negotiations very often, what determines leverage?

In general, the parties with more control over resources—future decisions, budgets, services, and staff—enjoy the most leverage in idea-selling negotiations. And take note: this is not always the person with the highest rank or most prestigious title.

At another point in the bureaucratic bickering that surrounded the Apollo program, James Webb got into a fight with the White House science adviser, Jerry Wiesner, over a technical issue related to the program. A British diplomat, hearing of this disagreement, asked President Kennedy how the dispute would come out. "Jerry's going to lose," the president said. "It's obvious."

"Why?" the diplomat wanted to know.

"Webb's got all the money," Kennedy rejoined, "and Jerry's only got me."

In addition to controlling resources, you gain leverage whenever you make the other party more *dependent* on you. We once interviewed a financial adviser by phone for a research study we were doing. We happened to catch him on his car phone and asked where he was going. To our surprise, he said he was driving from his home in western Virginia to a small town in the neighboring state of Tennessee—a three-hundred-mile drive—to fix a computer belonging to one of his investment clients. "Are you a computer consultant on the side?" we asked. "No," he replied, "but this guy has ten million dollars with me, so I try to make myself as indispensable as possible." The adviser was, in short, building leverage within this important relationship.

Thus, as part of an effective preparation, you should always assess your leverage and see if it can be improved before you begin the negotiation. What do you control that other people need? What could you withhold that they might miss?

In Oppenheimer's case, he had leverage over Teller as the director of the Manhattan Project. But he did not have *all* the leverage: he needed Teller's genius to keep the mission moving forward. Thus, some sort of interest-based compromise was the best solution for everyone. Oppenheimer's secret to success in using his leverage was his skill in managing volatile emotions and quirky personalities, not his ability to hammer on the table. Like John D. Rockefeller in chapter 2, Oppenheimer was an effective Chess Player.

## Stage 2: Probing

The second stage of negotiation is the reciprocal exchange of information about the problem under discussion. This stage generally begins, as do many persuasion encounters, with rapport building based on similarity and liking. It then proceeds to an exchange of information on what the agenda is before narrowing to the issues that the parties have to resolve.

As this chapter has suggested, smart negotiators realize that the most important part of information exchange is the search for interests that can be used to help resolve the issues in conflict. Thus, they defer the discussion of these difficult issues until they have had a chance to find out if the other side has problems or concerns that can be used to enrich the bargaining mix.

Unless time is very short, therefore, always begin the information exchange stage of negotiation by asking questions about the current situation facing your counterpart and what might be done to improve it. The more you know about the other side's problems and needs, the better you will be at structuring a wise concession strategy. The opposite is also true: the quicker you get to the issue in conflict, the less likely it is you will get beyond it to other interests. Once people begin bargaining over what they disagree about, they have a harder time seeing what they have in common—much less looking for new things they might be able to do together.

## Stage 3: Proposing

Stage 3 of negotiation begins with the first concrete proposal that offers a solution to the issue in conflict—either on its own or wrapped in a package that includes other issues and interests. It continues until the parties either reach an agreement or break off discussions because they cannot make a deal.

The initial tactical question that arises in negotiation relates to openings. Should you make the first offer or wait for the other side to propose something? There are possible advantages and disadvantages either way.

If you make the first offer, you get the benefit of what negotiation scholars call the "anchor effect": you set the other party's expectations about the range of final agreements that may be possible. Teller was trying to anchor Oppenheimer on his demands when he framed his opening offer as "Let me work on the hydrogen project or I'll quit!"

There is an art to opening. If your demands are ambitious but still plausible, you get the benefit of the anchor effect. If they are too extreme, however, you lose credibility—a price you cannot afford in relationship-sensitive, organizational negotiations.

Here is how the anchor effect works in a traditional, price-based negotiation. Suppose you are being recruited for a job and the salary ranges from £100,000 to £125,000. If you open at £130,000 (an ambitious but still plausible request), the employer is likely to anchor on your high opening, and his or her expectations will shift toward the higher end of the possible range. On the other hand, if you guess wrong about the range and open at £150,000, you will probably discourage the employer from countering at all—leaving you with the awkward choice of either walking away or apologizing for your aggressive opening. Lesson: the more you know about the range of "fair" outcomes, the better luck you will have constructing an opening and taking advantage of the anchor effect.

Letting *the other side* go first also has a big advantage: you get information about what your counterpart is willing to do before showing your own hand. We were leading a negotiation seminar for a major bank once and covered this point about openings in the morning session. After lunch, one of the executives returned with a story. He had had an important meeting with the divisional vice president over the lunch break to discuss a major reorganization the bank was going through. Staff cuts were on the table and the question on our executive's mind as he went into this meeting was, "Should I open with an offer of the cuts I would be willing to take—and try to anchor the discussions on my numbers—or should I hear the vice president out first?"

He decided to let the vice president make the first proposal. "I figured that he knew a lot more than I did about this whole process," he said, explaining his decision. "I had no idea what he might have in mind for our unit." The decision paid off: the vice president proposed *fewer* cuts than our executive would have opened with.

In general, the less you know about the range of appropriate solutions, the more you gain from letting the other person make the first offer. But when you let the other party go first, protect yourself against the anchor effect. If they put a surprisingly aggressive opening on the table, take a break before responding. Go back to your research and re-anchor yourself on your own goals and perspectives about what is fair. Otherwise you may unconsciously modify your expectations of what is possible.

With the opening round over, there are three standard methods for managing the actual give-and-take part of the negotiation process.

First, you can follow a "concession bargaining" procedure. This is the conventional ritual used in simple market transactions such as car sales, where each party stakes out optimistic opening ground and concedes slowly to some point between the two opening offers.

As common as this process is in transactions, it often looks clumsy and even a little disrespectful to your counterpart when ongoing relationships are important. You are negotiating to sell an important idea, after all—not buy or sell a used car. You can lose credibility when you bring the tactics of the bazaar into the executive suite. Oppenheimer showed both patience and skill in choosing not to respond to Teller's opening "I quit" gambit with an equally extreme "you can't quit because you're fired."

As ill-fitting as concession bargaining may be for structuring an entire idea-selling negotiation, however, you may come down to a mini-version of this procedure on small matters that are relatively unimportant to the overall proposal. Quick-and-easy strategies to "split the difference" or round up or down to the nearest focal point may then be perfectly appropriate.

A second way to manage the bargaining process is to offer a "package deal" containing several elements, some of which address conflicting interests and some of which address shared interests. The parties can then move the pieces in the package around until they find an arrangement that suits them both. This is what Oppenheimer and Teller did. Oppenheimer conceded on both of Teller's issues—but not 100 percent. With some tweaking about just how much time Teller could spend on his pet project and exactly how they would work out the weekly meetings, the two men were able to reach an agreement on the package.

The third way in which the proposal stage is handled in an idea-selling environment—and this happens surprisingly often in organizations—is for there to be no haggling or tweaking whatever. The opening proposal is assumed to be a good-faith attempt to incorporate everyone's needs, the justification for its elements are viewed by everyone as perfectly legitimate and fair, and everyone agrees that time can be saved—and relationships preserved—by putting a first, firm, and fair proposal together that solves the matter.

The success of this last procedure depends on there being relatively clear precedents and standards available that assure the parties they are working within a comfortable zone of agreement. It also presumes some degree of initial trust and continuing oversight that can be relied on to provide for adjustments should the original agreement later prove to be unfair or unworkable.

### Stage 4: Closing

The closing stage of negotiations secures the agreement and confirms everyone's commitment to the deal. We will discuss commitments as part of idea selling in chapter 9. For now, suffice it to say that a commitment at the end of an idea-selling campaign is designed to achieve the same goal as one at the end of a negotiation: you want other people to carry through on their agreements. Putting the agreement in writing, having witnesses who know what everyone agreed to, announcing the deal, having performance benchmarks, and reviewing progress periodically all help to secure a negotiated agreement and make it stick.

## Best Practices for Uncovering Shared Interests

As we have seen, discovering and appealing to shared interests helps to both frame proposals that are attractive to the other side and negotiate package deals when conflicting interests are part of the mix. How does one go about discovering these interests?

The first step is to make the search for shared interests a regular part of your planning and preparation. Research by two English social scientists—Neil Rackham and John Carlisle—confirmed that one of the best practices of the most skilled negotiators is to make this search a routine part of planning. The best negotiators in their study spent 40 percent of their planning time on the search for shared interests, compared with only 10 percent for less skilled negotiators.

One obvious way to do this is by seeking background intelligence on the situation your counterpart faces—his problems, concerns, and constraints. In organizational persuasion encounters, you can sometimes gain surprising amounts of such intelligence by chatting with lower-level staff in the person's division or asking for input from colleagues.

Another tool is a role reversal. Ask a friend to play you—while you sit in your counterpart's chair for a few minutes and play him or her. Role-play an encounter similar to the one you hope to have and see what arguments and feelings arise as you hear your own idea pitch coming at you. Your skills in understanding other people's perspectives will be an important part of making this effort productive.

Finally, as you make your pitch, do not be afraid to search for information that can help you confirm your assumptions about the other person's interests and, even better, uncover new concerns. Make comments that open the door to learning about the other side's needs. "It has been hard to think clearly with all the changes going on," you might say as you start your pitch for a new work-life balance program. "Our group is more stretched than ever with the most recent layoffs, but I was not sure if your division had been affected the same way."

The same Rackham and Carlisle study that revealed interest-based planning behavior among skilled negotiators showed an equal attention to interest-based questioning during the negotiation process itself. Skilled negotiators spent about 40 percent of their time at the bargaining table asking questions, testing for understanding, and summarizing—while average negotiators devoted only 20 percent of their time to these behaviors. The rest of their time was spent proposing, arguing, defending their positions, and haggling—activities that discourage the candid flow of interest-based information.

## Conclusion

This chapter concludes our look at Step 2 of the Woo process. Your audience's underlying goals and interests are the final barriers that may block your idea from receiving a fair hearing on the merits. By the same token, if you can position your idea as helping your audience to solve an urgent problem, you achieve four important goals.

First, you will have your audience's attention—a crucial, scarce resource in today's busy world. As Andrew Carnegie's nephews taught us, people pay closer attention to your communications when they think they might have something to gain.

Second, your audience is likely to become biased in favour of your idea. Once people see an idea as furthering their own agenda, they do not press as hard for reasons, evidence, or logic. They already *want to buy* your idea. You just have to supply them with justifications to do so.

Third, you will gain valuable leverage in any negotiation that subsequently takes place to resolve disagreements over your proposal. You now have a "positive" to place in the scales against any "negatives" that others may put there. And your shared interest may be enough to overcome the conflicting ones that later surface.

Finally, as we will see in chapter 9, shared interests are the glue that holds political alliances together in tough organizational battles over resources, implementation, and control. The more problems and needs you address, the wider the base of support you can build within the organization.

As this chapter showed, the negotiation process can help overcome barriers when interests collide. Negotiation is a structured way of handling disputes that begins with preparation and probing and ends with proposing and closing. Your ability to manage the six foundations of negotiation—bargaining styles, goals, standards, relationships, interests, and leverage—will greatly increase your success in selling ideas. And the more resources you control and dependencies you create, the better your outcome is likely to be.

With your audience's interests in mind, you are now ready to move to Step 3—*Make Your Pitch*. In the next two chapters, we will help you make your best argument and then put some "snap" into your ideas to give them special appeal.

chapter seven

# State Your Case: The Proposal

A problem well stated is a problem half solved.
—Charles F. Kettering, inventor

Strong reasons make strong actions.
—King John in William Shakespeare's *King John*

Imagine that you work at Google, one of the world's most successful Internet companies, and that you have a hot new idea you'd like to sell to senior management. Following the advice we've given you so far, you would devise a stepping-stone strategy, build a broad base of support, and move carefully up the chain of command to the decision maker.

Only at Google, all of that would be a complete waste of time.

Because, unlike most companies, Google has an explicit "geek culture" process for selling ideas that is structured, direct, and non-political. As Google vice president Jonathan Rosenberg has put it, "Everyone spends a fraction of [the] day on R&D." Google believes in cutting straight to the content of proposals. They are big believers in the kind of idea-selling culture that Alfred Sloan instilled in General Motors in the 1920s and Sam Walton insisted on at Wal-Mart in the 1960s and 1970s.

Not long after Google was launched, its senior leadership had a realization. As the director of technology said, "We always had great ideas, but we didn't have a good way of expressing them or capturing them." So Google created a system for getting ideas circulated and vetted. A Stanford-trained computer scientist named Marissa Mayer—Google's twentieth employee—developed an intranet site that is the center of the process, and targeted it to appeal to the typical Google employee: a quiet, introverted engineer who has lots of ideas but who feels much more comfortable writing them down than talking about them. Now anyone who has an idea can post it on a separate Web page, where it gets thoroughly discussed by Google colleagues.

This is a Darwinian, survival-of-the-fittest process. As one ex-employee has commented, the discussions on the Google idea board exhibit "geek machismo": employees vie for the honor of being the person who delivers the smartest electronic "zaps" that support, modify, or even kill an idea.

If an idea gets enough support on the Web board, its originator wins a face-to-face meeting during "office hours" with Ms. Mayer. At this point, says Mayer, "I can get [my engineer] to come out of his shell." But here, too, Google culture dictates that participants dispense with pleasantries, flashy slide shows, and long-winded presentations. When a Google employee steps into Mayer's office to sell an idea, he or she gets no more than *ten minutes* to make the case. And Mayer can be as ruthless as a TV reality show judge. When managers fail to impress her, the interview is over.

The final idea-selling stage is a formal product-review session with Google's top brass. At these sessions, nobody gets away with statements such as "most people like this" or "the majority prefers that." Google's leaders worship data and want to know exactly what information led the idea sellers to their conclusions. From the ideas that make it through this top-level forum, Google selects the ones in which to invest.

Imagine, then, that you are in Marissa Mayer's office at Google and you have ten minutes to woo her on your idea. How should you proceed?

First, you need a template for making the most powerful argument possible in the shortest amount of time. This chapter provides you with such a template. Second, you need to support your argument with the most relevant, convincing evidence—so the last part of the chapter deals with how to select and present such evidence. Finally, you need devices that will make your audience sit up and take notice—a subject we will treat in chapter 8.

## An Introduction to Practical Reasoning: The Power of "Because"

When all is said and done, the two most reliable ways to persuade people are the most traditional: offer them solid reasons to say "yes," and back those reasons up with evidence. The soundness of the reasons required and the depth of evidence, however, vary with the circumstances. When people don't care much about the issue under discussion, are unqualified to evaluate it, or are already inclined to agree based on their own beliefs and interests (see chapters 5 and 6), the arguments need not be rigorous. Indeed, the simplest of statements such as "I think this is a good idea because . . ." may be enough to make a sale if you say it with conviction and credibility.

Research has demonstrated that the word *because* has a special power in human interaction. A Harvard psychologist named Ellen Langer once decided to test just how powerful this word could be—especially in informal, everyday settings. She set up an experiment at one of Harvard's libraries. Her assistant waited until there was a line of people waiting to use a popular photocopy machine and then attempted to cut into the front of the line to make her own copies. See if you can guess (in rough percentages) what the assistant's success rates were for each of the following persuasion attempts. For example, if you think the assistant was successful about half the time using the first statement, you would write "50%" in the space below. In the first three statements, the assistant asked to make only five copies. In the last two, she told people she had twenty copies to make. Read through all five statements before making your guesses.

1. "Excuse me, I have five pages. May I use the Xerox machine?" Success rate: _____

2. "Excuse me, I have five pages. May I use the Xerox machine because I am in a rush?" Success rate: _____

3. "Excuse me, I have five pages. May I use the Xerox machine because I have to make copies?" Success rate _____

4. "Excuse me, I have twenty pages. May I use the Xerox machine?" Success rate: _____

5. "Excuse me, I have twenty pages. May I use the Xerox machine
   because I am in a rush?" Success rate: _____

First, if you guessed that the assistant had better luck cutting in
line when she had five pages than when she had twenty, you were
correct. The more you impose on someone, especially strangers, the
harder it is to obtain a favour. But once you hold the number of
pages constant, the assistant's success improved dramatically when
she offered a "because" statement to justify her request.

In the experiment, the success rate for statement number 1 was 60
percent, but jumped to 94 *percent* for statement number 2. And, interestingly, the wording of the offered reason made no difference
whatever. When the assistant offered a nonsense reason ("because I
have to make some copies") in statement number 3, people let her
cut ahead in line 93 percent of the time. And the pattern of responding more willingly to a "because" statement held true even when the
assistant was asking for a bigger favour—to cut in line to make
twenty copies. The success rate for statement number 4 was only 24
percent, but almost doubled to 42 percent for statement number 5.

Conclusion? Simply offering a reason to justify the request increased the assistant's success rate dramatically. The assistant could
have said something elaborate like, "I have a professor waiting outside in the car and he is double parked," but "I am in a rush" and "I
have to make copies" did the trick. The listeners unconsciously filled
in the blanks of a possible story behind the assistant's request and let
her cut in front of them.

Langer called this "mindless" compliance and wrote an entire
book about it called *Mindfulness* in 1989. But we think the phenomenon she discovered might better be called a "civility" or "reason-
ableness" response. When it comes to small favours that people ask
of each other in everyday life, most people want to be helpful when
they can—so long as it does not greatly disrupt their own needs, and
provided that people make the requests in a polite, civil way. Offering reasons—even when the reasons are pretty thin—dignifies the request and shows a little respect for the people you are imposing on.

In the more formal persuasion settings you encounter at work, the
strength of your reasoning matters more. In addition, reasons that

point to external factors you do not control ("my professor is double parked, so I need to cut in line") tend to carry more weight than ones pointing to your own convenience ("I am in a rush"). But even here you will face two distinct levels of scrutiny, as we saw in chapter 6. When your audience is motivated by its own interests to support you—or when it does not care about or understand your idea—little more than "plausible" reasoning is required. "The salary I am offering is well above the average range for this type of position in the industry," an employer might say. If the employee wants to take the job and the salary level suggested meets her needs, the employer's "it's more than fair within the industry" explanation provides a good way to close the sale. There is no need to engage a consultant to discover exactly what the industry norms are. When asked by her friends why she accepted the offer, the employee has a face-saving story to tell: "It was above the industry standard."

Psychologists call this sort of relaxed reasoning "peripheral" or "heuristic" processing. Credibility (chapter 4) and accessibility (the next chapter) count for a great deal in such cases. The audience scans the proposal for reassuring signs of familiarity, fairness, expertise, or personal trustworthiness and, finding such signs, says "yes."

Sometimes, especially when presenting a technical idea to a nonexpert audience, you need to work hard to find a "hook" in the audience's ordinary experience to trigger this "yes" response. Otherwise, people may resent your expertise instead of deferring to it—interpreting your lack of effort to explain your idea as a lack of respect for them.

For example, thousands of consumers recently sued the pharmaceutical company Merck, alleging that a pain-relief medicine called Vioxx caused them or loved ones to suffer life-threatening heart attacks. The first case to go to trial was brought in Texas, and Merck put on a vigorous scientific defense. The company showed the jury all of its drug studies, explained how these studies were done, called its researchers to testify about methodology, and discussed how scientists reason with statistics.

The plaintiff's lawyer, by contrast, told a story of the plaintiff's innocence, suffering, and loss. This is a time-honored courtroom strategy followed since Roman times, when plaintiffs' lawyers would hire professional "wailers" to come to court and weep as the injured victim told his story. In the Merck case, the plaintiff's legal team explained how the plaintiff had gotten Vioxx from his doctor, taken it as recommended, suffered a heart attack, died, and left a grieving widow and family. The lawyers then showed how Merck had failed to report certain findings related to heart attack risk, had resisted disclosing this information even when pressed for it, and had made billions of dollars selling the drug to the public. In short, there were good guys and bad guys—and Merck was the bad guy.

The jury found for the plaintiff. Merck's arguments about statistical significance fell on deaf ears. A juror named John Ostrom later commented, "We didn't know what the heck they were talking about." Whenever Merck was up there, Ostrom said, "It was wah, wah, wah." But the jury could understand the story about an innocent victim and a profit-hungry corporation. So the jurors based their decision on what they understood.

Unfair? Perhaps. But Merck's lawyers made a bad call: they offered a research seminar to a nonexpert audience. They should have been telling a story of their own: how the plaintiff died because of a bad heart, not because of bad medicine. In subsequent Vioxx trials, Merck put the science in the background and did a much better job making its case on a human level that juries could understand. Merck's success rate rose substantially.

So much for practical reasoning when the audience is biased, uninvolved, or unable to follow a technical pitch. Now it is time to return to Marissa Mayer's office hours. What is the best way to structure a high-stakes, ten-minute argument in a Google-like environment—when your reasoning is sure to be challenged by an attentive, well-informed group?

## Wooing an Engaged Audience: The PCAN Model

Our template for making a tight idea-selling case to an involved audience has four parts:

- a short, concise statement that defines the problem your idea solves (or the need it addresses),

- an explanation of the cause of this problem or need,

- your solution—or answer—for the situation, and

- a summary of why your answer is the best available, all other options considered.

We call this the PCAN model—the acronym stands for **P**roblem, **C**ause, **A**nswer, and **N**et Benefits. We use this model in our executive programs and consulting projects. Managers start with a set of issues identified as important to a company's strategy. Over the course of a program, they take each issue apart, discuss how to define the underlying problem, and then move on to possible causes, solutions, and assessments of net benefits. The PCAN model concentrates people's attention, producing sharp, practical recommendations.

It also gives you a structure within which to use all the information you gathered as you grappled with the five potential barriers. It is here that you can select the arguments and evidence that address other people's interests, reinforce their beliefs, and accommodate their preferred vocabulary for discussing your issue.

We wish these four PCAN factors were original with us, but they go back to the ancient philosophers of rhetoric, who identified this structure as the best way to debate questions of policy (that is, debates seeking answers to the question "What shall we do?"). There are other structures for investigating questions such as "What is morally right?" or "What do we mean by this term or word?" But we will focus on the "What shall we do?" question because it is the stock-in-trade of people within organizations—from sales departments trying to attract customers to senior leaders arguing over whether to enter a new market or close an old factory.

The PCAN model works at both an intuitive and a formal level. In his book *Perfect Pitch,* for example, advertising executive Jon Steel tells a story of a five-minute meeting he had in 1997 with Apple CEO Steve Jobs. Apple's communications VP had invited Steel and a colleague to come to Apple, meet with Jobs, and pitch their company for an advertising engagement. They had brought a full-throttle presentation to sell Jobs on using their services.

Jobs kept Steel and his partner waiting in a conference room for almost two hours before he finally came in wearing his signature outfit: jeans and a black polo sweater. Steel and his partner were ready to start their pitch, but before they could get up from their seats, Jobs went to the front of the room and picked up a marker pen.

"Okay," Jobs said. "This company is in deep shit. But I believe that if we do some simple things very well, we can save it and we can grow it. I've asked you here today because I need your help."

In rapid strokes on a white board, Jobs made fourteen boxes to represent fourteen current projects, all of which carried hundreds of millions of dollars in investment. Then, one by one, he crossed through all but two of them. "I'm going to bet the future of this company on them," he continued, pointing to boxes labeled "G4" and "iMac."

"Now, what do I want from you?" he continued.

What he wanted, Jobs explained, was a cost-effective plan to communicate a huge "thank you" to Apple's core customers—the people who had stuck by the company during the recent, grim days when it looked as if Apple had lost its way and might even go bankrupt. He wanted to reconnect with these customers and prepare the way for the launch of the two "bet-the-company projects" that were what stood between Apple and oblivion. With that, Steel and his partner were asked to deliver a proposal ASAP and shown the door.

Steel left the meeting with two thoughts. First, Jobs was something of a jerk. He kept them waiting for two hours, never apologized, and never let them get a word in. Second, despite his arrogance, Jobs was a brilliant, efficient idea seller.

Do you see the structure embedded in Steve Jobs' intense, five-minute presentation?

**Problem:** Apple was in deep financial trouble.

**Cause:** Fourteen projects with millions in sunk costs were bleeding the firm dry.

**Answer:** Jobs was betting the company on the G4 and the iMac, and needed advertising help to reconnect with his customer base to set the stage for these two products.

**Net Benefits:** Jobs' focused, two-product strategy was, by implication, the best of the many alternatives the Apple leadership team had considered as ways to save the company.

Jobs' presentation also illustrates several "best practices" to keep in mind when making a powerful, compressed pitch.

First, lead off with your best arguments and evidence rather than hiding them for a surprise at the end. Jobs got right to his main points and nailed them down tight. Your audience's attention is a prize worth winning. If you do not impress people right away with the urgency and importance of your problem, you may not get a second chance.

Research on the so-called Primacy Effect shows that, given a list of things to remember, people tend to recall the first few items much better than the items in the middle or at the end. By contrast, when you are selling your idea over a longer period of time, people are subject to the "Recency Effect" and recall better the points you make near the end of the persuasion process and that are therefore most top of mind. To get the benefit of both effects, make your best points early, then summarize them briefly again at the end.

Second, make your conclusions explicit. Don't hide the ball. Jobs summed up his company's situation in his first six words: "This company is in deep shit." We will talk about a number of devices in chapter 8 to keep and hold your audience's attention. And several of these involve getting your audience to participate in your presentation by asking them to guess or speculate about where your argument is headed. But never leave your conclusions ambiguous for long. Show your audience where you stand.

Finally, keep it simple. Even smart people like to have ideas boiled down to the most concise, practical form. This makes your case easier for them to remember, categorize, and fit into the pattern of their mental maps and experience. Reduce your statement of the problem to the length of a Chinese cookie fortune slip. Summarize your data in one hundred words rather than one thousand. Capture your recommendations in one or two phrases. But don't forget to bring all the data. You want to be able to defend your case if you are called upon to do so.

You now have a model for how to handle a Google-styled, ten-minute idea pitch. But the PCAN model is just as powerful when you find yourself in a more formal presentation setting or must plead your case to a series of audiences, each with its own special interests. To illustrate the power of the PCAN model in these more complex situations, we have chosen a fateful White House meeting that took place on May 13, 1940—roughly a year and a half before America entered World War II. If Steve Jobs' company hung in the balance at his meeting in 1997, the future of the free world was at stake at this White House meeting. As you will see, a well-structured, ten-minute pitch covering the first two PCAN factors got this idea sale started. It then took a series of presentations over several weeks to cover the "A" and "N" factors and close the deal.

## Making the Case for War

In May 1940, the Army Chief of Staff, General George C. Marshall (later to take charge of the entire Allied war effort against Germany and Japan), and several senior cabinet officials asked for a meeting with President Franklin D. Roosevelt to protest recent military spending cuts by Congress. They wanted the president to demand that Congress restore these cuts. In the back of Marshall's mind, like distant thunder, were thoughts of the war in Europe.

Three days earlier, on May 10, Hitler had launched his "blitzkrieg"—or lightning war—against northern Europe, invading the low countries and driving toward France. Nevertheless, strange as it now sounds, Roosevelt and his political team were more worried about winning the upcoming November 1940 presidential election than they were troubled by what was happening in Europe. Public sentiment in the United States was strongly isolationist and the country was still a major exporter of steel to Japan. Talk of war was unpopular with the press and unwelcome in the White House. As one angry Marshall staff assistant had put it prior to this meeting, "They'd rather lose a war than lose a vote."

The meeting was scheduled for 11 A.M. As Marshall, Secretary of the Treasury Henry Morgenthau, and several other officials entered the Oval Office, Marshall immediately noticed that the president was distracted. "It was quite evident," Marshall later commented, "[that he] was not desirous of seeing us." Morgenthau plowed ahead anyway, launching into a detailed presentation about military equipment and budgets. Roosevelt cut him short, telling him he had heard enough. Well then, said Morgenthau, "Will you hear General Marshall?"

The president was curt. "I know exactly what he will say," Roosevelt replied. "There is no necessity for me to hear him at all."

As Marshall later recounted the situation, Roosevelt's offhanded way of dismissing him and his senior advisers suddenly brought home to him the full emotional weight of his responsibility for correcting the "desperate situation" the United States faced militarily. "I felt that he might be president, but I had certain knowledge that I was sure he didn't possess or which he didn't grasp," Marshall later said.

He then made his move. "Recalling that a man has a great advantage, psychologically, when he stands looking down on a fellow, I took advantage—in a sense—of the president's condition [Roosevelt was confined to a wheelchair with polio]. When he terminated the meeting, I, having not had a chance to say anything, walked over and stood looking down at him and said, 'Mr. President, may I have three minutes?' " Marshall's voice carried the strain of strong emotions held in check.

Roosevelt, used to being approached by military advisers in subdued, deferential tones, was caught short by Marshall's intensity.

"Of course, General Marshall," he replied.

Marshall then stated his case—and, because of the feelings of genuine frustration surging within him, he painted his ideas on a broader canvas and with more passion than he had planned. The military situation was more than serious, Marshall said. It was "catastrophic." The evidence was everywhere. Hitler had invaded Denmark and Norway in April and taken them virtually without a fight. A mere three days ago, Hitler had invaded Luxembourg, Belgium, the Netherlands, and France with stunning swiftness and success. These actions revealed not only Hitler's plan to conquer Europe but also the power and strength of his modern war machine.

America, meanwhile, was barely prepared to defend its own coastlines, much less take on an enemy of such ferocity. Its war equipment dated from World War I. Its force strength was below even peacetime standards—a fraction of what would be needed if Hitler used his newfound leverage to cut America off from its markets and vital economic supply lines. Commanders were complaining bitterly about the poor state of readiness and equipment.

"I just came here in the first place about a [funding] cut," Marshall continued. But the stakes were much, much higher.

"I don't quite know how to express myself about this to the president of the United States, but I will say this to you." And here Marshall's emotions tumbled out: *"You have got to do something and you've got to do it today."* (The emphasis is in the transcript of Marshall's audiotaped recollection of this meeting.)

Let's pause the story for a moment to see where Marshall is in terms of stating his case.

### PCAN: Define the Problem

The first question on an audience's mind when you are selling an idea is the most basic one: *so what?* Why should anyone be spending time with you? President Roosevelt's distracted demeanor made this question explicit for Marshall, but it is always lurking in the background when you pitch an idea. Marshall's first move was therefore to identify, define, and document the urgent problem that the president needed to address. Marshall used his three minutes to paint a high-definition picture of the military crisis the United States faced on the brink of war. And the emotion he brought to the encounter drove his message home.

As our lead quote for this chapter notes: "A problem well stated is a problem half solved." And according to noted communications expert David Zarefsky, "definition is the key to persuasion." By providing a crisp answer to the question "What is the problem?" you establish the context in which your idea will be evaluated. Cognitive psychologists call this the act of *framing,* and it powerfully affects people's perceptions, the standards they will call to mind, the evidence they will consider relevant, the emotions they will feel, and the decisions they will ultimately make. As the American journalist and commentator Walter Lippmann once said, "For the most part, we do not first see, and then define. We define first and then see." How you state the problem defines what your audience will see in its mind's eye.

At the World Economic Forum in Davos, Switzerland, in 2005, social activist Bono (whom we met in chapter 5) sat on the main stage with British Prime Minister Tony Blair, former U.S. President Bill Clinton, President Olusegun Obasanjo of Nigeria, President Thabo Mbeki of South Africa, and Microsoft CEO Bill Gates to discuss the problems of Africa. Bono listened as the others detailed all of the difficulties Africa faced in overcoming AIDS, poverty, and political corruption. Then the moderator asked Bono what he would like to see changed.

Instead of continuing with the panel discussion, however, Bono decided to reframe the issue. What he wanted changed, he said, was "the tone of the debate." And he continued:

> Here we are, reasonable men talking about a reasonable situation. I walk down the street and people say: "I love what you're doing. Love your cause, Bon." [But] I don't think six thousand Africans a day dying from AIDS is a cause; it's an emergency. And three thousand children dying every day of malaria isn't a cause; it's an emergency.

Bono's message got through. The audience of corporate executives, government ministers, and cultural luminaries burst into loud applause. Poverty and AIDS in Africa were not business-as-usual issues for public officials and bureaucrats. They were global "emergencies." Emergencies require action, not analysis. They affect everyone, not just specialists.

We once witnessed a similar act of problem reframing at a meeting between community representatives and local university officials. The meeting had been called to discuss a crime wave around the campus. A neighborhood activist took the floor and launched into a litany of complaints about how the university had failed to follow through on various promises made in the past to help the community. The officials, who were new to the university and had had nothing to do with any of these failures, began looking frustrated and impatient. But the activist raged on.

Sensing the officials' frustration, a college professor who lived in the neighborhood interrupted and pointed out that none of these past failures had happened on these administrators' watch. Moreover, the professor said, the current situation was more urgent than any in the past and touched more directly than ever on the university's core interests. He then told a story of an armed assault on a new member of the faculty that had happened a week earlier a few blocks from the campus. The traumatized faculty member was now considering leaving the university. "The problem," said the professor, "is not what the university may or may not have done ten years ago, but what it can do to protect the safety of its students, staff, and faculty *tonight*."

The officials perked up immediately. "This is what we came to discuss," the top administrator present said. "What actions do you think the university should be considering?"

## PCAN: Explain the Cause of the Problem

Marshall had brought home to the president a crisp, urgent definition of the problem. The question now naturally arose: how had this situation gotten so out of hand?

The second stage of an idea sale answers the question "Why do we have this problem—what caused it?" An investigation into causes usually points the way toward solutions. After all, what better way to eliminate a problem than to remove the conditions that brought it about?

But this question put Marshall in a delicate position. Roosevelt had been in office for most of the 1930s and was, therefore, directly responsible for the weak state of the military. If Marshall made this part of his argument explicit, he would offend the president, shutting down any hope of gaining Roosevelt's support. So Marshall finessed this issue. He let Roosevelt fill in the blanks for himself.

Secretary Morgenthau would later reflect on this meeting in his personal diary, noting that Marshall had acted with notable courage by even raising the military preparedness problem with Roosevelt. "The President has to take a great deal of the responsibility that the Army is in as bad shape as it is. . . ." Morgenthau wrote. "[I was] tremendously impressed with General Marshall. He stood right up to the President."

Thus, in the second stage of the PCAN process, you want to explore—as Steve Jobs did when he showed the fourteen projects at Apple that were draining cash—the causes of the problem. But you may sometimes need to do this diplomatically, in a way that avoids assigning *blame*, especially if your audience helped to create the situation.

## PC*A*N: What Is My Answer to the Problem?

Perhaps Roosevelt realized that he was at least partially responsible for the depleted state of the military, because Marshall's message struck home. As Marshall and Morgenthau turned to leave, Roosevelt stopped them.

"Oh, General," the president said casually. "Come back and see me tomorrow. And bring me a list of your requirements."

Marshall did so, and the next day presented the third part of his case: his answer to the military's needs. He wanted tens of thousands of new airplanes, an increase in defense appropriations from the current five hundred million dollars per year to tens of billions in the next two years, an increase in manpower to bring the Army to 280,000 men, and a strong new emphasis on industrial and material production for military purposes. With these actions, Marshall said, America would be in a position to meet the Nazi challenge.

The president agreed to each and every one of Marshall's requests.

The third part of the PCAN model is the payoff section. Here you get to outline your proposal, show how it will solve the problem, and demonstrate that it could work in the real world.

The question of feasibility is central to this stage of your argument. Sure, you have come up with an answer for a problem—but will your idea *really work*? Idea sales in technical fields often get hung up at this stage. For example, George W. Ferris, a bridge builder from Pittsburgh, Pennsylvania, almost lost his chance to invent the "Ferris Wheel" for the 1893 Chicago World's Fair because he stumbled at this stage of his idea-selling campaign.

Daniel Hudson Burnham, the chief architect for the fair, had issued a challenge to America's engineers, asking them to design something "novel, original, daring and unique"—similar to "the Eiffel Tower at the Paris Exposition"—to serve as the fair's iconic image and uphold American engineering as a profession of "prestige and standing."

Ferris later said that his richly detailed idea for a giant revolving wheel had come to him "like an inspiration" almost as soon as he heard Burnham's challenge. After weeks of intense calculations, Ferris and his team concluded such a wheel could be built, and with Burnham's endorsement, the fair's Ways and Means Committee approved the idea.

But the very next day, the Committee reneged. As word got out about the Ferris Wheel project, former supporters began calling Ferris's design a "monstrosity" and engineers derided it as both unworkable and unsafe.

Undaunted, Ferris pushed on. He created more detailed specifications, put twenty-five thousand dollars of his own money behind the effort, and recruited prominent investors, including an engineer who had helped build the Canadian Pacific Railway. After five months of effort, he returned to the Ways and Means Committee with greatly enhanced documentation that proved his design would work and a checkbook that showed that he had enough money to make his massive wheel a reality. This time the committee's approval stuck and the wheel was the hit of the fair.

"There is nothing in the World's Columbian Exposition that compares in genuine novelty and sensationalism with the great vertical wheel which stands in the very center of the Midway," a journalist wrote. "[T]he Eiffel tower . . . involved no new engineering principle, and when finished was a thing dead and lifeless. The wheel, on the other hand, has movement, grace, and the indescribable charm possessed by a vast body in action."

### PCAN: Does My Answer Provide Net Benefits Compared with Alternatives?

In the fourth and final section of an idea sale, you must prove that your idea is better on a cost–benefit basis than both the current situation and any alternative solutions that might be available. This is where the hard work of comparative analysis among feasible solutions gets done.

It is often the most challenging part of your argument. Solid evidence that your idea is actually superior to available alternatives may be hard to come by. You will need to rely on speculation, probability, and inference. For this reason, proposals for experiments, trial balloons, pilot projects, and market tests—versions of the "one small step" procedure we discussed in chapters 5 and 6—are popular methods for concluding a good, policy-based idea pitch. These are ways of gathering evidence to test which of several solutions might work best in practice.

Marshall faced the challenge of presenting this part of his argument when Roosevelt tapped him to testify before Congress on behalf of his military buildup. Marshall's defense of the plan was masterful, and he got almost everything he asked for. Within a year, appropriations were coming faster than the Army could spend them: eight billion dollars by the end of 1940 and an additional twenty-six billion dollars in 1941. By the time the Japanese attacked Pearl Harbor on December 7, 1941, Congress had already spent more for Army procurement than it had for both the Army and the Navy during all of World War I. General Marshall's "three minutes" had assured that America would be ready to fight the biggest war in its history.

## Using the PCAN Model with Maximum Credibility

Jim Collins writes in his bestseller *Good to Great* that one of the best practices of the best companies is a willingness to gather data, analyze it, and "confront the brutal facts." Sounds simple. But as the story about George C. Marshall and his meeting with President Roosevelt shows, this advice is much easier to give than to follow. The situation in the Army was an "inconvenient truth" within a White House focused on reelection. Nobody wanted to talk about it and the president tried to dismiss the messengers bearing this unwelcome news.

Thus, in using the PCAN model, you must constantly remind yourself that your audience's point of view is much more important than your own. You need to return to the questions we raised in chapter 3:

How does the audience see you? Do you have credibility? It was the force of Marshall's personality, his emotional presentation, and his reputation for integrity—coupled with sound reasoning—that prompted the president to sit up and listen.

In using the PCAN model, you must balance two important credibility factors: (1) your need to come across as a committed advocate who is sold on the merits of your own idea, and (2) your objectivity as an expert who has considered all sides of the issue. The following are some "best practices" for balancing these two factors when you are presenting to attentive, knowledgeable audiences.

**Present Both Sides: Steal Their Thunder.** When former Charles Schwab, Inc. CEO David Pottruck first joined Schwab, he was an enthusiastic, dynamic presenter. But his boss eventually had to take him aside.

"Your colleagues don't trust you," the boss said.

"Why not?" asked Pottruck, shocked at this blunt feedback.

"When you come in to present an idea," the boss continued, "you present all the reasons why that idea should happen and none of the reasons why it shouldn't happen. You never present both sides." Pottruck took this advice to heart and changed his idea-selling strategy.

When your audience thinks you are biased, you lose credibility—especially if there are strong arguments against your point of view and you act as if they do not exist. Do not be afraid to argue your opponent's case. Summarize the strongest points against your idea, and then meet those points one by one. Stealing your opponent's thunder adds credibility to your presentation.

**If You Have a Conflict of Interest, Admit It.** If you come to an argument with an obvious conflict of interest, address this conflict right up front. When a sales manager argues for hiring more salespeople or when marketing people want bigger ad budgets, the people in charge of the budget apply a discount factor. These self-serving arguments lack credibility unless they are supported by data from objective sources.

Your job is to anticipate this factor and address it. Admit that you might lack objectivity. This sign of self-awareness shows you know about your apparent bias and, by implication, have done what you can to overcome it. "Everyone knows that I have mentored John," you might say in defense of promoting him; "But I hope that does not disqualify me from listing his qualifications." Collect and summarize expert opinions on John's behalf that are more objective—outside letters of commendation from customers, for example. Best of all, give someone with less of a conflict of interest the starring role in presenting your views.

**Don't Oversell Weak Arguments.** It may be tempting to gild your case by offering glib supporting arguments that an uninformed audience might accept but that turn out, on closer inspection, to be flawed. Avoid this temptation. As we noted above, you can actually gain credibility by acknowledging the possible weaknesses in your own arguments before presenting them, whereas you will lose credibility if you present a weak argument and your audience punches holes in it.

**State Your Assumptions.** Finally, be careful with your assumptions. Make them explicit so your audience will see where your argument is coming from. If you are assuming the audience shares your belief about the nature of a problem, say so. If they do not, they will tell you. If they do, you will get credit as someone who advances his case only with *his audience's* permission.

## Mediums: Another Look

Another factor that can affect how your case will be received is your choice of delivery medium. Our assumption so far has been that you are in a face-to-face meeting with Marissa Mayer at Google. But let's not forget that Google's idea-selling process begins with public comment on a Web site. The question therefore arises: which medium—meetings (formal or informal; large or intimate), memos, e-mails, telephone calls, or video conferences—should you use to make your best case?

There are no simple rules for answering this question. Organizational culture, the constraints imposed by being in large, global enterprises, the availability of colleagues at any given time, and your own strengths and weaknesses as a communicator all factor into a wise decision. But we can briefly identify some of the important considerations to keep in mind if you have the luxury of a choice.

**Communication Bandwidth.** As we noted in chapter 4, face-to-face, informal meetings offer the widest bandwidth for purposes of building relationships. They also provide many advantages as platforms for making your case. When you are sitting down with someone, you can convey nonverbal cues such as voice tone, body language, and emotional emphasis. George Marshall's meeting with Roosevelt worked because he displayed spontaneous emotions (something we will explore more fully in chapter 8) that contrasted sharply with his normal demeanor. He connected with Roosevelt on a personal level. No memo or telephone call can substitute for this wide-open channel of communication. When you want to deliver the most personalized information in the shortest amount of time, therefore, informal meetings are optimal. In descending order of bandwidth, the other mediums of communication stack up as follows: video conference, telephone, instant messaging, paper-based communication, and e-mail.

**Two-Way or One-Way Messages? Opportunity for Feedback.** If you are focused entirely on making a presentation—with no feedback—a formal meeting or memorandum is the best medium. If you want immediate feedback from your audience as part of your idea sale, informal meetings and, to a lesser extent, telephone calls are the best choice.

The Google system of Web postings can also be a great way to elicit comments and improvements as you polish an idea because there is no need to gather a group at the same time and place. The difference between personal and electronic forms of feedback is important, however. Feedback received in meetings or on the phone contains spontaneous emotional content, which may enable you to more accurately measure the intensity as well as the direction of the messages you are getting.

**Control over Your Argument.** Formal written memos provide the best way to convey a set of ideas that are tightly linked and hold together as a package. In the later stages of an idea sale, when your thinking has crystallized and you have tested your arguments to find the best ones, it can be helpful to reduce your idea to written form and rely on that as the formal proposal on which you seek a decision. Brad Garlinghouse's "Peanut Butter Manifesto" at Yahoo (see chapter 1) provides a good example of the role formal documents play in an idea campaign.

**Potential for Wide Dissemination.** With the advent of the Internet, it is possible to widely disseminate almost any form of communication about an idea—from a formal conceptual document to an informal podcast or videoclip of experts discussing your idea. Face-to-face meetings, by contrast, allow you to better maintain confidentiality. Be especially careful of using e-mail when confidentiality is important.

## PCAN's Roots: Evidence

To be persuasive, each of the four factors in the PCAN model needs to be rooted in evidence—no matter which medium you use. Below we explore what your evidentiary options are so you can come prepared with the demonstrations and proofs your particular audience is most likely to find persuasive. In general, there are five different forms of evidence to choose from when making a policy argument.

### 1. Data-Based Statistics

General Marshall came to his meeting with statistics on the relative strengths of the German and American armies, and these formed the foundation for his definition of the problem America faced. But, as British Prime Minister Benjamin Disraeli is reputed to have said (this comes to us via Mark Twain), "There are three kinds of lies: lies, damned lies, and statistics." You should be just as concerned with the credibility of statistics as you are with the credibility of the people presenting them.

There are many standards regarding data, ranging from the most rigorous scientific standards for peer-reviewed, double-blind medical studies to seat-of-the-pants surveys done by Web sites to determine user preferences. You should determine the standards your audience expects. In a surprising number of cases, even unscientific surveys can carry considerable weight within business organizations because there is so little time to make decisions.

For example, in 1995 the top leaders of Yahoo—Jerry Yang and David Filo—were trying to figure out how to turn their new Web indexing system into a business. The big question was whether to accept consumer advertising on the site as a source of revenue. Reuters news service had approached Yahoo about running ads next to news stories, but Yang and Filo were afraid the ads might offend Yahoo's community of users, who tended to be Internet "purists."

What tipped them in favour of accepting ads? A survey done by Randy Haykin, a Harvard MBA who had just been hired as vice president for sales and marketing, and his marketing team. They posted a poll on Yahoo's home page asking how users would feel about registering personal information and viewing ads, news features, and promotions. Haykin had expected to get five thousand to ten thousand responses. Instead, he got ninety thousand surveys back—with slightly more than half of them stating that the user would be comfortable with ads. Was the cup half empty or half full? Yang and Filo basically wanted the money paid advertising would bring, so they elected to read the study as favouring the ad idea. Yahoo gained twenty new paying sponsors in the first three months after the ad program was launched and fifty more in the three months after that. Yahoo's users, meanwhile, stuck with the site. Yang and Filo became fully committed to a profit model—and Yahoo took its place with advertisers and investors as a major player in the Internet economy.

## 2. Specific Examples

In addition to enumerating statistics, Marshall provided the president with a specific example of the German threat—Hitler's April 1940 attacks in northern Europe. Were these attacks a sign of further aggression to come against the United States? Hitler denied it. But Marshall thought so. Examples are like that—they look rock solid as facts. But what they mean is always a matter of interpretation.

Examples play a key role in almost every good idea sale, as master persuaders have demonstrated throughout the ages. According to one scholar, Abraham Lincoln "never asked an argument to do what an illustration could achieve more easily." And humanitarian Albert Schweitzer put it this way: "Example is not the main thing influencing others. It is the only thing." It is for this reason that charities often select poster children to be the human faces for the diseases and social problems they seek to cure.

Scientists tend to reject examples as a form of proof because they are mere "anecdotes"—usually selected to confirm a speaker's existing biases and beliefs. But even in scientific circles, vivid examples can be helpful in making a persuasive case.

In the ordinary world of organizations, meanwhile, examples are the door openers of persuasion. The average managerial audience can get its teeth into a specific example much more easily that it can take apart a statistical assessment. When you argue that something is a problem, therefore, most audiences' first thought—even at Google—will be "show me a typical example." If you can do that, you have set the stage for presenting a more detailed case.

And sometimes a single example sells an idea—as it did in our earlier story about the faculty member and the university administrators. Whether there was a "crime wave" around the campus or not, the fact that a professor had been mugged at gunpoint in the local neighborhood created a situation the university had to respond to.

### 3. Direct Experience—Demonstrations and Tangible Objects

Direct experience is a powerful source of evidence. If you are trying to win someone over to a new idea, few things convince more quickly or thoroughly than a "show and tell" demonstration. That is why car dealers woo customers with test drives in new cars and consumer companies distribute free samples of products they are launching.

Tangible objects can also be very persuasive. Had Marshall been able to produce a decoded telegram showing that Hitler intended to invade the United States, he would not have needed any elaborate statistics on relative air power. Roosevelt would have immediately seen the need to prepare for war. Evidence you can hold in your hand speaks louder than many other forms of proof.

For example, in the 1970s, when Intel physicist-turned-engineer Dov Frohman was deciding how to convince his boss, Gordon Moore, to invest in an idea for a new semiconductor chip, he realized that the best way to explain it was a demonstration. So he created a three-dimensional mock-up of the device that would show how it worked.

Then, in a ten-minute demonstration, Frohman opened Moore's eyes to a whole new method for computing. As Frohman himself described it, "We put together a 16-bit array with primitive transistor packages sticking out of the sixteen sockets. There were red bulbs to indicate the bits. . . . We showed Gordon that by pushing the button you could program the device, and we demonstrated that it would hold a charge." A new product was born—and sold to the boss in ten minutes because he could see, touch, and feel it.

## 4. Personal Testimony

If your audience cannot directly experience your proof, the next best thing is to bring in people who have, and get them to testify about it. Legal proceedings are based in large part on testimonial evidence, with lawyers for both sides bringing their best witnesses. And many businesses depend on focus groups, customer interviews, field trips by senior managers to talk with line employees, and a host of other techniques that help them gain access to the actual testimony of customers and employees. The informal survey Yahoo did to help it decide whether to take ads was an aggregation of the personal testimony of each user. Yahoo could have gone further and invited several survey participants to come present their views in person. In fact, survey professionals often like to perform personal interviews when interpreting survey results to help them contextualize the data they gather.

Another, especially powerful form of testimonial evidence is the recommendation of a trustworthy expert. When a doctor tells you that, based on her knowledge and experience, she would take the same medicine—or undergo the same operation—that she is suggesting for you, you are getting a very strong dose of testimonial evidence.

## 5. Social Consensus

The fifth and final form of evidence is the most elusive: social consensus. "Everyone knows," this form of argument goes, "that our customers are style-conscious and like an upscale shopping experience."

It follows that your colleague's idea for plain-Jane uniforms for store employees makes no sense and that your idea for trendy, high-concept outfits is a better solution. You could, of course, go out and survey your customers on this question, but resources and time are limited in the real world. So you rely on generally accepted truths that you and your audience share to support your case. This form of evidence is especially popular because it is so easy to assert. But it is often the least convincing to attentive audiences. Who really knows what "everyone thinks"? One year's conventional wisdom is the next year's outdated belief. Automobile manufacturers in the United States were recently unable to sell hundreds of thousands of gas-guzzling sport utility vehicles and trucks that "everyone knew" Americans loved—until "everyone knew" they were dinosaurs.

## Conclusion

Step 3 of the Woo process—*Make Your Pitch*—gives you a chance to apply all the intelligence you gained in Steps 1 and 2. If you want to convince an audience to do something new, you usually have to provide them with reasons supported by some form of evidence. And the best arguments address an audience's interests and beliefs. But, as we have seen in this chapter, what counts as a sufficient reason in one setting may not count in another. Understanding the intensity of the environment you are working in is therefore the first step to using practical reason as a persuasion tool.

This chapter has provided you with a simple, powerful template—PCAN—for anticipating objections and making your case whenever your idea addresses the general question "What shall we do?"

Step 1—Define the problem.

Step 2—Analyze the causes of the problem.

Step 3—Present your answer.

Step 4—Argue the net benefits of your answer compared with alternatives.

As we saw when Steve Jobs met with his advertising executives, the PCAN model can structure an intensive discussion lasting as few as five or ten minutes. But it can also form the basis for making a case over several weeks' time before several different audiences—as George Marshall showed in selling first the president and then Congress on the crisis of military preparedness in May 1940.

As you argue the points in the PCAN model, you need to deploy appropriate forms of evidence to support each element. What proof do you have for your claim that there is a problem? What evidence supports your argument about what caused it? Can you really show your solution will work? And who—besides you—says your answer is the best one, all things considered? The chapter investigated the five forms of evidence available to answer these questions: data-based statistics, examples, tangible objects and demonstrations, personal testimony, and social consensus. As chapter 5 argued, you should always tune to your audience's preferred persuasion channel and select your evidence with that channel in mind, even if you would be more convinced by something else. And give some thought to your choice of communication medium, paying close attention to your bandwidth needs, how important it is to get feedback from your audience, the degree of message control you want to exercise, and how widely you would like your presentation to be disseminated.

Our next chapter completes our study of Step 3 by reviewing the ways you can make your ideas and arguments not only clear but also memorable. Even Google appreciates a good slogan ("Don't Be Evil"), image (an uncluttered, white home page with a single, dominant "Google" on it), and ad campaign ("You're Brilliant—We're Hiring" was a recent Google human resources pitch). And President Roosevelt was not only impressed with Marshall's argument, he was moved by Marshall's passion. Memorable words and images can capture a complex idea and communicate it with lightning speed.

chapter eight

# Make It Memorable: The Personal Touch

There is science, logic, reason; there is thought verified by experience. And then there is California.
—Edward Abbey, author of *The Monkey Wrench Gang* (1975)

The heart has its reasons which reason knows nothing of.
—Blaise Pascal, French mathematician and physicist (1623–1662)

Consider the following two facts of modern organizational life:

- According to the *Wall Street Journal*, roughly thirty million PowerPoint presentations are delivered in the world every day, and

- Seventy-eight percent of surveyed executives report they have slept during a recent corporate presentation.

We think these facts are related to each other. This chapter is our attempt to save you and your pitch from the idea graveyard—where all the tombstones are decorated with clip art and all the graves are dotted with bullet points.

When you make a solid case on the merits of your idea, you are appealing to people's rational side—the human calculator that adds up the benefits and costs of your proposal and weighs them. This is an absolutely necessary part of idea selling, and your problem statement, the evidence you cite, and the arguments you make form the foundations on which your audience builds explanations about why it might say "yes" or "no."

But a problem remains.

That calculator does not make the actual decision. Something deeper and more interesting is involved.

Remember what both the brightest business leaders and the top cognitive researchers taught us in chapter 1 about how people make real-world decisions. The hyper-rational Andy Grove put it this way: "Drive into the data, then trust your gut." Alfred Sloan, the inventor of the modern business corporation, advised his executives to review the relevant facts and arguments, then listen to their "intuitions," where the "final act of business judgment" takes place. The unconscious mind, as Malcolm Gladwell taught us in *Blink,* takes the logical and factual information gathered by the conscious mind, locates the patterns in the data, and folds these patterns into insights based on experience. These insights—not the logic of your case or the strength of the evidence—are what ultimately produce the decision to accept or reject a new idea.

So you really have two audiences in every persuasion event: your audience's rational calculator and its intuitive decision maker. You must present arguments and evidence to the former, but unless you also make your ideas easily accessible to and actionable by the latter, you will lose the sale.

This chapter explores eight specific pathways leading to this intuitive decision maker—techniques for grabbing your audience's attention and keeping it firmly focused on your idea. You do not need to be a marketing or creative genius to use these methods. You need only ask yourself the following question as you prepare: *Which of these eight ways to make my idea memorable seems appropriate given the specific circumstances?* Identify as many or as few as you like. Then, as the last step in your preparation, brainstorm the images, stories, emotions, or personal touches that might add flavor to your case. The pathways are:

1. Make it vivid.

2. Use demonstrations and symbolic actions.

3. Put your heart into it.

4. Tell a story.

5. Personalize it.

6. Make it a puzzle.

7. Build bridges with analogies and metaphors.

8. Force your audience to think.

## Pathway Number 1: Make It Vivid

Bacterial infections are a serious problem in hospitals, with thousands of people dying each year from germs carried from one patient to another on the hands of doctors and nurses. But getting hospital staff—especially physicians—to wash their hands after each examination is surprisingly difficult, even though everyone knows it is the right thing to do. Hospital hygiene poses, in short, a classic idea-selling problem, similar in many ways to persuading people in any complex organization to adopt a new "best practice" when old habits are deeply ingrained.

Why is hand washing such a hard sell? *Freakonomics* authors Stephen Dubner and Steven Levitt investigated this question in the *New York Times Magazine*. Their story focused on the experience of Cedars-Sinai Medical Center in Los Angeles. At Cedars-Sinai, there were several causes for lax hand washing: physicians said they were too busy, the sinks were not always conveniently located, and, most surprisingly, the doctors actually believed they *were* washing their hands. There was a touch of arrogance in this final factor. Each physician was convinced that "someone else" was the source of the bacteria problem.

This presented administrators with a delicate issue of organizational politics: how could they sell doctors on the idea of washing their hands without insulting or alienating them? Administrators tried both data-based and inspirational appeals using e-mails, faxes, and posters, but hospital staff assigned to spy on the doctors reported no change in behavioral habits. The hospital then switched to the self-interest persuasion channel and offered doctors ten-dollar gift certificates at the local coffee shop when they were seen washing up by hand-washing "spies." This program had a moderately positive effect, but compliance still fell far short of what the hospital needed to protect its patients.

Finally, the hospital decided to try a vivid, visual way to deliver the hand-washing message. At a formal luncheon for the senior medical staff, the administrator in charge of the hand-washing initiative surprised everyone by bringing out a set of lab trays and asking the doctors to press their hands into these trays to record the bacterial cultures residing on their hands at that moment. The hospital used these hand prints to create full-color, graphic images of the bacterial colonies residing there. They made sure these pictures were as disgusting as possible.

Their final step was to transform these images into screen savers and load them on every computer in the hospital. Thus, no matter where physicians were, these images stalked them. Compliance with the hand-washing rule immediately shot up to nearly 100 percent and stayed there. The pictures of the actual bacteria on the doctors' own hands, as Dubner and Levitt put it, were worth not only the usual one thousand words, they were "worth 1,000 statistical tables."

This story is an extreme example of a more general truth about human perception: people respond to ideas that are easy to visualize because they can be recalled from memory more readily. Psychologists call this the "availability" phenomenon. As we were investigating the research on this important facet of persuasion, we ran across an interesting example that illustrated how an entire industry has been built on this principle.

Arizona State psychologist (and best-selling author) Robert Cialdini once attended a training program for insurance salesmen as part of a research project on social influence. The attendees were given an article titled "Add a Picture—Make a Sale" that laid out some of the most successful selling strategies in the industry. The instructor explained this technique to his new recruits as follows:

> If you are selling auto insurance, start by getting 'em alone in a quiet place and making 'em imagine that they just totaled the

car. If you are selling health insurance, first make 'em suppose that they're laid up in the hospital too sick to work. If you're selling theft, get 'em to think how it would be to come home from vacation and find everything gone. And take 'em through every picture, every step along the way.

This selling system works because, regardless of the statistical likelihood, people tend to think that things they can easily visualize are more likely to happen. If an airplane crashes or a hurricane blows ashore, the sale of flight and flood insurance goes up because people have recent, vivid images in mind that planes sometimes go down and big storms sometimes cause severe damage.

Moreover, the more "available" an idea is, the more people believe it to be true. The beauty of the Cedars-Sinai screen savers was that the bacteria displayed actually had been found on the physicians' hands. But vividness can trigger belief even when no proof is available. Doctored photographs of unidentified flying objects inspire beliefs that our planet has been visited by people from outer space. Memorable, oft-told tales of miracles inspire religious worship. And visually compelling advertisements provoke beliefs that a new shampoo or aftershave lotion can truly improve one's romantic life. To see is to remember, and to remember is to believe.

Before grabbing just any visual image you find compelling and associating it with your idea, however, make sure it is an image *your audience* will respond to in the way you intend. A sales manager in one of our executive programs told us a story about a CEO who forgot this important caveat and—in a misguided attempt at humor—selected an image for a presentation that cost him his credibility.

This man kicked off a presentation at a national sales meeting by flashing a large picture of a skunk on the screen. "What is that?" he barked at his audience of account managers. Nobody spoke.

After a few beats, he gave the answer.

"That's you," he declared. "You stink."

A deadly silence followed.

In three seconds, he had destroyed his standing as the leader of the sales group. From that moment on, he was vividly associated in his employees' minds with this insulting picture, and a year later he was drummed out of the company.

There are two lessons in this story. First, humor can often be found in exaggeration—but not in exaggerating other people's failures. Second, when you use a vivid image to communicate your point, you had better be sure you are tuned to your audience's channel because a tone-deaf presentation will live in your audience's imaginations for a long, long time.

## Pathway Number 2: Use Demonstrations and Symbolic Actions

Nothing is more vivid than an object your audience can see and touch or an experience they can feel. Thus, assuming the corporate culture permits them, demonstrations and symbolic activities are an excellent way to make an idea memorable.

In his book *The Heart of Change,* Harvard professor John P. Kotter features a story that illustrates the power of a demonstration. A senior procurement officer named Jon Stegner was trying to drive a major cost-cutting initiative through his multinational firm. Each factory had its own suppliers and its own negotiated prices for inputs, and Stegner's analyses suggested he could squeeze out as much as one billion dollars in costs by centralizing purchasing. But the business unit leaders were not buying his idea. They did not want to give up autonomy and control over procurement and did not believe that savings of the sort Stegner was talking about were feasible.

To make his case, Stegner had a student intern investigate the purchasing practices for just one item that all the factories bought—gloves used by workers on the factory floor. The intern's report was a shocker: the factories were sourcing 424 different kinds of gloves for the same basic job at prices ranging from three to seventeen dollars per pair. This fact alone was a compelling statistic, but Stegner wanted to make his point memorable, so he had the student acquire a sample of each of the 424 types of gloves and tag each one with its price, the factory it was used in, and the division the factory was part of. Then he called a meeting of the division presidents.

As they filed into the boardroom, the business unit chieftains found themselves looking, as Stegner later reported, at "a large, expensive table, normally clean or with a few papers, now stacked high with gloves. Each of our executives stared at this display for a minute . . . It is a rare event when these people don't have anything to say. But that day, they just stood there with their mouths gaping." Stegner turned his collection of gloves into a traveling road show to sell his cost-cutting initiative throughout the company. The firm ended up saving hundreds of millions of dollars in procurement costs.

A more obvious role for demonstrations comes when a company is launching a new product and naysayers within the firm need to be convinced. Edwin Land, the visionary entrepreneur who founded and ran Polaroid, was having trouble in the early 1970s persuading executives in his company that his idea for an instant camera with self-developing film was technically feasible. Even longtime colleagues thought the project was too complex and the resulting product would be too cumbersome for a mass market of consumers.

So, when he thought he had finally solved the riddle, he invited a group of Polaroid's leaders to his office and made a show of placing a rubber frog, a paper tiger, and a multicolored blanket around the room. Next, he slipped off into a side room, where a chemist and a photographer were preparing Land's prototype cameras for their debuts, and returned with the first SX-70 cameras to be used outside the lab. The group then began snapping pictures. As images of the frog, tiger, and blanket emerged from the cameras with its characteristic "whirring" sound and in full color, his executives were sold. They had seen and touched the future of the company, and the SX-70 went on to become a runaway hit.

Asking people to take symbolic actions related to your idea can also engage them in memorable ways. Moreover, research on a psychological phenomenon called the "foot in the door" technique (we will revisit this in chapter 9) has shown that once someone takes a concrete, physical action that is consistent with holding a value or belief—such as putting a political candidate's sign in their front yard—they are more likely to actually adopt that belief. Corporate rituals sometimes try to exploit this effect.

Top executives at America Online once constructed a huge wooden T-Rex dinosaur representing Microsoft and displayed it at an employee retreat. The message: Microsoft's new network service was a vicious monster about to devour AOL's core business. Hundreds of employees then "signed on" for the fight against Microsoft by writing their names on the T-Rex. The president of AOL, Ted Leonsis, later admitted that "the dinosaur thing was a bit of hyperbole, but I . . . believed it. I was asking, 'Are you going to let Bill Gates do this?'"

Asking employees to take symbolic actions that rally them behind a new plan to fight the competition is fairly common. But this technique also finds its way into the C-suite when major corporate change initiatives are on the table. For example, when David Pottruck (whom we met in the preceding chapter learning to make two-sided arguments) became the CEO of discount broker Charles Schwab, he wanted to commit the company to the world of Web-based trading. He developed a "one low price" online business strategy, then devised a campaign to sell this idea to his senior executives.

First, he called an all-day retreat for the company's top 130 leaders where he gave a soup-to-nuts presentation on the strategy, complete with tables, charts, bullet points, and data. At the end of the meeting, however, he switched modes. Buses picked up the entire team and headed for the San Francisco end of the Golden Gate Bridge. Once there, a professor told the group about how the builders of the bridge had overcome an array of organized opponents in 1937 to create one of the most striking landmarks in America. Pottruck then spoke, making the connection between this literal bridge and the one his team needed to build that led from the old to the new economy. The meeting ended with the team making the two-mile walk across the span, symbolizing the journey they would take together.

Asking senior people to take this sort of symbolic action can be risky—you had better be sure your audience is ready for such drama. Moreover, good metaphors do not guarantee good business strategies. Not long after Pottruck asked his team to take the Golden Gate Bridge walk, the dot-com bubble burst and founder Charles Schwab returned to rescue the company from the Internet strategy that Pottruck had championed. The firm survived—by (figuratively) walking part of the way back across the bridge toward the old economy.

## Pathway Number 3: Put Your Heart into It

As we noted earlier in the book, people will be more inclined to believe your arguments if you show that you, yourself, believe in them. What convinces is conviction, especially if that conviction is backed by genuine feeling. Emotions give an electric charge to a presentation that says: *this idea matters to me*. Studies show that in the right setting, if you have credibility and don't go overboard, emotions can also send a parallel message to your audience: *this idea should matter to you*.

In the example we used in chapter 7 to illustrate the PCAN model—General George C. Marshall's presentation in May 1940 that convinced President Roosevelt to begin preparing for World War II— the pivotal moment came when Marshall let his emotions show. "I don't quite know how to express myself about this to the President of the United States," Marshall told the president. "But I will say this to you: *you have got to do something and you've got to do it today.*"

As a general rule, you should reserve your emotional displays for your most urgent ideas. Otherwise, people will stop listening. But do not be afraid to reveal your feelings when the issue is important and when your audience does not seem to be "getting it." And within ongoing relationships, where your style is known, the more reserved you are normally, as was the case with General Marshall, the greater the impact of a candid display of intensity.

For people at the "Driver" end of the persuasion styles spectrum (see chapter 2), by contrast, emotional displays are part of everyday business. As Donald Trump once described his passionate style of persuasion, "When [someone] says no, sometimes you can talk him out of it. You rant and rave; and he rants and raves back, and you end up making a deal."

Legendary entrepreneur Colonel Harlan Sanders, founder of Kentucky Fried Chicken, knew just what he was doing when he relied on emotion: "I used to bang on the counter to emphasize my point," he once said. "That, in addition to my fancy cussin', sure scared the hell out of them franchisees who weren't living up to their end of the agreement." His colleagues got wise to this tactic because Sanders used it so often. But it worked on people who did not know him well. "The

Colonel was just crafty," said a wise observer. "When he walked into a store and raised hell, he shook people up, but they did a better job."

## Pathway Number 4: Tell a Story

As we saw in chapter 7, examples are a staple form of evidence used to support an idea pitch. Audiences have a much easier time following you when you proceed from a specific example to a general point than they do when you proceed the other way around. The most vivid and effective way to present an example is to tell a story.

A research study was once conducted to test different forms of persuasion. One group of high school teachers was presented with a written argument, complete with statistical tables, showing that a new science curriculum had led to greater learning and higher test scores over a number of trials in different schools. Another group of teachers heard about the same new curriculum from a single teacher who had used it and who told an inspiring story about its success. Which group of teachers do you think was more eager to try the new curriculum? The one that had heard the success story.

Stories have many virtues. First, they engage your audience immediately, giving them something concrete to imagine. Second, a story has many moving parts, all of which affect one another. This makes it possible to illustrate something as complex as teaching a new curriculum within a single, straightforward narrative. That sort of integration is hard to achieve with mere description.

The key difference between a simple example and a story is something scholars call *movement*. When you tell a good story, the audience starts wondering what plot twists lie ahead. We have seen this effect many times. As you settle into a story, you suddenly become aware that the room has fallen silent. People who were fidgeting moments earlier are now following each word you say with the rapt attention of children at bedtime. If you have integrated your idea pitch into the story in a compelling way, you can be sure that the intuitive decision maker you are trying to reach will be listening.

When you are pitching an initiative, you want your audience to understand not only your idea but also the process that led you to it. This enhances your credibility by showing your thoroughness and objectivity. It also gives you a chance to tell a special kind of story—the story of the hunt.

The hunt story starts by presenting the problem quickly and neatly. Then you lead your audience on the quest you followed to find the best answer. If you are using presentation software, don't give away the answers. Have just a few slides with a provocative word or phrase on them: "THE PROBLEM," "HOW WE GOT HERE," "OUR QUEST FOR OPTIONS," and so on.

Then tell your audience your story. What made the problem difficult to solve? Why hadn't it been solved before? Then have your answer emerge just the way your thinking evolved. Where did you look for an answer? What alternatives did you pick up and then reject? Why?

Don't take too long. Just pace your story as a search. Show them how you found the diamond amid all the glittering pebbles. Get them to help you find it.

A special version of the hunt story is the mystery. When you tell a mystery, you introduce some false leads to get your audience wondering "Who (or what) did it?" Mysteries can work especially well in creative contexts such as selling advertising campaigns, marketing programs, or book ideas.

Take a lesson from Hollywood, where idea pitching has been elevated to a fine art.

When acclaimed art-film director David Lynch offered his idea for an off-beat TV show called *Mulholland Drive* to a couple of senior executives at ABC Entertainment in 1999, he and production partner Tony Krantz used a "mystery story" approach.

The meeting took place in Steve Tao's ABC Entertainment office in Hollywood. As Lynch sat on a sofa drinking black coffee and fingering an unlit cigarette, Krantz launched into a description of the opening shots of the show they were proposing. We will tell it in the present tense, just as they did.

"Darkness," Krantz intones. "Distant sounds of freeway traffic . . . Then the closer sound of a car—its headlights illumine an oleander bush and the limbs of a eucalyptus tree. Then the headlights turn—a street sign is suddenly brightly lit. The words on the sign read 'Mulholland Drive.' The car moves under the sign as it turns and the words fall once again into darkness."

Krantz pauses. "The car is a black Cadillac limousine," he goes on. "The driver stops and pulls a gun on a beautiful brunette sitting behind him. Seconds later, [another] car races around the corner and slams into the limo. The woman staggers out of the wreckage and weaves down the hill into Hollywood."

Lynch picks up the story here, describing how the woman—named Rita—stumbles into the parking lot of an apartment complex and discovers a mysterious wad of £125,000 in her handbag. She has lost her memory in the crash and does not remember who she is.

Enter a new character, Betty, an aspiring actress from Canada, who takes Rita under her wing and leads her up to an apartment. As the two women start trying to piece together the fragments of Rita's mind, the camera cuts to distant parts of the city where police officers and two shady-looking men begin separate quests to find the lost woman.

At this point in the presentation, Lynch stopped and lit his cigarette. He sat in silence, took a long drag, and stared at a low table in front of the sofa where he was sitting.

Steve Tao couldn't contain himself.

"What happens next?" he blurted out.

"You have to buy the pitch for me to tell you," said Lynch.

And that's exactly what ABC Entertainment did. Television pilots usually fetch a few hundred thousand dollars. But the studio bid four and a half million to develop Lynch's treatment of *Mulholland Drive*. Although the show later stumbled over artistic differences during the production phase, Lynch reconceived it as a film, and it was released theatrically.

"It was the best kind of pitch," Steve Tao said afterward, "[the kind] where you're on the edge of your seat."

## Pathway Number 5: Personalize It

When Winston Churchill sat down to write about the end of World War I from his vantage point as First Lord of Admiralty, he swept his audience into the text by placing them at the center of a dramatic moment—standing next to him at his window as the Great War ended: "It was a few minutes before the eleventh hour of the eleventh day of the eleventh month," he wrote in 1927 in *The World Crisis*. "I stood at the window of my room looking up Northumberland Avenue towards Trafalgar Square, waiting for Big Ben to tell that the War was over." What better way to draw readers into a detailed historical analysis of the Great War's conclusion than to share a personal moment of what it felt like to be in London on Armistice Day?

Alluding to specific, real people facing actual problems and experiencing concrete feelings and thoughts turns your audience's imagination on like a light bulb. Charities have known this for decades. Would you rather send a hundred dollars to buy three months' worth of food and clothing for Karnees, a ten-year-old boy living in the war-torn African country of Sudan—or contribute a hundred dollars to a billion-dollar fund managed by the United Nations to help refugees throughout the world?

When you are selling more conventional ideas, the most persuasive stories are the ones people can relate to from their own personal experience. The audience visualizes, embellishes, and surrounds your story with its own context—making your point of view more vivid, believable, and easier to recall later.

A Mexican American friend recently had an experience that illustrates how this process works. He had been awarded a prize for his legal work in the Mexican American community and had been asked to give a speech at a dinner honoring him at New York's Waldorf-Astoria hotel. He decided to speak about immigration policy and recent moves to build a fence along America's southern border to keep Mexicans from crossing into the United States. As our friend warmed to his topic, he paused to tell a number of stories of his own family's struggle to get from Mexico to America, of his grandfather's enlistment in the U.S. Army during World War II, of the grandfather's death as a soldier on the beaches of Normandy, and of his father's hard work to keep the family together and make a brighter future possible for his children. Immigrants, our friend argued, may sometimes start out as "illegals," but rapidly become strong supporters of American values.

His audience gave him a standing ovation after the talk, but the evening was not over. As he got up to go, he realized that a line of people had formed to shake his hand and tell him *their own stories*.

As they had listened to his talk, they had been flooded with memories of their own families, struggles, and histories. The room had been filled with hundreds of vivid images aroused in hundreds of different minds. The speech succeeded because each member of the audience provided his or her own personal proof of the policy ideas our friend was trying to sell.

There are many ways to personalize a presentation. Talk about specific things a customer or employee shared with you about the problem your idea addresses. Give these people names and place the story in a specific location at a particular time of day. Share an example of how you yourself have suffered from the situation you are trying to solve. A first-person approach to persuasion can transform even the most casual decision-making process and mark it with a memorable moment.

Personalized examples can also change the tone and direction of the most formal proceedings. For example, a few years ago the U.S. Supreme Court heard a case about a law in Virginia that makes it a crime to burn crosses as a method of communicating political views. Cross burning was once a favorite activity of the Ku Klux Klan in their campaigns of racial hatred against blacks, and the Virginia law banned this symbolic act to protect public order. The legal challenge, however, was based on the absolute First Amendment protections in favour of free expression—especially politically motivated expression. The Virginia Supreme Court had ruled that cross burning was constitutionally protected speech, and it was widely expected that the Supreme Court, which had previously said that burning an American flag was protected by the First Amendment, would affirm the Virginia decision.

In the middle of the oral argument about the cross-burning law, however, Justice Clarence Thomas spoke up. Thomas, the Court's quietest member and its only African American, expressed with unexpected passion what cross burning meant to him and to blacks. This symbolic act, said Thomas, spoke of nothing but "one hundred years of lynchings" and a "reign of terror." It had no political content beyond pure racial hatred—and had a "virulent effect" on its intended audience. He concluded by stating that the burning cross was "unlike any symbol in our society."

His personal story about the meaning of this symbol in his life (Thomas was raised in Georgia during a time when segregation laws were enforced) and its brutal impact on African Americans prompted his fellow justices to speak out in his support, with some suggesting that a burning cross was as threatening as a loaded gun and others reinforcing his point that a burning cross was a uniquely hostile symbol.

When the case was decided a few months later, the justices let the anti-cross-burning law stand. Thomas's personal narrative had trumped all the legal precedents that usually apply (the evidence for this was in the fractured coalitions and multiple opinions that were written in the case to reach the result everyone desired). Had he not spoken, the result would almost certainly have gone the other way. And had anyone other than a black justice made this point, it would not have carried the power that it did.

While personal perspectives and narratives can convey strong convictions, there are risks. First, you must have standing as someone who can speak to the issues you address. If Justice Thomas had not been a black man raised in poverty, his speech might have been seen as "over the top." Second, when you rely on the authenticity of your story, you put your veracity in play. If people do not believe you, you have lost your credibility.

But there is a silver lining. If you can pass the truth-telling test, you will hit the equivalent of a persuasion home run. People will respect your character. The grandfather of all persuasion scholars, Aristotle put it this way: "We believe good men more fully and more readily than others; this is true generally whatever the question is, and absolutely true where exact certainty is impossible and opinions are divided . . . [the speaker's] character may almost be called the most effective means of persuasion he possesses." We will be talking more about this issue in chapter 10, when we conclude the book.

There is an entire industry today of storytelling consultants—people who offer coaching services to leaders at all levels to help them construct narratives to sell corporate change initiatives, inspire and motivate employees, and persuade others to adopt new strategies or enter new markets. You may or may not need the assistance of these high-priced helpers. But you should never underestimate the power of a good, personalized story to sell an idea.

## Pathway Number 6: Make It a Puzzle

People like puzzles because they pose mental challenges. And in groups, you can sometimes engage your audience in a mini-contest to see who can be the first one to figure the puzzle out.

Here is an example of a puzzle we use when teaching business people about law: how is a baseball like a whale? If you ask a question like that, people will immediately be curious. How *could* a baseball be like a whale? After a few stabs at an answer they will demand that you reveal the solution. And while all this is going on, you have their attention. Your idea will always be a little easier for them to remember because they will associate it with your puzzle.

Of course, now that we have raised this question, we should probably explain the baseball-whale puzzle or you won't believe there is an answer (see how powerful this device is?). The solution involves a case about a home run that San Francisco slugger Barry Bonds—also famous for his alleged steroid use—hit during the last game of the 2001 season. As that baseball soared out of the park, Bonds set the all-time Major League Baseball single-season home run record at 73. The hit also set in motion a complex lawsuit over who caught the million-dollar ball.

Two fans—a health-food restaurant owner named Alex Popov and a software engineer named Patrick Hayashi—claimed ownership. The ball initially fell into the webbing of Popov's glove as he leaped to catch it, but then it somehow slipped out in the melee that followed and ended up in Hayashi's hands. Popov sued Hayashi to get the ball back, and Popov's lawyer cited several hundred-year-old cases about whale hunting to support his client's claim. Under whaling conventions, the first hunter to get a harpoon into a whale got to keep it, even if other whalers subsequently harpooned it or another whaler made the kill. Popov's lawyer argued that this home run baseball was just like a whale—Popov got his glove on it first (there were videotapes showing his catch), so he ought to have the right to keep it even if a bunch of rival "hunters" knocked it out of his glove and grabbed it.

Of course, Hayashi's lawyers argued that baseballs are nothing like whales because they cannot swim away. Neither man won—the judge ordered them to sell the ball and split the proceeds. We use the puzzle to introduce how lawyers argue about prior cases when they debate each other in court—the essence of a specialized form of analysis called "legal reasoning."

In pitching ideas to people in organizations, look for puzzles embedded within the problems you are trying to help them solve. Which is more important: customer satisfaction or brand awareness? How can you make more money by doing less work? The puzzle device works best when the solution to the puzzle is exactly what you want the audience to remember about the idea you are selling.

For example, how is corporate strategy like a tree? A tree's roots and a company's core competencies both power growth. This image could be useful if you are trying to persuade people to invest more in one of your company's key products rather than "branching" into riskier new markets.

How is a city like a pond? Each has a delicate ecology—one human and the other of plants and animals—that must be maintained for them to survive. If you were selling an idea related to stemming the loss of skilled professionals from a city, this metaphor might get your audience's attention and help them think about your proposals.

## Pathway Number 7: Build Bridges with Analogies and Metaphors

As the puzzle device suggests, metaphors and analogies are excellent ways to make your pitch memorable because they build conceptual bridges. When you are talking about something the audience does not know much about, you need to start with something it does know and build from that toward your subject. Physicists speak of "black holes" in space (areas of enormous gravitational pull from which even light cannot escape) because few people can grasp the mathematics needed to describe these phenomena more precisely. But everyone can conjure up an image of a large, black hole sucking everything around it into a whirlpool-like vortex. By coming up with a good metaphor, physicists studying these phenomena have made it easier to obtain funding, to write books, and to go on television for interviews.

When Bono wanted to get Jesse Helms's attention (see chapter 5), he used a metaphor equating AIDS with the biblical plague of leprosy. This helped Helms make a quick leap from something he knew (the Bible) to something he did not know that Bono wanted him to understand (the plight of people in modern Africa). This metaphor, in turn, triggered associations with several memorable stories in the Bible about how Jesus dealt with lepers in the New Testament, healing them, comforting them, and encouraging his followers to treat these untouchables of Hebrew society with love and compassion. The metaphor brought Helms to an inevitable conclusion: what better way could Helms serve God than by helping poor Africans with AIDS?

Metaphors can also help trigger self-concepts, such as competitiveness, that spur an audience to action. Sports and battle metaphors are obvious, if overused, examples. But any image that challenges an audience to think of itself as under threat can work. Early in the history of America Online, the company faced a make-or-break decision about whether to enter into talks with Microsoft to be acquired. At the board meeting called to make a decision on this, opinion was sharply divided. As the discussion grew heated, a board member named Doug Peabody spoke up.

"Do we want to be a footnote on Bill Gates's résumé?" he asked. "Or do we want to be the king of the online industry?"

The idea of being just one more item on Bill Gates's vita captured the competitive spirits of the swing voters on the board, and they voted to remain independent—a decision that yielded AOL shareholders hundreds of millions of dollars a few years later when AOL was acquired by Time Warner at the top of the dot-com boom.

When it comes to analogies and metaphors, the simpler and more widely understood the image, the greater its hold on the imagination. History (including the history of your organization) provides a rich source of metaphors and analogies when people try to persuade one another about issues of strategy. There is even a book, called *Thinking in Time: The Uses of History for Decision Makers*, describing how historical metaphors have helped to shape important government policy decisions. If you can argue that your preferred strategy is similar to a prior historical success or that your opponent's strategy is like a prior failure, you can build an effective, analogy-based case for your preferred outcome.

For example, when President John F. Kennedy and his senior leaders met for the fateful "thirteen days" that defined the Cuban Missile Crisis in 1960, one of the options that military leaders favoured was a surprise attack on Cuba to destroy the Russian missile sites. But President Kennedy's brother, Attorney General Robert F. Kennedy, provided an anchor for those who opposed this option by comparing it to the Japanese sneak attack on Pearl Harbor. He slipped his brother a note as the attack option was under discussion. The note read, "Now I know how Tojo felt when he was planning Pearl Harbor." The analogy became a heated topic for debate during the next few days, ultimately helping to tip the balance in favour of the more moderate plan for a naval blockade.

## Pathway Number 8: Force Your Audience to Think

As we argued above, analogies and metaphors build easy-to-cross bridges between what your audience knows and the case you are trying to make. But our final set of tools for making a presentation memorable focuses on jarring your audience—forcing it to think about the unknown and unfamiliar. We have borrowed these techniques from Andrew Abbott, who discusses them in his book *Methods of Discovery* as ways scientists use to advance thinking in their disciplines. These moves can be risky if your audience is not ready to step "outside the box" with you, but we offer them for the moments when they may be useful.

**Question the Obvious.** By questioning the obvious, you can sometimes get people thinking about old issues in new ways.

Is the purpose of college really to get an education? Maybe it is just an elaborate way for parents to get troublesome teenagers out of their homes at a time when young people need to engage in—and get over—risky, experimental behavior. If so, that may explain why universities have such lax disciplinary rules.

Is the real purpose of a business to serve its shareholders or keep its suppliers in business? The first of these two views supports the usual profit-driven view of the firm. But what about the second? Someone opposed to an initiative to buy from high-priced (but local) suppliers might use it to force people to confront the implications of a "buy local" program.

**Reversals.** Turn things upside down and ask your audience to consider what this upside-down world might look like. How could your organization increase sales by *raising* prices? If your audience sells, ask them to think of themselves as *buyers*. If you are talking about how to improve team performance, ask people what the firm could do to make team performance *worse*.

**Let's Pretend.** Make a radical assumption and get the audience to explore what the world might look like if that assumption were true. The best assumptions are ones that take an existing trend and push it to an extreme, looking for insights that might apply to your current situation.

If you are selling an idea related to work–life balance, ask the audience to throw out the conventional workweek and optimize the time available for work and leisure. See what the week ends up looking like.

Assume gasoline is twenty dollars per gallon. What does your business look like under this condition?

Assume compulsory education extends to the age of twenty-six. How could your organization exploit that with your service?

**Reconceptualize.** This is a favorite of corporate strategists and "visionaries." Ask the audience to rethink a basic purpose or mission as part of your idea sale.

The Disney Company revolutionized its relations with its employees at its theme parks by reconceptualizing them as "cast members" instead of workers. Xerox became a different place when it started expanding into financial services and other far-flung businesses. It got back to its roots by reconceptualizing itself as "the document company." Electric utilities have reconceptualized themselves as "energy" companies, thereby opening up a broader array of services and activities than were formerly relevant.

## Conclusion

Step 3 of the Woo process—*Make Your Pitch*—is showtime. Moreover, every time you sell an idea, you need to make your pitch at two levels: the rational and the intuitive. Chapter 7 gave you the tools to appeal to the rational side of your audience. This chapter gave you eight ways to appeal to the intuitive side: vivid images, demonstrations, emotions, stories, personal experiences, puzzles, metaphors, and outside-the-box mental exercises.

You must strike a balance when you attempt to make your ideas memorable. Too little attention to this part of your presentation, and you may lose your audience by putting it to sleep. The statistics cited at the beginning of this chapter suggest this is all too real a risk in many work environments.

On the other hand, too much effort to make your presentation entertaining will detract from your message. People will remember the bells and whistles in your presentation but forget what you said.

The tools we introduced to you strike that balance. They help you make your sale by engaging people's imaginations but minimize the need to dazzle people with special effects. By bringing ideas to life, devices such as personal stories and vivid metaphors connect your ideas to your audience's experience. They are the "hooks" people will use to recall your ideas quickly and easily.

In a world where standardized presentation software dulls people's thinking and reduces their expectations, surprise your audience. Turn off the computer. Speak directly to the people in front of you about the problem your idea addresses and the difference your solution will make to someone specific.

Paint a picture. Bring people into the idea-selling process so they help fill in the gaps with stories and experiences of their own.

With Step 3 behind you, the time has come to close the sale. In chapter 9, we move to the last and sometimes the most complex stage of the idea-selling process—Step 4: *Secure Your Commitments*. This means obtaining actions, not just promises, from the decision maker and then overcoming the organizational obstacles that always seem to get in the way of implementation. Whenever people work in groups, they bring problems of turf, incentives, personalities, and control with them.

So bring your campaign buttons and get ready to stage a rally for your idea. It is time to deal with politics.

chapter nine

# Close the Sale: Commitments and Politics

An ounce of performance is worth pounds of promises.
—Mae West

Those who are too smart to engage in politics are condemned
to being governed by those who are dumber.
—Plato

Charles F. Kettering was one of America's most talented inventors
and engineers. In 1909 he cofounded the Dayton Engineering Labo-
ratories Company (better known as Delco). Seven years later, he sold
it to General Motors. In making the purchase, senior GM leaders announced at a meeting of the Finance Committee that Kettering "is
the center of the situation. [Obtaining] Mr. Kettering's entire time
and attention is of prime importance."

History has confirmed the wisdom of their judgment. Today, most
people enjoy the benefits of Kettering's creativity in some part of
their lives, and historians consider Kettering on a par with Thomas
Edison as one of America's true geniuses. A partial list of Kettering's
automotive inventions includes the automatic transmission, electric
ignition, safety glass, and shock absorbers. He also produced several
important innovations in the medical field and, with his GM boss
Alfred Sloan, cofounded the Sloan-Kettering Cancer Institute in
New York. He was featured on the cover of *Time* magazine in
January 1933. Yet for all his dazzling talents, Kettering failed to
close one of his most intriguing idea sales while he was at GM—an

air-cooled automobile engine that he thought would revolutionize the industry.

His story illustrates the two topics that will bring our journey through the Woo process to an end: the need to obtain specific commitments and the challenges of organizational politics.

The air-cooled engine was Kettering's bid to knock Henry Ford's Model T off the automotive bestseller list. It promised a GM vehicle that would have fewer parts, less weight, reduced cost, and much better performance in the winter, when water-cooled engines such as the Model Ts had trouble starting. "It is the greatest thing that has ever been produced in the automobile world," he proclaimed. And it was timely. Rumors were flying that Henry Ford was close to completing a version of the same engine.

Kettering's air-cooled engine was timely for another reason, too. A sudden, sharp downturn in the automobile market in 1920 prompted GM's board to fire the company's freewheeling, visionary CEO, William Durant. Two buttoned-down organizational men replaced him: Pierre S. du Pont and Alfred P. Sloan. Sloan had been lobbying Durant to adopt a reorganization plan that included putting "Boss Kettering" (as his staff called the no-nonsense scientist) at the head of a centralized R&D department. Durant's abrupt departure provided just the opportunity Sloan had been looking for to implement this plan.

The Boss wasted no time putting the full weight of his new job title behind the air-cooled engine, writing a letter to GM's leadership that stated, "The air-cooled engine of the . . . type [Ford is developing] is now ready to push toward . . . production." Kettering then invited GM's leaders to Delco's labs in Dayton, Ohio, where he put on a demonstration of the new engine to "make it memorable."

Sloan and his team were impressed. Kettering followed up with a "one small step" strategy, asking for funding to produce a limited number of cars with the prototype air-cooled engine. GM's Executive Committee gave the go-ahead.

It was at this point that Boss Kettering made his mistake. Having closed his idea sale, he turned his focus to technical issues and left potential political problems to others. The Executive Committee, meanwhile, surveyed its available choices for getting the test cars built and decided to hand the assignment to the head of the Chevrolet division, K. W. Zimmerschied. The Chevrolet group, which had enjoyed managing its own affairs under Durant, was not consulted about this decision. It was, Sloan later noted, "virtually an order."

Management problems immediately emerged. Fearing that head-quarters was betting the future of his division on unproven technology, Zimmerschied openly criticized the project. His attitude spilled over to his engineers, who expressed their skepticism that the engine could ever be made to work. They suggested GM send the project elsewhere.

But the Executive Committee held firm. In response to queries by Kettering, senior executives told him to ignore the "wiseacres" and "know-it-alls" and get on with his work.

Next came the problem of "buzz." Pilot projects of new technologies always face a "cup half full" versus a "cup half empty" image problem. When the buzz is positive and expectations are high, early setbacks for new initiatives are seen as normal parts of developing any new idea. But when the buzz is negative, each new problem, however small, confirms everyone's expectations that the project will fail.

The latter problem now began to plague the air-cooled engine. Engineering trials showed that in warmer temperatures the air-cooled engine misfired and lost power. Kettering set to work to fix the design, but support for the project, already low in the Chevrolet division, started slipping in other parts of the company. The rumor mill began to churn.

Kettering felt victimized by the mounting opposition and went to Sloan to air his grievances. "I am perfectly sure that we can take any proposition and make out of it a 100 percent success, provided we do not have to overcome an organized resistance within the corporation," he told his boss. Kettering begged the Executive Committee to use its formal authority and "force through an order" committing Chevrolet to the project.

But the momentum had shifted and the Executive Committee refused to issue the order. Too much time had been wasted debating the pros and cons of the new engine and not enough progress had been made toward perfecting it. Sloan acknowledged that there was a "difference of opinion" about why the effort had stalled, but he nevertheless pulled the plug. Kettering was given a stand-alone business unit to continue with his research, but with no car division willing to partner with him, the program was doomed. The operating divisions had defeated R&D. Detroit had beaten Dayton. And with the GM project no longer a threat, Henry Ford also dropped out of the race. It took until the 1960s for the Volkswagen Beetle to introduce the first air-cooled engine in a mass-produced car.

## Newton's First Law of Organizations

Kettering's story illustrates an important lesson: to succeed at the closing stages of selling ideas, you need to remember Newton's First Law of Motion. It reads:

> An object at rest tends to stay at rest and an object in motion tends to stay in motion with the same speed and in the same direction unless acted upon by an external and unbalanced force.

If we leave the word *unbalanced* to one side (Newton meant a force that is not canceled out by an equal and opposite one), this law can be restyled as *Newton's First Law of Organizations* because it applies to people as much as objects in the natural world. In closing an idea sale, you must first overcome "decision inertia"—that is, get decision makers who are "at rest" to move in your desired direction. Then, through persistence, you must add organizational "push" to maintain your idea's momentum so it will "stay in motion . . . in the same direction," eventually becoming reality. As Kettering's saga shows us, you can't quit after the first push. The internal forces working against change—fear of the unknown, competing interests, politics, and concerns over turf—will bring your initiative to a grinding stop unless you keep applying pressure.

## Overcoming Decision Inertia

Your first job in closing a sale is often the hardest: overcoming the natural inertia that keeps people locked into the tried and true. Scientists have a name for this phenomenon: the "status quo" bias. Change requires effort, so people tend to maintain the status quo, provided it works "well enough" to satisfy their interests.

Two states, New Jersey and Pennsylvania, unwittingly ran a test of this theory not long ago. Citizens in each state were offered two, almost identical ways to handle claims for car accidents: a pricey option with higher premiums that provided they could sue for full damages in the event of an accident, and a less expensive option that restricted their litigation rights.

Although the two options presented to drivers were identical in both states, the manner in which drivers were asked to decide between them was not. In New Jersey, the law stated that drivers would get the more expensive coverage by default unless they specifically opted for the cheaper one. In Pennsylvania, the reverse held true: people were told they would get the *less* expensive option by default unless they specifically opted for the more expensive one.

Decision inertia prevailed in both states. An overwhelming majority of Pennsylvania drivers (80 percent) elected to stay with the cheaper coverage, while a similar number of New Jersey drivers (75 percent) decided to use the more expensive insurance. Numerous other examples of decision inertia can be observed in the world around you, from the way people make contributions to retirement plans (they contribute more money if the contribution is set as the standard operating procedure) to whether they become an organ donor (they "volunteer" much more often if that is the default choice made for them on their driver's license application).

How can you overcome decision inertia and gain commitment to your ideas on an individual-by-individual basis? Kettering actually did a good job of this, as evidenced by his initial success selling the air-cooled engine idea to Alfred Sloan and the GM Executive Committee.

He had all of the critical Woo factors working for him. First, through his relationship with Sloan, he had access to the C-suite. Second, he had credibility as one of the nation's top inventors. Third, in terms of interests and values, his initiative gave Sloan a chance to show off how GM's new organizational design could help speed innovation and keep the company ahead of its competitors—especially hard-charging Ford. Finally, Kettering did a good job presenting a problem-based argument for the idea and making the argument memorable with a vivid demonstration.

To cap all this off—and get us into this chapter's concerns—he asked for and received specific funding commitments to support defined actions: the mandate to launch his experimental program at an operating division. Let's pause here for a moment to examine exactly what makes a commitment different from a mere promise or agreement inside organizations.

## Gaining Individual Commitment

As Mae West advised in her quote that opened this chapter, it takes "pounds of promises" to equal an "ounce of performance." Unless you enjoy a Trust-Level relationship with the other party and can take their word to the bank, you need to close your sale by asking for performance-based rather than promise-based commitments.

Psychologists tell us that to engage the commitment process, you need the other party to:

1. Take a concrete action that

2. Requires effort,

3. Is freely chosen, and

4. Is observed by or known to people other than you.

The action the other party takes can be as simple as sending an e-mail to a group list endorsing your idea or as complex as allocating millions of dollars and hundreds of staff to your initiative. Either way, you can now count on that person as an ally. As psychologist Robert Cialdini has put it, commitment "grows its own legs" through specific actions that satisfy the above four conditions. Small actions seed commitment to bigger ones.

As we mentioned in chapter 8, sales professionals know this as the foot-in-the-door phenomenon. If a salesman can get his foot in the door, a prospect will generally let him all the way into a home or office to make his pitch.

Psychologists have repeatedly documented this process. In one study, researchers convinced a large number of homeowners to allow a massive, poorly designed public-service billboard to be erected on their lawns. The key to their agreement was a visit made two weeks earlier. Other researchers posing as volunteer workers had visited their homes and asked the owners to display a small, three-square-inch sign that said: "Be a Safe Driver." Once they agreed to this request—which they did freely, publicly, but with only a modest amount of effort—they became willing to display the larger, ugly sign that proclaimed: DRIVE CAREFULLY. In fact, 76 percent of the group that had agreed to display the small sign agreed to erect the big one, compared to only 17 percent of a control sample who had not received the earlier visit.

It all sounds deceptively easy. Just get your decision maker—as Kettering did—to agree to take one small step in your direction and you are done. But, of course, it is not so simple. A number of problems remain. We deal with the individual-level issues below, saving the political problems for later.

First, other people are smart. They instinctively know that even modest concrete actions commit them, so they resist taking such steps. We were advising a major health care institution on a change initiative recently and one of the senior leaders had strong reservations about the program. In an effort to get him on board, we asked him if he would lead a meeting to debate the recommendations and start it off by reading them out loud so everyone could focus clearly on the issues. He agreed to lead the meeting but he refused to read the recommendations aloud, saying that even this small step was more than he was comfortable doing. We had to rely on the underlying merits of the ideas and some concerted wooing by his colleagues to win his reluctant support.

Second, you may fear being seen as "too pushy." This can be especially difficult when you are up against a high-powered, hard-to-pin-down decision maker. For example, the famous Hollywood producer Peter Guber was known for scattering promises everywhere he went. According to the book *Hit and Run: How Jon Peters and Peter Guber Took Sony for a Ride in Hollywood*, "half the people in Hollywood" thought they had an agreement to do a project with Guber at any given time—but few were willing to force his hand by asking for a true commitment. He would dash from office to office, dazzling people with his nonstop enthusiasm and his talk of "Let's do this; let's do that." But an encounter with Guber usually left people looking around the room and asking, "What just happened at this meeting?"

To close an idea sale with such people, you need to take a lesson from Sue McFarland (chapter 2) and the way she handled her over-the-top boss, Andy Grove. Meet assertiveness with assertiveness. As she put it, "He [Grove] would tend to treat people like doormats, [but only] if they behaved like doormats." Stand up for your idea—don't let a hyperactive boss give you the runaround. And if he or she refuses to respond to your request for concrete action, understand that this is really a "no." Finally, if you don't have the personality to ask for a commitment from a person like this, look for an ally who does and bring this person along for support.

A third problem is the fear of rejection. This can interfere with the closing stage of even the most conventional sales process, and idea selling is no different. During a negotiation seminar we were teaching recently at a manufacturing company, a sales manager reported on his plan for his first visit to a new, very large distributor in South Africa. The distributor had asked for the meeting so it could be approved to carry the company's premium products.

The sales manager explained how he intended to position the firm's products, introduce his company's system of doing business, and communicate the firm's expectations for sales volume over the first twelve months of the relationship. He was concluding his presentation when his boss, who was also in the group, broke in.

"And then you are going to ask him for an order, right?" the boss queried.

The salesman looked surprised. "Won't our sales volume number make it obvious how much he will be buying?" he asked.

"You want a sign of commitment," the boss said. "Don't leave until you take his first order."

Why was the sales manager reluctant to take the order? He did not want to spoil the first meeting by raising even the remote risk that this new customer might say "no" to him. So he planned to finesse this key question. Yet the customer had requested the meeting and obviously wanted the product. All the salesman had to do was ask. If the fear of hearing the word *no* can paralyze even an experienced salesman when he has this much leverage, it is no surprise that people selling ideas in less secure situations are reluctant to pull the trigger.

The answer: get over it. If the other person says "no" when you ask him to take a specific step to further your idea, use that as a springboard for finding out the objections that lie beneath this response. Search for shared interests and common beliefs that might provide the platform for reframing your proposal.

## The Problem of Shifting Priorities

A final difficulty: shifting interests and priorities may supersede those that were on the table when the other party first made his or her promise to help you. These problems can arise even when you have closed the sale and gotten the other party to take a specific commitment step.

Organizational life presents a moving target for idea sellers. Programs that were Priority number 1 last week can shift to Priority number 5 next week because new orders have come from headquarters, people have been reassigned, or unexpected events have intruded. When your decision maker can keep only two of last week's five commitments—all equally important and legitimate—what steps can you take to assure that your idea remains a priority?

**Reaffirm Shared Interests.** The more your idea furthers important interests of the other party, the more likely he or she will stick with it in the face of changing circumstances. So reinforce those interests as often as possible.

**Rely on Relationships.** Your relationship with the decision maker will often be important in her decision on which commitment she keeps. The closer and more interdependent your relationship—that is, the more you enjoy Trust-Level dealings and the more she needs your assistance to help with *her* plans and initiatives—the more likely she will be to pick your program as one of the two that survive the shift in priorities. An especially favorable situation arises when she owes you an explicit, major favour in the reciprocal exchange system we talked about in chapter 4.

**Create an Important Audience.** At the initial commitment stage, see to it (with her support, of course) that high-ranking, influential people in the organization—especially people she wants to impress—are the "audience" observing her concrete action that furthers your idea. When priorities shift, the presence of this audience will weigh in favour of keeping your idea on the active list.

**Build In Accountability.** The ideas that have the most accountability built into them—that is, the ones tracked by monitoring systems, performance benchmarks, and deadlines—tend to be the ones that survive when subsequent events make it impossible for people to keep all their commitments. You can easily test this in your personal life. If you are planning a barbeque dinner at your home for a community or office group and you want everyone to come, assign each person to bring something that is absolutely critical for the overall event to work—things such as utensils, napkins, cups, and so on—and tell each person that *no one else will be bringing that item.* When the date draws near and other priorities intrude, they will not be able to rationalize skipping the dinner by telling themselves "nobody will miss me." Instead, they will feel a sense of responsibility to provide their essential ingredient for the event's success.

Keep this in mind when selling ideas: assign people specific, unique, and important roles in implementation. Inspire them to feel accountable for the entire effort by making them responsible for something nobody else is doing. Then add some specific deadlines for their parts of the project. When competing priorities intrude, your colleagues will be much more likely to keep working on your idea than on projects that have no deadlines and where their contributions—or lack thereof—will go unnoticed.

## Organizational Commitment—Managing Politics

So much for the problem of gaining individual commitment. Now on to politics. The second part of Newton's First Law of Organizations suggests that once you set people in motion, they will stay on the course you chart unless they are acted on by some countervailing force. There is good news and bad news about this part of the law. The good news is that organizational momentum can carry your idea a fair distance once you get decision makers to take concrete action and the wheels of group commitment begin to roll. The bad news:

there are many countervailing forces that can slow or stop this momentum. If you want your idea to succeed, therefore, you must remain an active and energetic advocate.

As the story about Kettering's air-cooled engine showed, selling ideas sometimes sparks large-scale disputes between organizational units. When this happens, serious issues of corporate strategy, resources, careers, and turf can stop an initiative. Of course, you can expect people who disagree in good faith over the merits of a proposal to do battle over it. The solution to such disputes lies in your making the best possible case to the most influential people—in short, in following all of the Woo Steps we have discussed so far.

But often the battles are less about the merits of an idea and more about the effects your idea will have on the existing distribution of power, resources, and status. When this happens, political strategies become paramount.

There is plenty of evidence showing that politics is a reality in most workplaces. As we mentioned in chapter 2, studies have found that some political activity takes place in nearly all organizations. And in nearly half, it takes place to a "very great" or "fair" extent. In other words, Plato was right: if you consider yourself "above" office politics, you condemn yourself to being dominated by those who are willing to get into the trenches and fight.

Kettering did some things right in this regard, but he and his champions also did a few things wrong—and the mistakes were enough to kill his idea. Below, we will examine the two most important political risks that can derail your idea and then look at some ways to overcome, or at least mitigate, these risks.

## The Territorial Imperative: Turf

The most important political problem facing any new idea is the possibility that someone, somewhere in the organization, will see it as a threat to his or her turf. Bertrand Russell, a Nobel Prize–winning philosopher, summed up this fact of organizational life very well: "In every organization there are two purposes: one, the ostensible purpose for which the organization exists; the other, to increase the power of its officials." Kettering and Sloan did not properly appreciate just how much the air-cooled engine experiment—coupled with Sloan's radical new design for running GM—would threaten the Chevrolet division's autonomy.

Humans are ego-sensitive creatures who can be counted on to defend their territorial interests, whether it is a cubicle or a kingdom. For example, Michael Eisner—the former CEO of the Walt Disney Company—once hired a Hollywood super-agent and power broker named Michael Ovitz to be president of the company. As part of the deal, Eisner promised Ovitz that the two of them would be "co-heads" of Disney and that Ovitz would be first in line to succeed Eisner as CEO.

The day Ovitz was hired, Eisner invited him to his house for dinner to go over the press release that would come out the next day. When Ovitz arrived, he was greeted by Eisner, CFO Steve Bollenbach, and Chief Legal Counsel Sandy Litvak. Unbeknownst to Ovitz, Bollenbach had been lured to Disney under the assumption that *he* would be the next president. Eisner had made the same promise to Litvak.

Worse still, Eisner had delayed telling these two about Ovitz's hiring until that very afternoon. As Ovitz entered Eisner's home, Bollenbach greeted him with a blunt reminder of the territorial imperative in organizations.

"Welcome to the company," he said. "I just want you to know that I'll never work for you."

Litvak piled on. "Me too. I'm not going to report to you."

Ovitz looked at Eisner with alarm, but Eisner said nothing and managed to get the group past this awkward moment and on with the business of drafting the press release. Later in the evening, he whispered to Ovitz that he would deal with the situation after wounded egos had had a chance to heal. But he never did, and Ovitz's tenure at Disney turned into a soap opera that featured a £140 million severance payment to Ovitz followed by an embarrassing and ultimately unsuccessful lawsuit by shareholders to get this money back.

In her executive memoir *Tough Choices*, Carly Fiorina, former CEO of Hewlett-Packard, coined the phrase "one thousand tribes" to describe the organizational territories she encountered when she took over HP. Soon after arriving at the firm, she asked her CFO where the company stood with respect to its quarterly targets, and he replied that he didn't know. There were four other people with the title "CEO" in addition to Fiorina, he explained, and each one had his own CFO. The other CEOs did not think it was their job to "improve the company's overall results—their jobs were to deliver against their own plans." Each business unit had its own marketing strategy, with its own budget and distribution channels. In a very real sense, there was no such thing as "HP."

While Fiorina ultimately failed as the leader of HP for reasons that went far beyond its "tribal" culture, what she observed there is typical of many organizations. Indeed, sometimes merely labeling a group or unit is enough to generate turf-defending behavior. Groundbreaking research conducted by social psychologist Henri Tajfel has shown that subjects randomly assigned to groups and given separate identity labels display immediate bonding behaviors. People feel friendlier toward others who share their label and exaggerate trivial differences as signs of group distinctiveness. Multiply these effects by hundreds of factors and you can begin to understand why business units sometimes square off against one another even when there are relatively few genuine conflicts of interest between them.

## The Strategic Imperative: Momentum

In the face of organizational opposition, the most important thing idea sellers can do is gain and maintain positive momentum for their initiatives. This is easier said than done because in most political battles, "losers are louder"—those who stand to lose power, control, resources, or head count can be counted on to fight vigorously to preserve the status quo. Never underestimate the zeal of an opponent in protecting his or her interests.

Underlying this pit-bull phenomenon is a powerful psychological principle described in numerous scientific studies—the scarcity response. People react more forcefully to the possibility of loss than to the prospect of an equivalent gain. Unions will bargain hard for wage increases, but they will go on strike if you attempt to cut even one benefit. Similarly, business units may lobby to gain new resources, but they will fight like warriors to keep the resources they already have.

Kettering's opponents in the Chevrolet division reacted immediately to being "stuck" with the new air-cooled engine and did not let up until the burden was lifted. Meanwhile, of course, there were no consumers or dealers clamoring for the new car because it had not been built yet and people had no conception of what they stood to gain by it. That left the battle lines drawn between GM's most successful operational unit—Chevrolet—and an R&D group with no allies that was based in another state and had no direct control over what Chevrolet would do with the project.

The "losers are louder" phenomenon explains many political puzzles—such as why it is hard to find places to bury nuclear waste or build prisons (the Not In My Back Yard—NIMBY—problem), and why countries block low-priced imports by raising taxes and tariffs (local manufacturers and labour unions face an immediate loss of market share and they are louder than the great mass of consumers who might benefit from the lower prices). The people who would be better off with such things as lower cost imports and well-managed nuclear waste facilities are not organized for political action, but the potential losers from cheap foreign goods or a nuclear dump near their town are—and they make a lot of noise.

There are several solutions to this problem, as we will see below. The most effective answer is to design open, above-the-board forums for the discussion of new ideas. This way the potential winners and losers can hash out their differences in public, and turf-related concerns can be identified and branded as illegitimate—that is, not related to the overall interests of the organization. Alfred Sloan took this approach in the wake of the air-cooled engine saga and made formal idea selling within and across divisions a recognized corporate practice. "What was needed," he said, "was a place to bring . . . men together under amiable circumstances for the exchange of information and the ironing out of differences." Executives could then listen to all sides of an issue, weigh the arguments and interests, and make good business decisions. As we saw in chapter 7, Google has designed a modern, Web-based version of Sloan's open-forum idea-selling system.

In the absence of such an enlightened practice, however, you will need to master some basic political maneuvers to avoid Kettering's fate. Below, we examine some specific tactics that can help you gain and maintain political momentum for your ideas when you face determined opposition.

## Best Practices for Managing Politics

Winning political battles within organizations is not all that different from winning traditional political fights. Instead of television advertising, however, you may be using group e-mails. And rather than assembling coalitions such as Mothers Against Drunk Driving or the Alliance for Responsible Trade, you might be gathering supporters from marketing, sales, and planning to back your initiative. Below we survey some time-tested political tactics that can help you win. Before we get to these, however, it may be helpful to review an example of someone using them skillfully to overcome organizational inertia and gain genuine commitment to a new program.

## Archie Norman Rides to the Rescue

In 1991, when Archie Norman took over Asda Group PLC, a failing chain of big-box supermarkets in the United Kingdom, he held the fate of a broken company in his hands. The company had had a successful run serving value-conscious shoppers, but recent senior-level decisions had brought it to the brink of ruin. Several powerful competitors posed a threat to Asda's traditional strongholds in the northern, working-class parts of the country; a string of poorly chosen and badly financed acquisitions had turned sour; and the company was saddled with expensive layers of bureaucracy. Employees had stopped making suggestions to improve performance for fear they would be sacked for criticizing central management. Short-term debt was putting such serious pressure on cash flow that bankruptcy was a distinct possibility.

On his first day at the helm, Norman signaled his determination to change this dysfunctional culture by articulating a simple, clear theme. At the 9:00 A.M. senior management meeting called that day, Norman announced:

Today is Day Zero in our recovery program. This business is in poor shape and must change. . . . There will be management re-organization. My objective is to establish a clear focus on the stores, shorten lines of communication, and build one team. I want everyone to be close to the stores. We must love the stores to death. That is our business.

The managers in front of him greeted this speech with stony silence—not a word was spoken and not a question was asked. The company was such a political minefield that no one dared speak up. But Norman had struck a chord. He had articulated a simple theme for his plan to turn the company around: *love the stores*. And this phrase became the rallying cry for his allies in the months ahead as Norman moved to isolate his opponents and gain momentum for change.

To underscore the urgency of the situation, Archie Norman took some immediate actions. Less than an hour after his 9:00 A.M. talk, he fired the widely discredited CFO who was responsible for let-ting the firm's finances slip so badly. And during the next few days he started "walking the talk" by visiting some stores. What he heard confirmed his fears. One manager stated he was "so tired of trying to get Asda to listen to [his] problems in the store . . . that he just stopped trying. He felt like he was treated as if he was an idiot . . ." In political terms, Norman could see that corporate head-quarters had considered the people running the stores to be the enemy—and its own splashy and expensive acquisition strategy to be the solution.

So Norman underscored his commitment to "love the stores" by unloading Asda's recently acquired businesses—a carpet and furniture chain as well as a property development company—and letting go of the people who had masterminded these deals. In his announcement of these actions, he reinforced his theme. "My objective," he said, "is to establish a clear focus on the stores."

Next, Norman instituted an initiative he called the "Store Renewal Program," under which managers at the worst performing sites re-ported directly to him. Norman worked closely with these managers to turn around their operations, mandating that every innovation that worked—whether it was a new way of baking bread or of tracking sales—be quickly copied by all the stores. These practices—a series of small wins that were broadcast widely—became known as the "Asda Best Way." In time, store managers began to compete for the honor of contributing to it.

The result? In five years, Asda's foot traffic in the stores rose by 50 percent, sales increased by a third, and the stock price quadrupled. Moreover, 120 stores had been renewed, and headquarters staff had been reduced by half. As one analyst put it, Norman "had transformed the very nature of how the company worked."

### Political Move Number 1: Find a Simple Theme That Captures Your Idea

Let's review Archie Norman's story to see what political moves helped him to succeed where Kettering and Sloan fell short. His first step was the most familiar: find a simple way to summarize and communicate his idea.

We have seen this advice before in both our discussion of how to make a good case in chapter 7 and in thinking about ways to make your idea memorable in chapter 8. The bigger the group of people you need to communicate with regarding your idea, the larger the payoffs from having a simple, clear theme that captures the essence of what you want to get done. To succeed in politics, you need a slogan.

Herb Kelleher, former CEO of Southwest Airlines, became a corporate superstar by creating an entire culture around a single theme: low-cost air travel. He demanded that every corporate decision be put to a simple test: Does it help us maintain our industry leadership as the low-cost carrier? The beauty of a simple theme is that people can remember it, use it in conversation, and pass it on to others with a minimum of complex explanation. This can give your idea wings to help sustain it when the winds of political opposition begin to blow.

Archie Norman handled this political necessity well, creating a simple catchphrase in his first speech—*Love the stores*—that instantly communicated what he wanted everyone to focus on and that strengthened the bonds of the people who were ready to sign on as supporters of his new program.

### Political Move Number 2: Get Your Idea on the Agenda—Create a Sense of Urgency

In every organization there are more ideas than there are places on the agenda. The question is: which ideas will get considered? A good stepping-stone strategy (see chapter 3) will eventually move you up the chain of command to the decision maker. But you may still need something extra to turn people's attention to the problem you are trying to address. And nothing works quite as well as being able to show people that your idea addresses an *urgent* need. Deadlines, external threats, and mandates from higher authority can all be useful ways to make your idea a priority.

Sometimes external events can create urgent conditions that favour a given idea. History is replete with examples of this phenomenon, which political scientists call the opening of a "policy window." For instance, the American space program, which had languished on the back burner throughout the 1950s, was suddenly thrown into high gear when the former Soviet Union orbited its first *Sputnik* satellite. An entire set of plans and initiatives that had gone begging for resources now had money thrown at them. Similarly, the attacks of September 11, 2001, bolstered the advocates inside organizations who had been arguing for greater attention to corporate security. In the GM story, Boss Kettering injected a sense of urgency into his air-cooled engine proposal by referring to the imminent threat of Henry Ford coming up with an air-cooled engine of his own.

So once you have crafted your idea, stay on the lookout for events that can help you gain political leverage for it. These need not be front-page news stories. They need only be items that your decision makers will consider both urgent and important. If your idea will help cut costs, a downturn in profits in your division or a major new corporate initiative to slash overhead will make cost-cutting initiatives especially attractive—and urgent—to your boss. If your competitor is in the news with a big product announcement, you can argue that your proposed initiative would give your boss something concrete and immediate to announce in response.

### Political Move Number 3: Score Small Wins Early and Broadcast Them Widely

When new ideas are working their way through an organization, it helps to create some buzz for them. Small wins, broadcast widely throughout the organization, give your idea momentum. In addition, when people see positive results from their actions, their commitment deepens, generating organizational goodwill that can carry you through the inevitable trial-and-error period to come.

Archie Norman followed this rule explicitly. He fired Asda's CFO on Day 1. And his "Store Renewal Program" produced a series of small wins that became the "Asda Best Way." The accumulated goodwill created by these actions helped him overcome internal skeptics and sustain his turnaround plan.

### Political Move Number 4: Form Key Alliances to Broaden Your Base

At the beginning of any idea campaign, it is especially helpful to form alliances with the people who have three key powers: the power to decide, the power to fund, and the power to implement. Norman had the power to decide and the power to fund in his own office, so he focused all his attention on the people with the power to implement—the managers in the stores.

In addition to personally visiting the stores and setting up direct-report relationships with some store managers, he instituted "Archie Monday Night Football," a weekly soccer game between his senior executive team and store employees and managers, to strengthen his bonds with line employees. After mixing it up on the field, everybody would hobble off to a pub for beer and pizza. Another less athletic but no less colorful alliance-building activity were meetings where field people got to give senior managers candid comments and feedback. Here senior managers had to "walk the plank"—step up on a board thrown between two chairs in the middle of the room. Each time a senior manager was unable to answer a criticism, he had to take a step on the board. With sessions such as these, there was no doubt which of the two factions—headquarters or field employees— was in charge of the company.

One of the most famous cases of building momentum for a project by broadening its support base comes from a campaign waged by a group of five military contractors—including Northrop, General Electric, and Boeing—to gain congressional budget approval for the B-2 "Stealth" (radar-evading) bomber in the 1990s. To assure that it would win, the contractors spread lucrative contracts for B-2 bomber work to companies in forty-nine states. These subcontractors then brought intense political pressure on their representatives in Congress to pass the funding bill. Today, at two billion dollars per plane, the aircraft is the most expensive flying machine ever built. Opponents of the plane, who thought they had the votes to kill it on numerous occasions, tipped their hats to the political skills of the defense industry—and took note of the virtues of broadening one's base of support for selling any idea.

### Political Move Number 5: Create a Snowball Effect

At a certain point in an idea campaign, momentum becomes self-sustaining. Ever-increasing organizational support and commitment creates a "snowball effect" as the number of people who back the idea increases and the pressures build on opponents to get out of the way. Once you have a sufficiently broad coalition, your opponents— rather than you—will appear to be the "extremists."

The same effect can be generated on a smaller scale with specific projects. Consider the story of how Lloyd Braun, ABC Television Group Chairman, created the hit television series *Lost*. When Braun first read an outline of the *Lost* story, he detected the makings of a major hit. He announced to one of his assistants: "This, my friend, is *ER* [the mega-hit hospital drama]." But Braun's bosses had a different point of view. "A crazy project that's never going to work," said Disney CEO Michael Eisner (head of ABC's parent company). "A waste of time," said Bob Iger, Eisner's number two.

Braun pushed ahead anyway. He decided he would try to create a snowball effect—generating so much momentum for the program that it would be impossible to kill. He approved a twelve-million-dollar budget before there was even a final script. Eisner and Iger were furious when they got wind of the price tag, but Braun pushed on. Supremely confident of his eventual success, he told his colleagues: "If we are pregnant enough, they won't shut us down."

Eighteen million viewers watched the first *Lost* episode, the biggest success for the network in the previous four years. Twelve Emmy nominations followed, and the show topped the charts internationally. The snowball effect had worked—but Braun himself was not around to enjoy the fruits of his success. His heavy-handed tactics had earned him enemies, and he failed to follow our next piece of political advice.

### Political Move Number 6: Be Flexible—Respond and Adjust

The French philosopher Montaigne once said, "In their beginnings, it is we who guide affairs and hold them in our power; but . . . once they are set in motion, it is they which guide us and sweep us along." So it is in organizations when it comes to new ideas and initiatives. Once you achieve organizational momentum, your ideas will take on a life of their own as more people become involved and they attract a larger set of corporate interests. When this happens, you need to show flexibility if you and your idea are to survive politically.

This is exactly what Lloyd Braun did *not* do on his way to getting ABC "pregnant enough" with his *Lost* show to guarantee that the program would be produced. His stubborn, defiant way of jamming the program through the corporate hierarchy at Disney made him powerful enemies. As filming for *Lost* got under way in Hawaii, Braun heard through the grapevine that he was being fired, and before the first episode aired, he was gone. He made too much of the fact that he was "right" and too little of the fact that every corporate initiative is a team effort. Lesson: the goal is not just for your idea to win, *it is for you to succeed*. In managing politics, flexibility is necessary for survival.

It did not have to work out this way for Braun. For example, an executive we once worked with at a large corporation was charged with implementing the company's "Six Sigma" program—a system of complex statistical management tools designed to enhance quality.

The system had worked well at the corporate level in a financial crisis, but line managers were resisting the heavy-duty statistical training, which had a bureaucratic, check-the-box feel.

The executive succeeded in selling the Six Sigma idea further down the chain of command by refusing to be dogmatic about it. He conducted structured interviews with key business unit leaders and used his findings to craft a simple campaign theme—"Focus it where you need it." He then changed the Six Sigma model so it was more flexible and required less statistical training. Finally, he gained some small wins by targeting situations where the revised program could actually add value. As the new program rolled out, people across the units began asking for it and adapting it to their individual needs. The Six Sigma concept, in other words, found its legs by adjusting and adapting.

### Political Move Number 7: Lock It In

Once you have generated organizational momentum, you need to lock the idea into the organizational matrix through budget lines, job descriptions, incentives, and other standard operating procedures. Your new initiative now becomes part of other people's careers, creating the sustaining force it needs to survive. This is the stage when formal authority becomes especially useful—either your own or that of your idea champions—because only people with authority can authorize actions with budgetary implications.

An executive we worked with at a large company followed just this strategy when he was charged with redesigning his firm's information systems support function. There was no problem getting agreement that the function needed repair—everyone was complaining about it. The entire support area had become a fiefdom more worried about its own needs than that of end users. The question was what to do.

He helped himself politically by creating an open consultation process so people from every important constituency in the organization could be heard. This gave him the input he needed to design a new mission statement: "the user comes first." Next he launched a series of pilot programs designed to test how different support roles might work for different organizational units. A steering group of senior managers was set up to monitor the pilots and make budget and organizational recommendations to him. Finally, he asked this group to make a series of "lock-in" recommendations, asking for specific budget lines, job titles, salary bands, incentive plans, and other official policies to assure that the new user-friendly focus for IT would become the standard procedure. Without this last step, it would have been all too easy for IT's "technology first" culture to reassert itself.

In addition to illustrating how the lock-in process works, the way this firm handled its change initiative illustrates a critical point about the use of formal authority we made in chapter 1. Many people think of their position—whether it is a front-line supervisor or a general manager—as a bat they can swing to force people into adopting their ideas. But people in higher positions "possess" authority *if and only if* people in lower positions give it (implicitly or explicitly) to them. The executive we worked with had enough formal authority to order people to adopt any IT support system he wanted. But he chose to engage in a politically sensitive process that brought everyone affected by the decision into the process of making it. This meant that the final idea belonged to everyone—not just him. When he finally exercised his formal authority to implement this plan, he was doing exactly what everyone below him wanted him to do.

### Political Move Number 8: Secure Appropriate Credit

As you make the political moves outlined above, you need to consider how to get the credit you deserve for the ideas you generate. Here you confront a paradox. If you do not seek credit for your ideas, you may end up like Kumar Chandra, the software engineer we met at the beginning of chapter 1, whose career was stalled because his best ideas kept getting hijacked by his colleagues. But if you try too hard to get credit, you risk being seen as a pushy self-promoter—someone who does not "work well with the team." The bottom line: it can be surprisingly hard to strike the right political balance when it comes to this important facet of selling ideas.

The payoff for getting appropriate credit is very high. Social scientists have identified a phenomenon called the Matthew Effect, which attaches when you begin to acquire a reputation for innovation. The

Matthew Effect is named for a cold-hard-truth passage from the Gospel of Matthew which, paraphrased, reads, "To those who have—will more be given. And from those who have not—will be taken away even the little they have." Research on high achievers in science has shown that people who are already famous get much more credit for and attention to their work—even when they contribute relatively little to coauthored studies—than do other, less-famous scientists. Cumulatively, these honors add up to better chances of receiving top awards such as the Nobel Prize.

The same is true inside many organizations. People get put on the fast track by acquiring a reputation very early in their employment for delivering results—a reputation that may or may not be deserved, but which comes from gaining credit. This reputation then gives them access to better assignments and more face time with high-level executives, which in turn gives the fast-trackers more opportunities to shine. When the Matthew Effect kicks in, more opportunities are given to those who already have good ones—and those left behind find that the few responsibilities remaining are soon taken away from them.

There are several factors to keep in mind as you consider the politics of taking credit for ideas. First, if the initiative is important enough to you, you may actually want to let someone more powerful than you take the credit for it. Why? Because you add a powerful, interest-based incentive (see chapter 6) for the boss to champion your proposal, and, with a senior person's name on it, the idea will have more credibility.

In addition, organizational conventions may dictate that the senior member of your team get the credit for all ideas developed by the group. As noted above, this enhances the idea's chances for success. The practice also centralizes accountability for the idea in terms of budget, implementation, and what happens if something goes wrong.

But note well: if the idea proves to be a good one, a gracious, skilled team leader will be quick to point out at meetings and presentations that you were the real innovator. When you find yourself working for someone who refuses to give such public praise, you face a set of risky alternatives. If you keep quiet, you fall into Kumar's trap and your career grinds to a halt. If you let your frustration show by confronting the boss, you may make a powerful enemy. And if you try to gain credit by engaging in blatant self-promotion, research suggests that you can lose credibility. People do not like to hear others blowing their own horns.

So how can you strike the appropriate balance? Once again, as with so many topics related to Woo, the secret of success in gaining appropriate organizational kudos centers on relationships. If you cannot blow your own horn, you need others to blow it for you. And the people who will form the chorus line singing your praises are generally the ones who know you, like you, owe you, or trust you. If your boss or colleagues are hogging credit for your ideas, go to your network of allies and ask for advice. See if some of them can help you correct the record by whispering in a few well-placed ears what the "real story" is on how the new initiative got started. If even this seems too risky, then it is time to start looking for a new group to work with. Life is too short to spend it labouring for people who do not know how to give credit where it is due.

If, on the other hand, the boss is open to sharing the limelight, seek out opportunities to present the idea at meetings or speak on its behalf outside the group. Associate yourself—along with the boss— with the idea in e-mails, paper copies of the initiative that circulate widely, write-ups in newsletters, Web site mentions, and outside media interviews. Create a little branding campaign that gets people thinking of you in an appropriate, positive way as an agent of innovation. The Matthew Effect can work wonders for your career if you manage it skillfully.

## Conclusion

The writer George Plimpton tells a story about Muhammad Ali in the 1996 film documentary *When We Were Kings*. Both men were at a Harvard University commencement in the 1970s where Ali was giving an address. Near the end of Ali's speech, one of the students yelled out to him: "Give us a poem!" At the time, according to Plimpton, the shortest poem in the English language was a verse by an American poet named Strickland Gillian about fleas. It was titled "The Antiquity of Microbes" and it went:

Adam
Had 'em.

Muhammad Ali responded to the Harvard senior's request by breaking the record with the following verse:

Me?
*We!*

Although some people think Ali actually said "Whee!" rather than
"We"—and was therefore engaging in a bit of characteristic self-
celebration—we prefer our interpretation. Winning others over is a
journey from "me" to "we"—and the final steps in this process are
often the most difficult. It is all very well to have great relationships,
credibility, plans, and proposals, but if you cannot close the sale and
push your initiative through your organization, then you have failed.

Successful closing requires attention to two distinct problems:
gaining individual commitments and overcoming possible political
opposition. Both are captured in Newton's First Law of Organizations, which reads, as we have modified it:

A person at rest tends to stay at rest and an organization in
motion tends to stay in motion with the same speed and in the
same direction, unless acted upon by an external force.

*You are that force* and to gain the commitments that impart momentum to an idea, you need people to (1) take concrete actions that
(2) require effort, (3) are freely chosen, and (4) are observed by or
known to others. Mere promises, unless given by people you can
truly trust, will not suffice.

The commitment process requires you to overcome people's natural reluctance to act—their inertia—and to overcome your own fears
of appearing "pushy" and of hearing the word *no.* Finally, you need
to take steps at the very outset of your campaign to protect your
commitments from being washed away by the tides of shifting priorities. You can do this by reinforcing shared interests, relying on
strong, reciprocal relationships, creating influential audiences for

your commitments, and building in accountability features such as deadlines and specific deliverables.

Beyond the problem of securing and monitoring individual commitments lies the political process of committing your organization to your idea. Politics is not an optional activity for idea sellers—it is an essential aspect of the Art of Woo. Two imperatives present themselves: turf and momentum. Humans—especially in groups—are territorial. If your idea threatens someone's control, interests, or resources, you can be sure that it will trigger a defensive response. And the people who stand to lose under your new regime will usually be louder and more persistent than potential winners, so you should never underestimate the energy your opponents will bring to a political fight.

The antidote to turf problems is momentum—an overall movement by your unit or the organization as a whole toward your idea. To gain momentum you need to communicate your idea using an easy-to-understand theme, create a sense of urgency so the idea gets on the right agendas, form key alliances and broaden your base of supporters, score small wins and broadcast them widely, generate a "snowball effect," create lock-in, and respond and adjust as your idea integrates itself into the organization. Finally, to protect and enhance your reputation, which is the source of your credibility, take steps to secure appropriate credit for your initiatives.

All of this sounds daunting. But it is a small price to pay for the satisfaction of seeing your idea spring to life. Moreover, with these skills at your command, you can become a positive force for change in every part of your world—at work, at home, and in your community.

With Step 4—*Secure Your Commitments*—behind us, our Woo journey is over. But before we close, we need to revisit some basic questions that we raised at the very beginning of the book about best practices in persuasion. So we invite you to join us in the final chapter as we summarize the Art of Woo and conclude with some thoughts on Aristotle's favorite persuasion tool: personal character.

chapter ten

## Woo with Integrity: Character

As our book ends, we want to share one last idea-selling story to summarize the Art of Woo. It is a remarkable tale, not only because of the simplicity of the ideas involved but also because it shows how strategic persuasion can help you change people's lives, not just improve the way they work. We tell this story from the perspectives of those most closely associated with it.

### The Art of Doing Good

Our story begins with a man named Jack, who grew up in a working-class neighborhood in Philadelphia. He graduated from a local college with a major in education and enrolled in medical school, hoping to become a doctor. But he quickly realized that he had neither the passion nor the patience for medicine and dropped out.

Two formative events then took place. First, after holding down a few odd jobs, Jack finally found his calling in a nonprofit program dealing with drug abuse. Here he discovered that he liked the social sector with its emphasis on helping people. He also married and started a family.

Second, his father died, which affected him in a profoundly spiritual way. He joined a large church and became a dedicated member. Religion was to play an important role in the events that would soon consume his life. In addition, with the help of business and political leaders he met through his church, Jack launched two ambitious social service organizations, one in the drug-abuse area and the other in mental health. His successes were noticed. He became known throughout the region as a skilled fund-raiser for worthy causes.

That is when Jack's big idea came to him. In his fund-raising work, he saw that people were much more willing to give to a cause when their money was "matched" by others, thus doubling the impact of their gifts. The problem was that such "matching" opportunities were hard to find and develop.

His idea was to create a central organization—a foundation—that would identify anonymous donors who were willing to provide matching gifts to worthy causes. Jack would collect money from charities, pair up this money with new money from anonymous philanthropists, and then return the doubled money to the worthy cause. His foundation could be operated off the interest earned by his donors' money during the six months it would take to pair just the right charities with just the right anonymous donors. He gave his idea a name—New Concepts in Philanthropy—and created a case for it based on the problem (there was not enough money being raised for worthy causes), the cause (people were stuck in old-fashioned, laborious fund-raising techniques), his solution (a centralized, anonymous-donor foundation), and its relatively inexpensive method of administration (the interest earned from donations would be enough to cover operating costs).

Through his widening social network, he made a new friend at about this time—one of the top physicians at the area's leading hospital for children. And that man, in turn, introduced Jack to his father, one of the richest men in America and perhaps its most visionary and well-connected philanthropist. Jack impressed both men with his energy and new ideas. They set up an institute—with Jack as its director—to spread his fund-raising expertise and commitment to values. The father joined Jack's new matching-fund foundation as a trustee and the son helped him launch the new idea by recommending friends who could participate as donors.

To get his idea off the ground, Jack took one small step. With names given him by his physician friend, he let it be known that if he could get twenty people to donate five thousand dollars each to his new foundation, their money would be matched by an equal amount from a donor who wished to remain anonymous and the combined money would be given to some important local charities. When people saw who was affiliated with this new program, Jack had no trouble raising his first hundred thousand dollars.

In no time, the idea caught fire. Other people asked Jack if they could contribute and donations began to flow. And as they did, Jack's foundation began making substantial gifts to local causes from these monies. That, in turn, triggered interest from other groups that wished to receive grants from Jack's foundation. People lined up to get to know this new foundation and its founder.

Then Jack came up with his second and most original idea. He realized he could accelerate his program by opening the foundation to a whole new type of donation. If a nonprofit institution—say a college or university—placed part of its endowment in his foundation, then Jack saw that this money, too, could be matched by Jack's growing stable of anonymous donors, allowing the charitable organization to increase its endowment through matching gifts. Jack's new idea took hold, and Harvard, Princeton, and the University of Pennsylvania (among others) signed up to deposit funds. With these premier institutions on board, a host of smaller colleges, especially many religious schools that struggled to raise money, clamored to be included in the program.

Within a few short years, Jack's foundation was raising hundreds of millions of dollars and making large donations to many well-known, highly visible institutions, including the Red Cross, the Salvation Army, and top universities. Jack himself had become one of the most respected people in the philanthropic world.

Jack had found the secret of doing well by doing good—and it had all come about through his remarkable powers to leverage relationships, address interests, and implement his simple insight: people give more to causes when other people are matching their gifts.

## A Woo Review

Let's push the pause button at this point and review what Jack did right in terms of the Art of Woo. His strategy reflects an almost perfect execution of the four-step Woo process.

**Step 1—Survey Your Situation.** First, Jack did a great job on the "me" stage of Woo. He came up with a well-formulated idea and polished it using his extensive nonprofit experience. Second, he found and embraced his own personal persuasion style—an affable mix of other-oriented Promoter and Advocate roles coupled with an ability to project a sincere, committed belief in his idea. As he achieved early successes, he acquired confidence and that helped him to project credibility. Finally, he surveyed and mapped the philanthropic social network around Philadelphia and found his way, one stepping-stone at a time, to some of the nation's wealthiest and most open-minded donors. Jack's networking activity never stopped and was the source of an ever-widening set of contacts.

**Step 2—Confront the Five Barriers.** Jack also showed respect for and command of the five potential barriers to persuasion. Let's look at each one of them in turn.

- **Relationships.** Jack built and scrupulously maintained key, Trust-Level relationships. Jack had no trouble meeting and greeting people. And by selecting his most powerful friends to be the trustees of his foundation, he created the momentum he needed to both launch his idea and keep it expanding.

- **Credibility.** Jack's relationship skills and his proven track record gave him credibility. People trusted him and saw him as a reliable, competent expert in his field. Those who did not know him could rely on the reputations of the well-known people who were affiliated with him. Finally, he delivered on his double-your-donation promise time after time in very public ways.

- **Tuning to the Other Person's Channel.** Jack had a gift for communicating effectively with many diverse audiences. He excelled at the Visionary and Relationship communication channels, as did most of his charity-minded audience. Even the hard-nosed denizens of Wall Street he approached were inclined to shift to the visionary channel when it came to charity. With religious people, he spoke of religion. With educators, he spoke of education. With hospitals, he spoke of health care. Regardless of whom he spoke with, as one supporter put it, Jack had a way of finding the "key to their hearts."

- **Beliefs and Values.** Jack's mission was to advance people's values and beliefs by enhancing their ability to do good works. And he not only spoke of values, his life reflected them.

- **Interests and Needs.** It was in addressing this factor that Jack showed his touch of genius. Leveraging the power of matching gifts is an old idea—some say Benjamin Franklin invented it. But Jack took it to a whole new level and, in doing so, opened his foundation to many smaller institutions that had never had an opportunity to benefit from mainstream philanthropy. The president of the Coalition for Christian Colleges and Universities, for example, said that gaining access to Jack's stable of donors was "almost a gift from heaven, in a religious sense."

**Step 3—Make Your Pitch.** Early on, Jack constructed a powerful, PCAN-based case for his program. He gave his early backers reasons to say yes, and when he spoke to new donors, he could point to others who had doubled their money and received substantial gifts. He combined all his insights regarding his audience's beliefs and interests into his message.

There are no records of specific pitches Jack made, but his results suggest they must have been memorable. As a Christian, for example, he had Jesus' "Parable of the Talents," which teaches that people "to whom much is given" should multiply their assets rather than hoard them so they can provide the means to advance God's work. And as his organization grew, Jack had many stories and examples to offer from the lives of individuals who had been touched by his foundation's work.

**Step 4—Secure Your Commitments.** Finally, Jack was not content to gain promises of support. He demanded actions. A realist about human nature, he required concrete commitments from his donors—deposits of cash and agreements to leave it in his care for at least six months while he arranged the "match." And at the institutional level, he was skilled at overcoming occasional objections raised by naysayers—usually traditional fund-raising professionals—whose career or professional interests conflicted with his philanthropic model. As his program grew, he mounted true "campaigns" for his idea, creating a "snowball effect" within the charitable world as a whole. He built a broad base of enthusiastic supporters, and was widely credited for his innovations.

## Back to Jack

Given his success, you may be wondering how Jack's story ended. Did his foundation spawn similar institutions?

Jack's full name was John G. Bennett Jr. He lived in a suburb of Philadelphia in the 1980s and 1990s. His organization was called the Foundation for New Era Philanthropy. At the height of his fame, he counted as close friends the wealthy mutual fund magnate John Templeton and his physician son John Templeton Jr., former ABC news anchor Peter Jennings, former Treasury Secretary William E. Simon, former co-head of Goldman Sachs John C. Whitehead, philanthropist Laurance Rockefeller, and many other political, business, and cultural leaders.

And, as of this writing, Jack is finishing up a twelve-year sentence in a federal penitentiary for securities law violations and fraud.

The Foundation for New Era Philanthropy was a pyramid scheme. When New Era went down—as it did in May 1995 after five years of operation—it owed pledges of more than five hundred million dollars and had few assets with which to pay them. Jack never had or found any "anonymous donors" willing to give money—though many people had assumed John Templeton was the mysterious benefactor behind Jack's plan. Instead, he raised *all* his money from charities with his compelling "double your money" pitch and used the new money he raised to pay off the groups that had put money in earlier. His system required him to raise ever-increasing millions to stay ahead of his rapidly escalating obligations—a job made somewhat easier by the fact that many colleges and universities let their endowment money "ride" for multiple six-month cycles.

He returned just enough "doubled" money to keep everyone's confidence. Meanwhile, he pocketed millions of dollars from the interest earned while he held his victims' cash. He and his family bought expensive homes and Lexus automobiles, and they entertained lavishly.

An accounting professor from a small college in Michigan, worried that his own school was about to throw its endowment away by giving it to New Era, got hold of its 1993 federal tax return and discovered the fraud: the foundation had reported almost no interest income on its hundreds of millions of dollars in assets. The *Wall Street Journal* put the story on its front page, New Era's bankers called a £65 million loan, and the regulators swooped in.

Such is the power of reputations and beliefs, however, that even at this point Jack's backers refused to believe what they were hearing. John Templeton, reached by reporters in a London hotel, commented, "I think he will have good answers, and as people get to know him, I think people will have the same view of him that I do."

Jack was carted off to jail in 1997 after trying unsuccessfully to argue in court that the whole affair had been the result of brain damage he suffered in a 1984 car accident. He wept when he met with his staff to confess that he had made the whole thing up. "I betrayed you all," he said. "All I ever wanted to do was help people. There are no anonymous donors."

The biggest losers turned out to be those that could least afford the loss—the small religious colleges. Lancaster Bible College lost £16.9 million and John Brown University of Siloam Springs, Arkansas, lost over £2 million, 4 percent of its endowment. Other losers included hospitals, major universities, the Academy of Natural Sciences in Philadelphia, a program teaching English-language courses in Cambodia, and a long list of other charities.

Why did he do it? With his gift for Woo, Jack could have made a good living as a highly paid nonprofit executive. He gave a hint of his motivation just before he was sentenced. "As the years passed," he told the court, "the desire became a dream, the dream became a need, the need became an obsession, the obsession became a fantasy, and the fantasy became a delusion." In some ways, he was like the dieter who by day truly believes that he or she is on a diet, only to lapse into compulsive eating—in Bennett's case into writing himself checks—in the dark of night. An attorney specializing in nonprofit law and familiar with the New Era story had this to say about Jack: "I'm not sure Bennett set out to commit fraud. I think the situation got away from him. These things aren't necessarily set up to defraud charities or the public, but the philanthropic community is about power and reputation . . . not so much about money. And that's very exciting."

In other words, Jack longed to be a "player" in the world of the rich and famous. He craved a feeling of importance. As Winston Churchill warned in his quote that led this chapter, the "ambition . . . for fame" that "glints in every mind" led Jack to use his persuasion skills to con an entire community of very sophisticated people.

## What Matters Most: Character and Purpose

We saved this story for the last chapter because we want to make a point about persuasion skills. Like any powerful force, these skills can serve many purposes—some good and some not so good. The skills themselves are neutral. With these tools now in your hands, therefore, you confront the ethical problem of how you will use them.

When Richard was making the rounds of magazines and newspapers to promote his earlier negotiation book, *Bargaining for Advantage,* he spent an hour or so in the office of a *BusinessWeek* editor who was kind enough to see him. After some general discussion about business trends, the editor flipped through the pages of *Bargaining for*

*Advantage* for a minute and then looked up. "Isn't this just another book about how to manipulate people?" he asked.

"It depends on who the reader is," Richard replied.

Winston Churchill noted in his history of World War II that Hitler was, on a person-to-person level as well as at rallies, a very persuasive person. So was Churchill. These two men understood the Art of Woo in all its details.

The main difference between them was that Churchill had character: he was an honorable man who was committed to using his persuasion skills to achieve worthy goals.

Let's put it this way. An earnest and sincere lover buys flowers and candy for the object of his affections. So does the cad who seeks to take advantage of another's heart. But when the cad succeeds, we don't blame the flowers and candy. We rightly question his character. And in Jack Bennett's case, we should not blame the misery he caused on the persuasion tools he mastered. Instead, we should ask how we can avoid slipping—even a little—into the self-serving state of mind that led Bennett to his downfall.

The answer lies in paying attention to both your own motives and the effects of your actions on others when you sell your ideas. Almost all persuasion situations at work involve a mix of purposes—people want to advance their own careers and take care of their own needs even as they work toward their organization's goals. But you will face tough choices—people always do—when your needs conflict either with the organization's or with other people's as you advance your agenda. As a person of character, you have an obligation to think about the standards of conduct you will hold yourself to in these situations, or you risk joining Jack Bennett in the rogue's gallery.

One simple test is to avoid purposes and practices that benefit yourself by causing direct and substantial harm to others. For example, we object to some of the advice given in Robert Greene's *The 48 Laws of Power,* which teaches readers to obey such rules as "Get Others to Do the Work—While You Take the Credit," "Be Selectively Honest and Generous to Disarm Your Target," and "Crush Your Enemy Totally."

But even this test will leave you with unanswered questions in many circumstances. For example, suppose you are promoting a strategy idea that requires the organization to close an existing business unit and lay off hundreds of employees—but would also result in a big promotion and raise for you. Many worthy ideas involve actions that will make someone, somewhere worse off. And we don't think that makes them unethical.

For these cases, we recommend what we call the *Wall Street Journal* standard—a paraphrase of Richard's conclusion on negotiation ethics in *Bargaining for Advantage*.

It goes like this: "Persuaders who aspire to personal integrity should test their actions with a thoughtful set of personal values, based on widely shared social norms, that they could explain and defend to the *Wall Street Journal* were that paper to run a front-page story on the idea-selling strategy they adopted."

If you could not defend your actions on the front page of the *Wall Street Journal*, where Jack Bennett's fraud was revealed, then you should rethink your strategy. You may still go astray if the social norms you consult are controversial or if you give in to the temptation to delude yourself about your motives, but you will keep yourself out of a lot of trouble.

## Ten Questions for Would-Be Wooers

As you put this book down and return to the world of work with all its tough challenges, we thought it might be helpful to give you a set of ten questions to ask as you get ready for every idea-selling encounter. Consider these the preflight checklist for launching your idea. We have provided a more graphic, Excel-styled format for this checklist in Appendix C at the end of the book.

### 1. What Is the Five-Minute Summary of My Idea?

Before going into a meeting or sending an important message, review exactly what your idea is about. Scan quickly through the PCAN model: What is the problem? What are the causes of that problem? How does my idea answer the problem? How is my answer superior to the status quo or available alternatives? Recall a memorable image or metaphor that captures the idea clearly and positions it favorably against the background of its alternatives.

## 2. What Role Does This Person Play in the Decision Process?

Review why you have chosen to meet with or communicate with this person at this time. Which step are they in your stepping-stone strategy? How can he or she help you advance your idea?

## 3. What Is My Goal for This Encounter?

Think specifically about your goals. Useful goals include: getting feedback on your idea, gaining access to someone else, persuading this person to take a favorable attitude toward your idea, obtaining authorization for resources, gaining endorsements, making decisions, and getting help with implementation. Write down your goal and refer to it before as well as after the encounter. Did you achieve your goal? If not, why not?

## 4. What Is the Basis for My Credibility with This Person?

What relationships, references, credentials, past accomplishments, or competencies should you be prepared to mention or display to establish your credibility? If you think you have a Trust-Level relationship, this will be less of an issue. If it is a Reciprocity-Level relationship, you may need to be prepared to diplomatically remind the other person of who owes what to whom at this point in your interaction. If this is only a Rapport-Level relationship, concrete signs of credibility may be especially important.

## 5. What Persuasion Channel Will This Person Be Tuned To?

Be prepared to adjust your pitch so you are communicating on the other person's channel. If you think the Rationality channel is his dominant mode, be prepared with your analysis and evidence. If the other person is more conceptual, emphasize the larger purpose or framework within which your idea fits. Have a Plan B in case you need to shift to a discussion of interests (what is in it for him?), politics (how will it look to a larger audience?), relationships (how does this fit into your ongoing interactions?), or authority (who is in charge and is that authority being respected and used appropriately?).

### 6. What Persuasion Style Is Appropriate?

Be aware that your preferred persuasion style—Driver, Commander, Advocate, Chess Player, or Promoter—may not be the best way to appeal to this particular audience. Remember how Charles Lindbergh (chapter 4), a man who preferred the reserved and rational Commander style, bought a new suit, made an expensive telephone call, and took on the role of the Idea Promoter when he went to New Jersey to sell the busy aircraft executives at Wright Aeronautical Corporation on his plan to fly across the Atlantic. Once he had attracted a group of loyal and enthusiastic backers, he quickly shifted back to his more restrained, natural persuasion mode. But he was smart enough to adjust the way he presented himself to meet his audience's expectations.

Of course, different people have varying degrees of flexibility when it comes to personal style. If you try to adjust yourself beyond your stretch point, you will damage your credibility. Had Lindbergh taken the Promoter role too far—throwing parties and giving lavish gifts—he could not have sustained it and people would have wondered who he thought he was fooling. He was a mail pilot, after all, not a Wall Street mogul.

So make an effort to shift your presentation style in the right direction—turn up (or down) your volume and focus more (or less) on spinning your message to appeal to the audience. But remember that it is better to be a bit awkward—and authentic—than it is to try too hard to be someone you obviously are not.

### 7. Will My Idea Conflict with Any of This Person's Beliefs?

Will the other party be skeptical of the idea based on its feasibility? If so, how can you address that? Might your idea conflict with a basic value or norm the other person holds? Think of ways to minimize this conflict—such as mentioning the prior endorsement of someone who holds that same belief or value.

### 8. Might My Idea Conflict with This Person's Interests?

Imagine that you are sitting in this person's chair. Think of the interests the person may have—especially those related to control, resources, career, decision-making jurisdiction, and future opportunities—that your idea could conflict with. Then think of the interests you both might share that could help bridge the conflicting agendas that arise.

### 9. What Commitments Can I Ask For?

What specific actions do you want the other person to take to advance your idea? What audience should witness this action? If you have an endorsement goal, obtain agreement on the people you can notify about the endorsement. If you have a decision goal, request permission to notify others of the decision.

### 10. Can I Leave the Relationship Better Than I Found It?

Always remember that Woo begins and ends with positive, constructive relationships. Think about how you can conclude the encounter with a strong relationship intact. Be considerate of the other person's time. Ask if there are things this person needs that you can help with. Find ways to demonstrate your good faith and reliability. As story after story in this book has shown, there are few problems a good relationship cannot fix.

## Conclusion

We began chapter 1 with a story about Kumar Chandra, a frustrated information technology manager working for a large California company. "I just can't seem to sell my ideas" was his lament. *The Art of Woo* has been our response. We wanted to help Kumar and everyone like him become more effective idea advocates.

You need persuasion skills no matter what kind of organization you work for. And the higher you go, the more these skills matter. Most important, you need to think *strategically* about persuasion, with an eye on the moves that lie ahead as you decide which ones to take today.

We recently read about a Dutch traffic engineer named Hans Monderman whose theories of avoiding automobile collisions in urban environments resemble what we have tried to get across about designing and executing a good persuasion strategy. Monderman designs intersections with no stoplights, signs, painted centerlines, speed bumps, or defined pedestrian crossings. His idea is that people actually do a better job looking out for themselves—and each other—when they are given full responsibility for maneuvering than when they rely on systems and signals. Traffic lights, he says, are "the wrong story. People here have to find their own way, negotiate for themselves, and use their own brains."

Monderman calls this the concept of "shared space." Surveying his busy intersection, Monderman comments: "This is social space, so when Grandma is coming, you stop, because that's what normal, courteous human beings do." Tens of thousands of people cross paths every day at Monderman's intersections, and there has never been a fatal accident.

We are not sure Monderman's traffic theories would work so well outside the friendly confines of small Dutch cities, but we think that selling ideas in most organizations is quite similar to maneuvering through the traffic in one of his "shared spaces." The typical organization may have many traffic lights and stop signs, but these "standard operating procedures" are often ignored—and everyone knows they are ignored. To advance initiatives through these spaces, therefore, you have to navigate by keeping your eye on the right people and avoiding obstacles such as conflicting interests, hostile beliefs, cultural missteps, and political minefields that can come out of nowhere and cause collisions. *The Art of Woo* provides a road map for working your way through these dangerous intersections to safety and success.

Woo. Simple to say. Hard to do.

Now it's up to you.

# Appendix A

## Six Channels Survey

Without giving the matter too much thought (and without revising your answers for any reason!), please select the statement in each pair below that MOST ACCURATELY describes what you do to exercise influence. Pick ONE STATEMENT in each pair of statements and record the letter associated with that statement in the "I select ___" space.

There are two columns for recording your choices:

- Column 1 is for the statement that describes **what you feel you must do in your organization to be effective most of the time.**

- Column 2 is for the statement that describes **what you would feel more comfortable doing** and would prefer to do if you had complete freedom to act as you would like.

For both columns, select the statement you think is *more accurate*—even if you think neither statement is very accurate or both are very accurate. If you do not currently work for an organization, you can skip Column 1 and record your choices only in Column 2.

Please note that you can select the same statement for both columns if what you generally do at work to influence others is also what you prefer doing.

Warning: Do not pick the statement you "ought" to agree with—just pick the one your gut tells you is more accurate most of the time. In addition, some statements repeat, but you should not worry about answering consistently. Just keep going. All answers are equally "correct." Summarize your selections at the very end.

## Survey

|  |  | Column 1 | Column 2 |
|---|---|---|---|
|  |  | What I must do to be effective within my organization | What I would be more comfortable doing if I could choose |
| 1. | A. I sometimes assert my control.<br>B. I let the data do the talking. | I select ___. | I select ___. |
| 2. | C. I present the big picture.<br>D. I reach out to be friends with the people I need to influence. | I select ___. | I select ___. |
| 3. | B. I use detailed information to support my points.<br>D. I establish good relationships with others. | I select ___. | I select ___. |
| 4. | A. I use the authority I have to help me accomplish my goals.<br>E. I negotiate so everyone wins. | I select ___. | I select ___. |
| 5. | B. I show people the logic of my proposal.<br>E. I engage in a little give-and-take to get things done. | I select ___. | I select ___. |
| 6. | C. I try to inspire others.<br>F. I assemble coalitions when necessary. | I select ___. | I select ___. |
| 7. | E. I negotiate to obtain others' support.<br>C. I emphasize the broader goals of the organization. | I select ___. | I select ___. |
| 8. | A. I rely on whatever authority I have.<br>D. I do favours to create good relationships. | I select ___. | I select ___. |
| 9. | B. I construct a tight case to argue for my ideas.<br>F. I gather support by approaching key people. | I select ___. | I select ___. |

10. D. I get to know people personally.    I select ___.   I select ___.
    F. I work hard to make sure "people who matter" support my idea.

11. A. I use the authority of my position.    I select ___.   I select ___.
    B. I present the data, point to the precedents, and argue the pros and cons.

12. D. I socialize with people I want to influence.    I select ___.   I select ___.
    C. I show where my idea fits into the overall scheme.

13. E. I find ways to negotiate so everyone wins.    I select ___.   I select ___.
    F. I establish a wide network of organizational contacts.

14. B. I make my case with data and evidence.    I select ___.   I select ___.
    F. I focus on people and groups who can sway opinion.

15. B. I use reasoned argument.    I select ___.   I select ___.
    D. I reach out to understand how other people feel.

16. A. I use my position to get things done.    I select ___.   I select ___.
    F. I work behind the scenes to get support.

17. D. I rely on relationships to accomplish my goals.    I select ___.   I select ___.
    E. I sometimes ask for a bit more than I expect to get.

18. A. I get things done efficiently by using my authority.    I select ___.   I select ___.
    C. I inspire others to feel as I do about the proposal.

19. B. I present objective information to convince others.    I select ___.   I select ___.
    C. I remind people of what the organization stands for.

20. D. I win friends and influence people.    I select ___.   I select ___.
    F. I target key decision makers.

21. A. I use whatever formal authority I have.    I select ___.      I select ___.
    E. I seek the middle ground when there are disagreements.

22. B. I base my arguments on objective information.    I select ___.      I select ___.
    E. I negotiate so everybody wins.

23. E. I provide incentives to gain support.    I select ___.      I select ___.
    F. I build momentum by winning over key individuals and groups.

24. A. I assert the authority that goes with my position.    I select ___.      I select ___.
    C. I get people excited about the future.

25. B. I use data and logic to make my case.    I select ___.      I select ___.
    C. I emphasize our common purpose.

26. C. I frame my ideas in terms of our organization's goals.    I select ___.      I select ___.
    F. I take time to consult key individuals.

27. A. I rely on my formal position to get things done.    I select ___.      I select ___.
    D. I make sure that others know I care about their needs.

28. E. I give concessions and expect others to do the same.    I select ___.      I select ___.
    C. I remind people that what we do matters.

29. A. I assert my authority.    I select ___.      I select ___.
    F. I anticipate the politics and work around them.

30. D. I establish rapport and pay attention to feelings.    I select ___.      I select ___.
    E. I make deals that work for both sides.

## Results

Now add up all your "A", "B," "C," "D," "E," and "F" answers above and put those totals below:

| Column 1 | Column 2 |
|---|---|
| **What I need to do to be effective within my organization:** | **What I would be more comfortable doing if I could choose:** |

A's = _____          A's = _____
B's = _____          B's = _____
C's = _____          C's = _____
D's = _____          D's = _____
E's = _____          E's = _____
F's = _____          F's = _____

_____ TOTAL (should equal 30)          _____ TOTAL (should equal 30)

## Decoding Your Results

Your scores for the six letters represent your tendency to use each of the six important channels of influence inside organizations: authority (A); rationality (B); vision (C); relationships (D); interests (E); and politics (F). If you can determine which of these six come to you most naturally, which require the most effort, and which you can improve most readily, you will be well on the way to understanding your style. Below, we introduce each channel.

**A—Authority.** Your "A" scores denote your tendency to use influence moves based on authority—both your authoritative, formal position in your organization and your reliance on authoritative rules, regulations, and standards. Research tells us that, predictions of its demise notwithstanding, the Authority channel is the one most commonly used in organizations and has been since scholars began investigating organizational behavior. If you scored high (7 or above) for this role under Column 1 (what your job requires you to do), you probably occupy a position that requires you to give directions or orders—whether as the leader of a unit or as the designated enforcer of some set of rules. If you also scored high in this category under Column 2 for your personally preferred style, then we would say that you are probably comfortable using your authority as an influence mode and your job "fits" you well. If you prefer this role but your job does not offer you a chance to play it, you may feel frustrated by your lack of positional power. And if you do not prefer this role but are called upon to play it at work, you may feel some stress and conflict at having to issue blunt directives when you would prefer to use some other, perhaps more inspiring or consensus-based, method to gain others' cooperation.

B—Rationality. Your "B" scores represent your tendency to rely on data-oriented reasons to persuade, the second (along with authority) of the two most common persuasion styles used in organizations. Research suggests that this persuasion mode is most often invoked in "bottom-up" or "peer-to-peer" situations, when people try to influence others over whom they have no formal authority. Once again, the two different columns give you a comparative sense of how much your job requires this mode of influence and how much you prefer it irrespective of what your job demands.

C—Vision. Your "C" scores indicate your use of what we call the "visionary" channel. This mode is perhaps the most overtly emotional of the six. When you persuade others based on shared purposes, hopes, fears, and dreams, you are squarely in this role. If you are working in an organization that values Visionary persuasion, it helps to be enthusiastic about your initiatives. Otherwise, people may not take you seriously.

D—Relationships. Your "D" scores relate to the Relationship channel. People who have a strong personal preference for this mode enjoy establishing genuine one-on-one connections with others and like to call them "friends" as well as "coworkers." A relationship builder leverages the fact that people are much more inclined to say "yes" to others they know and like. Moreover, part of friendship is doing small favours in the name of the relationship. These favours tend to trigger feelings of gratitude and obligation on the part of people receiving them. Mutual obligation then forms the foundation for persuasive influence and helps explain why working relationships are the lubricants that make the gears of so many organizations turn more smoothly. People with high Column 2 scores in this category don't mind going to office social occasions, are likely to reach out to new employees on their own to make them feel welcome, and seem, more often than others, to be genuinely willing to help colleagues with extra work. People with low scores in this mode (0, 1, 2, or 3) are the opposite. They are more likely to see the social side of work as an obligation and need to be asked to do things others might volunteer to do in the name of good relationships. In an organization that places a premium on blending social life with working life, people who score low in this category will find corporate socializing tiresome and may acquire a reputation for being somewhat aloof.

E—Interests. Your "E" scores denote how much you refer explicitly to interests, needs, and incentives as a mode for getting things done. Some organizations with highly decentralized structures depend on daily horse trading within and between business units to advance their goals; others rely on processes that require relatively little bargaining. But virtually everyone who works will, at one time or another, need to negotiate to resolve some resource allocation problem or conflict involving salary, head count, work assignments, hours, or technology. If your Column 2 score for this mode is low, these bargaining moments may be sources of anxiety. As we noted in the introduction, nearly 50 percent of executives who come to Wharton workshops to sharpen their negotiation skills are struggling with inside-the-organization issues.

F—Politics. Organizations are, by their nature, political. There is only so much power to go around, so an inevitable amount of winning and losing comes with political battles. Your "F" scores indicate the amount of politics you see in your organization (Column 1) and your comfort level with maneuvering within your group to manage this aspect of organizational life (Column 2).

An inclination toward this form of influence may not be all that important in an organizational culture free of power games and turf wars, but research shows that this is more the exception than the rule. In an average corporate culture where politics forms at least a modest part of the background of everyday life, some willingness to use this channel may be necessary for success. And in highly politicized organizations, this is a survival skill.

People with high scores in this category tend to pay attention to the social networks that channel power and influence, know how to form coalitions within those networks, and realize the importance of gaining access to key decision makers. They also work harder to receive credit when it is due and push their priorities so they get on the right agendas. You should understand that brokering power is neither inherently good nor evil as an organizational activity. It is just one of the ways organizations operate.

## The Psychological Foundations for the Six Channels: Research Note

For those curious to know how we derived our six-channels framework, the following paragraphs provide a research path.

Different scholars have listed a variety of different influence taxonomies, all of which form the foundations for our six channels. One influential study of different persuasion moves identified sixteen distinct influence tactics: promise, threat, positive expertise, negative expertise, liking, pregiving, aversive stimulation, debt, moral appeal, positive self-feeling, negative self-feeling, positive altercasting, negative altercasting, altruism, positive esteem, and negative esteem. See G. Marwell and D. R. Schmidt, "Dimensions of Compliance-gaining Behavior: An Empirical Analysis," *Sociometry,* Vol. 30 (1967), pp. 350–364.

Perhaps the most widely cited study of influence moves started with 370 moves and, through subsequent analysis, reduced this list to eight: assertiveness, ingratiation, rationality, sanctions, exchange of benefits, upward appeal, blocking, and coalitions—a set they later classified into three groups: hard tactics, soft tactics, and rational tactics. See D. Kipnis, S. M. Schmidt, and I. Wilkinson, "Intraorganizational Influence Tactics: Explorations in Getting One's Way," *Journal of Applied Psychology,* Vol. 65 (1980), pp. 440–452; D. Kipnis and S. M. Schmidt, "The Language of Persuasion," *Psychology Today* (April 1985), pp. 40–46.

In 1982, Kipnis and Schmidt developed a profiler measuring six "upward influence" tactics called the "Profile of Organizational Influence Strategies," which surveyed rationality, ingratiation, coalition behavior, bargaining, appeals to higher authority, and assertiveness. The first five of these correlate, in a rough way, with our Rationality, Relationship, Politics, Authority, and Interest channels.

Professors Yukle and Falbe later reconceptualized Kipnis's work and added two dimensions we consider important: inspiration appeals (our "Vision" channel) and consultation (included mainly in our "Politics" channel). See G. Yulke and C. M. Falbe, "Influence Tactics and Objectives in Upward, Downward, and Lateral Influence Attempts," *Journal of Applied Psychology,* Vol. 75 (1990), pp. 132–140. We owe a substantial debt to all of these scholars and their empirical work, which provided the basis for our pragmatic list of six channels.

# Appendix B

## Persuasion Styles Assessment

### Step 1: Mark Each Statement Below as Follows:

0 = Rarely true for me
1 = Sometimes true for me
2 = Equally true and not true for me
3 = Usually true for me
4 = Always true for me

____ E. Other people often comment on how balanced I am.
____ A. I am known for saying exactly what is on my mind.
____ B. I am an enthusiastic, assertive person.
____ E. I seek compromises when opinions are sharply divided.
____ C. I have insights into others' feelings and needs that often surprise them.
____ E. I am equally assertive or restrained as the situation requires.
____ D. I let others do the talking at meetings.
____ A. I express my point of view, even if it means upsetting people.
____ C. I cultivate a wide network of contacts and relationships.
____ E. I am equally skilled at being candid and circumspect depending on the situation.
____ B. I am told I am very assertive.
____ D. I am quietly effective.
____ E. If need be, I can just as easily be blunt or diplomatic.

_____ B. I like to be out front, leading the charge.

_____ A. I devote more time to understanding ideas than to understanding people.

_____ E. I am equally likely to be assertive or reserved.

_____ D. I prefer a quiet conversation to interacting with big groups.

_____ C. I excel at understanding other people's feelings.

_____ E. I am good at both managing relationships and being forceful.

_____ B. I have an outgoing personality.

_____ A. I get right to the point without a lot of small talk.

_____ C. I can easily sense the other person's mood.

_____ D. People tell me I am reserved.

_____ E. I press my point of view but not to the point of endangering relationships.

_____ A. I concentrate on my message more than on the audience.

_____ B. I am outspoken and expressive.

_____ E. I give equal weight to what I think and what others think.

_____ C. I read other people's feelings accurately.

_____ D. When I speak, I do so forcefully but quietly.

_____ E. I can easily adapt my style to be assertive or restrained.

## Step 2: Add Up Your Scores

Now add up the total of the numbers you put next to the letter "A" statements. Then do the same thing for the letters "B" through "E." Your total scores for letters "A" through "D" should fall between 0 and 20. Your score for the letter "E" should fall between 0 and 40.

A = _____ (out of 20) This is a measure of your focus *on your own point of view*.

B = _____ (out of 20) This is your *social assertiveness* score.

C = _____ (out of 20) This is a measure of your focus *on your audience's feelings*.

D = _____ (out of 20) This is your *socially reserved* score.

E = _____ (out of 40) This is your *Advocate* score.

## Step 3: Discover Your Persuasion Styles

Add your letter scores from Step 2 using the system below to translate your scores into styles.

| STYLE | LETTER SCORES | TOTAL | RANK (top score = number 1) |
|---|---|---|---|
| DRIVER | _____ A + _____ B = | _____ | _____ |
| COMMANDER | _____ A + _____ D = | _____ | _____ |
| CHESS PLAYER | _____ C + _____ D = | _____ | _____ |
| PROMOTER | _____ B + _____ C = | _____ | _____ |
| ADVOCATE | _____ E = | _____ | _____ |

## Step 4: Note the Rank Order of Your Preferred Styles

Finally, rank your five styles in order from highest score (rank number 1) to lowest (rank number 5). The style with the highest total score is your most preferred. The style with the lowest score is your least preferred.

With your preferred styles in mind, return to chapter 2 and read the examples given there of the Driver (Andy Grove), Commander (J. P. Morgan), Promoter (Andrew Carnegie), Chess Player (John D. Rockefeller), and Advocate (Sam Walton).

## The Psychological Foundations for Persuasion Styles: Research Note

In defining these five persuasion roles, we drew on several streams of personality psychology. For those who wish to know more about the origins of our thinking, the following note explains our research path.

In making the distinction between "self-oriented" (the "A" statements) versus "other-oriented" (the "C" statements) personality-based perspectives, we drew on two related fields of research: self-monitoring and interpersonal orientation. Self-monitoring measures the degree to which people adapt their behavior to their social environment. High self-monitors are very adaptive and tend to "perform" to meet others' expectations. They walk into a room of strangers and ask themselves, "Who do these people want me to be?" Low self-monitors, by contrast, are less socially adaptive and more inwardly tuned. When they walk into a room of strangers, they ask "How can I communicate to these people who I am?" See Oliver P. John, Jonathan M. Cheek, and Eva C. Klohnen, "On the Nature of Self-Monitoring: Construct Explication with Q-Sort Ratings," *Journal of Personality and Social Psychology,* Vol. 71 (1996), pp. 763–776; Mark Snyder, *Public Appearances, Private Realities: The Psychology of Self-Monitoring* (New York: Freeman, 1987).

Interpersonal orientation (IO) comes from the field of negotiation studies. People with high IO tendencies—like high self-monitors—are "interested in, and reactive to, variations in the other's behavior." People with low IO scores are not so tuned to their social environment. See Walter C. Swap and Jeffrey Z. Rubin, "Measurement of Interpersonal Orientation," *Journal of Personality and Social Psychology,* Vol. 44 (1983), pp. 208–219. People with C scores closer to twenty (and A scores closer to zero) would tend to be, respectively, high self-monitors with high interpersonal orientation. By contrast, people with higher "A" scores (and "C" scores closer to zero) would tend to be low self-monitors with a lower interpersonal orientation.

For the "volume" dimension of the Persuasion Styles Assessment, we relied on two of the so-called Big 5 personality traits—extraversion and agreeableness (the other three traits in the Big 5 inventory are emotional stability, conscientiousness, and openness to new experience). For more on these five factors of personality and where they come from, see any standard textbook on personality psychology. For example, Sarah Hampson, *Advances in Personality Psychology* (Philadelphia: Psychology Press, 2000).

Extraversion measures a person's degree of social expressiveness, gregariousness, and assertiveness. Extraversion has been found to be associated with success in both sales and transformational leadership. See Timothy A. Judge and Joyce E. Bono, "Five-Factor Model of Personality and Transformational Leadership," *Journal of Applied Psychology,* Vol. 85 (2000), pp. 751–765. Promoters tend to be more highly extraverted and would have higher "B" scores and lower "D" scores. Commanders and Chess Players with "quieter" volumes tend to be less extraverted with higher "D" scores and lower "B" scores. Advocates are somewhere between these two.

We use the "agreeableness" dimension of the Big 5, along with the assertiveness dimension of extraversion, to help define the Driver. Agreeableness measures people's tendencies to be "easy to get along with," that is, to support others' opinions, accommodate, and cooperate. Drivers score low on agreeableness and high on assertiveness. Promoters would tend to score higher on both agreeableness and extraversion. Again, Advocates would fall between the extremes. See Dave Bartram, "The Great Eight Competencies: A Criterion-centric Approach to Validation," *Journal of Applied Psychology,* Vol. 90 (2005), pp. 1185–1203.

Readers interested in getting more nuanced information about their persuasion styles are encouraged to seek out the detailed psychological measurement devices associated with self-monitoring, interpersonal orientation, extraversion, and agreeableness. The latter two constructs, as noted above, form part of any Big 5 personality inventory.

# Appendix C

## The Woo Worksheet

## Step 1. Survey Your Situation

---

### The Idea

- What problem does my idea solve?

- What are the causes of this problem?

- What makes my idea better than the alternatives?

---

### Your Stepping-stones

- Who is the ultimate decision maker?

- Where does the person I am approaching fit into my stepping-stone strategy?

- What are my specific goals for this encounter (gain input, access, positive attitude, authorization, endorsement, decision, resources, implementation)?

- What medium (face-to-face, phone, e-mail, etcetera) should I use?

## Step 2: Confront the Five Barriers

- What characterizes my *relationship* to the person I am trying to influence? Can I improve that relationship?

- What is the basis for my *credibility* with this person? Can I emphasize this?

- *Communication*: What channels should I use (authority, rationality, vision, relationships, interests, politics)? Do I need to adjust my style?

- What *beliefs and values* does this person hold that could block or support my case?

- What are the other party's *interests* and how can I address them?

## Step 3: Make Your Pitch

Using information from Steps 1 and 2, frame the idea for maximum appeal.

- What is the five-minute PCAN pitch based on the problem *as my audience sees it*?

- What evidence will best resonate with the other person?

- How can I personalize the pitch and make it memorable?

- Link the pitch to key organizational goals and values.

- Address any potentially conflicting interests.

## Step 4: Secure Your Commitments

- What public actions can I request to obtain an individual commitment?

- What political objections may arise related to turf, resources, credit, or careers?

- How can I create momentum to generate a snowball effect?

- What alliances and coalitions should I develop to secure implementation?

# Acknowledgments

This book was several years in the making and benefited from the efforts of many people, all of whom deserve our earnest thanks. First comes Richard's spouse, Robbie Shell, editorial director of the Knowledge@Wharton Web site, who provided tireless and reliable editing at every stage of the project. We are grateful for her steady hand, patience, and practical, down-to-earth instincts when it comes to business writing. Second, thanks go to our literary agent, Michael Snell. Mike guided us from book idea to published product—brainstorming with us over the proposal, the book's title (the words "the art of woo" were spoken by him first), the contract, chapter titles, and other matters large and small. Mike is more than an agent; he is a true friend and partner.

At the crucial first-draft stage, several people took valuable time off to read the manuscript and give us comments. These included our Wharton School colleague Professor Maurice Schweitzer; Silicon Valley lawyer and Stanford Law School negotiation instructor Ralph Pais; Mario's friend Claire Batten; his father, Meyer Moussa; and Richard's mentor and friend Dr. Simon Auster.

As the project evolved, we benefited from the fact checking and probing comments of a number of people. Chia Tsay was a dedicated research assistant for Richard. Professor Angela Duckworth of Penn's Psychology Department and the Positive Psychology Center provided timely guidance on the persuasion-style profilers, as did Richard's Wharton colleague Bill Laufer. And several CFAR analysts, including Tim Riley and Matt O'Dowd, exhibited unflagging energy as they checked our stories and helped with digging up new examples.

Mario is expecially indebted to the members of the management committee at CFAR—Lynn Oppenheim, Mal O'Connor, Nancy Drozdow, Katey Watts, and Brian De Villa—for their guidance and support. And a particular thank-you goes to Tom Gilmore for being an unwavering friend and mentor.

To our families go our most heartfelt thanks. In the Moussa home, it was spouse Robin, son Miles, daughter Ella, and son Bix who cheered Mario through the days, nights, and weekends that were sacrificed to *Woo* drafting. Over at the Shells, sons Ben and Ned provided timely advice while spouse Robbie disappeared into the study to edit early drafts and emerge with encouraging words. *The Art of Woo* was a team effort in every way by both households—a true model of Trust-Level relationships at work. We could not have written this book without their support.

# Notes

Page

1 **a talent for "Winning Others Over":** Marcus Buckingham and Donald O. Clifton, *Now, Discover Your Strengths* (New York: Free Press, 2001), p. 116.

1 **in their latest James Bond film:** Kate Kelly, "With Bond Franchise, Broccoli Family Says Nobody Does It Better," *Wall Street Journal*, November 18, 2006, at A1. *See also* Harry Wallop, "Licensed to Sell," *The Daily Telegraph (London)*, Nov. 18, 2006, at p. 32 ("Barbara Broccoli, Cubby's daughter, takes a keen interest in all the 'sponsors' of the film, writing personal letters to Sir Richard Branson, for instance, to woo Virgin Atlantic, and helping to choose the Turnbull & Asser pajamas for M to wear.").

1 **to "woo" corporate recruiters to its campus:** The examples in the text came from a general search of the word *woo* in the Lexis/Nexis "Allnews" database conducted on November 21, 2006.

2 **"hoping she would marry him":** *The Oxford Modern English Dictionary, Second Edition* (New York: Oxford University Press, 1996), p. 1197 (first definition of "woo" is "court: seek the hand of or love of (a woman).")

2 **goddess of romantic love:** Find out more about the Roman goddess Suade and her Greek counterpart Peitho at http://www.loggia.com/myth/myth. html.

2 **"seeking favour and support":** *The Oxford Modern English Dictionary, Second Edition* (New York: Oxford University Press, 1996), p. 1197 (third definition of "woo" is "seek the favour or support of").

3 **"then to be understood":** This is the "fifth habit." Stephen R. Covey, *The 7 Habits of Highly Effective People* (New York: Free Press, 1989), pp. 235–260.

3 **"you can strike up a conversation":** Marcus Buckingham and Donald O. Clifton, *Now, Discover Your Strengths* (New York: Free Press, 2001), p. 116. Our idea of Woo extends to the entire process of relationship-based persuasion, whereas Buckingham and Clifton describe this talent

almost entirely in terms of establishing rapport. For example, Buckingham and Clifton quote someone called "Deborah C." as describing her talent for Woo this way: "I have made best friends out of people that I have met passing in the doorway. I mean it's awful, but wooing is part of who I am. All my taxi drivers propose to me." *Id.* at 116.

4   **at the Wharton School of Business:** *Bargaining for Advantage: Negotiation Strategies for Reasonable People, Second Edition* (New York: Penguin, 2006).

8   **Sun Tzu's *The Art of War:*** Sun Tzu, *The Art of War* (Ralph D. Sawyer, translator) (Boulder, CO: Westview Press, 1994).

## Chapter 1: Selling Ideas: How Woo Works

9   **"ideas won't get you anywhere":** We cannot vouch for this quote, but it is widely attributed to Lee Iacocca. See http://www.brainyquote.com/quotes/authors/l/lee_iacocca.html.

9   **"how to get people excited":** quoted in David A. Vise and Mark Malseed, *The Google Story* (New York: Delacorte Press, 2005), p. 18.

9   **how he thought about his job:** quoted in Jerry Vass, *Soft Selling in a Hard World, Second Edition* (Philadelphia: Running Press, 1998), p. 4.

10   **skill shrouded in mystery:** Ronald Alsop, "Off Course: If Sales Are So Important, Why Isn't It Taught?" *Wall Street Journal,* April 11, 2006, p. B8 (stating that "A company's sales force is its life's blood. But you wouldn't know it by looking at the typical M.B.A. curriculum.")

10   **what selling an idea looks like:** quoted in Sam Walton (with John Huey), *Made in America: My Story* (New York: Doubleday, 1992), p. 44. As Bogle tells the story, the two men were on a flight together, with Sam Walton at the controls. Walton handed Bogle some cards with various possible store names written on them and asked which one Bogle liked best. Bogle then wrote out WALMART on the bottom of one of the cards and made his pitch for it.

14   **close deals "in ninety seconds":** Jerry Vass, *Soft Selling in a Hard World* (Philadelphia: Running Press, 1998), p. 120 (describing the "90-Second Close"). Other examples of this genre include *The Science of Influence: How to Get Anyone to Say Yes in 8 Minutes or Less* (Hoboken, NJ: Wiley, 2005), p. 15 (describing the importance of the "first four seconds in a sales call") and Kevin Hogan and James Speakman, *Covert Persuasion: Psychological Tactics and Tricks to Win the Game* (Hoboken, NJ: Wiley, 2006).

15   **congressional committee in the early 1900s:** Ron Chernow, *The House of Morgan* (New York: Simon & Schuster, 1990), p. 154.

15   **once made this sort of mistake:** Laura Holson, "Fumbling the Plot: Can Katzenberg Redeem Dreamworks?" *New York Times* (July 25, 2005), p. C1.

16   **never get soldiers to man it:** This story is recounted in Robert T. Oliver, *The Psychology of Persuasive Speech* (New York: David McKay Company, 1957) p. 38.

17   **not in the way you would expect:** Ap Dijksterhuis, "Think Different: The Merits of Unconscious Thought in Preference Development and Decision

Making," *Journal of Personality and Social Psychology,* Vol. 87, No. 5 (2004), pp. 586–598; Eugene Sadler-Smith and Erella Shefy, "The Intuitive Executive: Understanding and Applying 'Gut Feel' in Decision Making," *Academy of Management Executive,* Vol. 18, No. 4 (2004), pp. 76–91; Benedict Carey, "The Unconscious Mind: A Great Decision Maker," *New York Times,* February 21, 2006, p. D1.

18 **"then trust your gut":** Richard Tedlow, *Andy Grove: The Life of an American* (New York: Portfolio, 2006), p. 123.

18 **"final act of business judgment is . . . intuitive":** Alfred P. Sloan Jr., *My Years with General Motors* (New York: Doubleday, 1963), p. xxi.

18 **"can get only through careful reasoning":** Akio Morita, *Made in Japan* (New York: E. P. Dutton, 1986), p. 196.

18 **research on how this process works:** Malcolm Gladwell, *Blink: The Power of Thinking Without Thinking* (Boston: Little, Brown & Co., 2005).

18 **"for everything one has a mind to do":** Benjamin Franklin, *The Autobiography,* reprinted in *A Benjamin Franklin Reader* (New York: Simon & Schuster, 2003) (Walter Isaacson, editor), p. 431; Robert T. Oliver, *The Psychology of Persuasive Speech, Second Edition* (New York: David McKay Company, 1957), pp. 274–293 (stating that rationalization is "a process of justifying ourselves, our groups and our beliefs" that is a "widespread habit" used "as a defense for our egos").

18 **"a good reason and the real reason":** Ron Chernow, *The House of Morgan* (New York: Simon & Schuster, 1990), p. 114.

19 **changing his company's business strategy:** Kevin J. Delaney, "As Yahoo Falters, Executive's Memo Calls for Overhaul," *Wall Street Journal,* November 18, 2006, p. A1.

21 **into three operating units:** Kevin J. Delaney, "At Yahoo, Rising Finance Chief Faces Host of Challenges," *Wall Street Journal,* December 7, 2006, p. B4; Miguel Helft, "Yahoo, Aiming for Agility, Shuffles Executives," *New York Times,* December 6, 2006, p. C1.

22 **"an organization its formal structure":** Herbert A. Simon, *Administrative Behavior* (New York: Free Press, 1945), p. 177.

22 **Authority gives you credibility:** Robert B. Cialdini, *Influence: The Psychology of Persuasion* (New York: William Morrow, 1984), pp. 208–236.

23 **an average of eight people:** Jeffrey Gandz, Victor V. Murray, and Martin Patchen, "The Locus and Basis of Influence in Organizational Decisions," *Organizational Behavior and Human Performance,* Vol. 11 (1974), pp. 195–221.

23 **selling ideas (and the birth of the modern corporation) this way:** Alfred P. Sloan Jr., *My Years with General Motors* (New York: Doubleday, 1963), p. 433.

24 **Sam was opposed to these high-tech solutions:** Sam Walton (with John Huey), *Made in America: My Story* (New York: Doubleday, 1992), p. 91.

24 **New Coke in 1985:** Constance L. Hays, *The Real Thing: Truth and Power at the Coca-Cola Company* (New York: Random House, 2005), pp. 105–121.

Chapter 2: Start with You: Persuasion Styles

27  "by a good salesman": this quote comes to us by way of the following Web site: http://www.creativityatwork.com/articlesContent/quotes.htm.

27  on joining his cabinet: We take this story from Doris Kearns Goodwin, *Team of Rivals: The Political Genius of Abraham Lincoln* (New York: Simon & Schuster, 2005), pp. 279–293.

28  "pre-eminently fit to be made": Lincoln's letter, dated December 8, 1860, can be found in the *Collected Works of Abraham Lincoln*, Vol. 4 (New Brunswick, NJ: Rutgers University Press, 1953), p. 148.

28  grasped Hamlin's hand: Charles Eugene Hamlin, *The Life and Times of Hannibal Hamlin*, Vol. 2 (Whitefish, MT: Kessinger Publishing, 2006), pp. 372–373 (reprint edition).

29  "person's angle as well as your own": Henry Ford is quoted as saying this in Dale Carnegie, *How to Win Friends and Influence People* (New York: Pocket Books, 1981), p. 37.

29  the postrevolutionary period: Dean Keith Simonton, *Who Makes History and Why* (New York: Guilford Press, 1994), pp. 78–81; P. Suedfeld and A. D. Rank, "Revolutionary Leaders: Long-term Success as a Function of Changes in Conceptual Complexity," *Journal of Personality and Social Psychology*, Vol. 34 (1976), pp. 169–178. There is a rich literature on cognitive complexity—sometimes called "integrative complexity," "interpersonal cognitive complexity" or "social perspective taking." See, e.g., Claudia L. Hale and Jesse Delia, "Cognitive Complexity and Social Perspective-Taking," *Communication Monographs*, Vol. 43 (1976), pp. 195–203; Walter H. Crockett, "Cognitive Complexity and Impression Formation," in *Progress in Experimental Personality Research Vol. 2*, Brendan A. Maher, ed. (New York: Academic Press, 1965), pp. 47–90; B. R. Burleson and S. W. Samter, "Effects of Cognitive Complexity on the Perceived Importance of Communication Skills in Friends," *Communication Research*, Vol. 17, No. 2 (1990), pp. 165–182; J. Liht, P. Suedfeld, and A. Krawczyk, "Integrative Complexity in Face-to-Face Negotiations Between the Chiapas Guerrillas and the Mexican Government," *Political Psychology*, Vol. 26, No. 4 (2005), pp. 543–552.

30  for the North, Ulysses S. Grant: P. Suedfeld, R. S. Corteen, and C. McCormick, "The Role of Integrative Complexity in Military Leadership: Robert E. Lee and his Opponents," *Journal of Applied Psychology*, Vol. 16 (1986), pp. 498–507.

30  respect from her superiors: Rebecca Santana, "OK, So She's West Point's First Woman General. So?", *Philadelphia Inquirer*, August 18, 2006, p. A8.

30  building the Blockbuster franchise system: Gail DeGeorge, *The Making of Blockbuster* (Hoboken, NJ: Wiley, 1996), pp. 136–137.

31  With self-awareness: Research confirms that self-awareness and the resulting ability to gain perspective on one's social environment is a key success factor for professionals. See Robert E. Kelley and Janet Caplan, "How Bell

Labs Creates Star Performers," *Harvard Business Review,* Vol. 71, No. 4 (July 1993), pp. 128–139 (finding that the ability to see one's self in the overall context of the organization, taking different points of view, was one of nine key factors that characterized star performers). Other success skills related to Woo revealed in this study include ability to network, to market one's ideas effectively, and to deal with organizational politics.

32 **discrete number of persuasion moves:** For deeper background on the six channels and where they come from, see the research note at the end of Appendix A.

33 **authority-based persuasion:** Authority is, of course, an enormous subject in its own right. Expanding on what we say in the text, note that there are at least three different foundations for authority—formal position (e.g., VP of Marketing), functional role (e.g., "the person putting the report together"), and various authoritative rules or standards (e.g., Title VII of the Civil Rights Act of 1964, which protects employees from race-based discrimination). See S. B. Bacharach and E. J. Lawler, *Power and Politics in Organizations* (San Francisco: Jossey-Bass, 1981), pp. 27–44.

34 **Nazi regime under Hitler:** For more on the famous Milgram experiments, see Stanley Milgram, "Behavioral Study of Obedience," *Journal of Abnormal and Social Psychology,* Vol. 67 (1963), pp. 371–378; Thomas Blass, "Understanding Behavior in the Milgram Obedience Experiment: The Role of Personality, Situations, and Their Interactions," *Journal of Personality and Social Psychology,* Vol. 60, No. 3 (1991), pp. 398–413.

36 **(95 percent) of the surveyed organizations:** Jan Wickenberg and Sven Kylen, "How Frequent Is Organizational Political Behavior? A Study of Managers' Opinions at 491 Workplaces" (2004). This is a working paper available at the Web site where these two scholars work. See Fennix at Chalmers University of Technology, http://www.fenix.chalmers.se (2004).

36 **to advance your ideas:** Research suggests that anyone who seeks to manage others' impressions as part of their organizational influence technique benefits from having political skills. See K. Harris, K. M. Kacmar, S. Zivnuska, and J. D. Shaw, "The Impact of Political Skill on Impression Management Effectiveness," *Journal of Applied Psychology,* Vol. 92 (2007), pp. 278–285 (supervisors rated employees who used impression management tools such as self-promotion and ingratiation more highly when these employees also had high levels of political skills, but opposite results were found—that is, nonpolitical people were more highly evaluated—when impression management usage at the workplace was low).

37 **of the twentieth century: THINK:** Richard S. Tedlow, *The Watson Dynasty* (New York: HarperCollins, 2003), pp. 105–106.

39 **"people we know and like":** Robert B. Cialdini, *Influence: The Psychology of Persuasion* (New York: William Morrow, 1993), p. 27.

41 **"other-oriented" persuasion:** For more on the distinctions between other-oriented and self-oriented perspectives in persuasion, please consult the research note at the end of Appendix B.

42 **"volume" they give to their message:** For more on the distinction between loud and quiet persuasion styles, please consult the research note at the end of Appendix B.

45 **"quantifiable set of relationships":** Tim Jackson, *Inside Intel: Andy Grove and the Rise of the World's Most Powerful Chip Company* (New York: Plume, 1998), p. 77.

45 **the "Driver" style in action:** Tim Jackson, *Inside Intel: Andy Grove and the Rise of the World's Most Powerful Chip Company* (New York: Plume, 1998), p. 240. Other candidates for the Driver category would be Donald Trump and Bill Gates. Trump once described himself as follows: "I can be a screamer when I want to be." Donald Trump, *The Art of the Deal* (New York: Random House, 1987), p. 161. And Gates was once described by one of his Harvard professors as follows: "He's an obnoxious human being. . . . He'd put people down when it was not necessary, and just generally not be a pleasant fellow to have around the place." Stephen Manes and Paul Andrews, *Gates* (New York: Doubleday, 1993), p. 58 (quoting Professor Thomas Cheatham). Needless to say, Trump and Gates both played the Driver role quite effectively in their business lives.

46 **"constructive confrontation":** Tim Jackson, *Inside Intel: Andy Grove and the Rise of the World's Most Powerful Chip Company* (New York: Plume, 1998), p. 110.

46 **his secretary, Sue McFarland:** Tim Jackson, *Inside Intel: Andy Grove and the Rise of the World's Most Powerful Chip Company* (New York: Plume, 1998), pp. 67–68.

46 **financial tycoon, J. P. Morgan:** This story comes from Ron Chernow, *The House of Morgan* (New York: Simon & Schuster, 1990), p. 75.

48 **"public at large":** David Nasaw, *Andrew Carnegie* (New York: The Penguin Press, 2006), p. 148. Nasaw comments elsewhere that Carnegie "was the classic Yankee promoter, the boomer, the salesman, the purveyor of success tales, writ large, but he was also a self-trained professional who knew how to construct prospectuses for bankers, who had heard it all before." *Id.* at 129.

48 **"engaged in at the moment":** David Nasaw, *Andrew Carnegie* (New York: The Penguin Press, 2006), p. 148.

48 **idea: wage reductions:** This story can be found in David Nasaw, *Andrew Carnegie* (New York: The Penguin Press, 2006), pp. 247–252.

50 **John D. Rockefeller, illustrates the difference:** The complete story of Rockefeller's maneuver to separate himself from the Clark brothers is located in Ron Chernow, *Titan: The Life of John D. Rockefeller, Sr.* (New York: Random House, 1998), pp. 82–88. On Rockefeller's character as a young man, see Grace Goulder, *John D. Rockefeller: The Cleveland Years* (Cleveland, OH: Western Reserve Historical Society, 1972), p. 115.

53 **"greeters" to meet customers as they enter the store:** This story appears in Sam Walton (with John Huey), *Sam Walton: Made in America* (New York: Doubleday, 1992), pp. 229–230 (quoting Tom Coughlin).

55 **"the limits of human endurance":** David Nasaw, *Andrew Carnegie* (New York: The Penguin Press, 2006), p. 68.

56 **"a second-rate version of somebody else"**: We found this quote at the following Web site: http://thinkexist.com/quotation.

56 **queen's closest advisers:** Sir Francis Bacon's journal entry comes from *The Letters and the Life of Francis Bacon,* in Francis Bacon, *Works,* collected and edited by James Spedding, Robert Leslie Ellis, and Douglas Denon Heath (London: Longman, 1857–74).

56 **"the situations they face":** Rob Goffee and Gareth Jones, "Managing Authenticity," *Harvard Business Review,* Vol. 83, No. 12 (December 2005), pp. 86–94.

### Chapter 3: Connect Your Ideas to People: Stepping-stones

59 **"is halfway reached":** Most Web sources attribute this quote to Lincoln, but some attribute it to motivational speaker Zig Ziglar. We prefer to think it was Lincoln. See http://www.bellaonline.com/articles/art20200.asp.

59 **"is a dangerous mistake":** The Web agrees that this quote is Peter Drucker's. See http://www.brainyquote.com/quotes/authors/p/peter_drucker.html.

59 **"Netflix" and sold it to investors:** Reed Hastings (as told to Amy Zipkin), "Out of Africa, Onto the Web," *New York Times,* December 17, 2006, Sunday Business, p. 11.

61 **as a leader in that new market:** Miguel Helft, "The Shifting Business of Renting Movies, by the Disc or the Click," *New York Times,* January 16, 2007, p. C1.

62 **"one good, nine bad":** John Keegan, *Winston Churchill* (New York: Lipper/Viking, 2002), p. 138.

62 *A Technique for Producing Ideas*: The text summarizes and slightly recasts the steps given in James Webb Young, *A Technique for Producing Ideas* (Chicago: NTC Contemporary Publishing, 1975) (reprint edition). The biographical details of Webb's life come from http://www.ciadvertising.org.

65 **"taking a trip to the future":** Thomas Gilmore and Gregory Shea, "Organizational Learning and the Leadership Skill of Time Travel," *Journal of Management Development,* Vol. 16 (1997), pp. 302–311

66 **during a single conversation:** Alfred P. Sloan Jr., *My Years with General Motors* (New York: Doubleday, 1963), p. 25.

67 **"the warder in one's section":** Nelson Mandela, *Long Walk to Freedom* (Boston: Little, Brown and Company, 1994), p. 365.

69 **informal social networks:** The sociology and psychology of social networks is a huge field of study. See, e.g., Joyce E. Bono and Marc H. Anderson, "The Advice and Influence Networks of Transformational Leaders," *Journal of Applied Psychology,* Vol. 90 (2005), p. 1306–1314; Charles Dhanaraj and Arvind Parkhe, "Orchestrating Innovation Networks," *Academy of Management Review,* Vol. 31 (2006), pp. 659–669; Jill E. Perry-Smith, "Social Yet Creative: The Role of Relationships in Facilitating Individual Creativity," *Academy of Management Journal,* Vol. 49 (2006), pp. 85–101. See the "Social Networks" heading in the bibliography at the end of this book.

70   **Robben Island is again instructive:** Anthony Sampson, *Mandela* (New York: Random House, 1999), p. 226.

70   **"finger out of your arse":** Anthony Sampson, *Mandela* (New York: Random House, 1999), p. 222.

72   **below the surface (see Figure 3.1):** We have adapted Figure 3.1 in the text from a related pair of figures contained in Rob Cross and Andrew Parker, *The Hidden Power of Social Networks: Understanding How Work Really Gets Done in Organizations* (Boston: Harvard Business School Press, 2004), p. 5. Cross's figures originally appeared in an article he cowrote, "Knowing What We Know: Supporting Knowledge Creation and Sharing in Social Networks," *Organizational Dynamics,* Vol. 30, No. 2 (2001), pp. 100–120.

74   *peripheral players*, **and** *subgroups:* We take the terms boundary spanners, connectors, peripheral players, and subgroups from Rob Cross and Andrew Parker, *The Hidden Power of Social Networks: Understanding How Work Really Gets Done in Organizations* (Boston: Harvard Business School Press, 2004), pp. 14, 74–76.

75   **"where he itches":** quoted in Michael and Deborah Singer Dobson, *Enlightened Office Politics* (New York: AMACOM, 2001), p. 47.

75   **power in these areas:** Miguel Helft, "It Pays to Have Pals in Silicon Valley," *New York Times,* October 17, 2006, p. C1; Joseph A. Slobodzian, "Real Leaders," *Philadelphia Inquirer,* October 15, 2006, p. E1.

75   **"Who is the Elvis here?":** Joshua William Busby, "Bono Made Jesse Helms Cry: Jubilee 2000, Debt Relief, and Moral Action in International Politics," Working Paper, Princeton University Woodrow Wilson School. See http://www.princeton.edu/~piirs/calendars/Busby%20paper.pdf.

76   **search engines—Google:** David A. Vise, *The Google Story* (New York: Delacorte Press, 2005), p. 37.

76   **use those ties to help you navigate inside them:** Deborah Tannen, *Talking from 9 to 5* (New York: Avon Books, 1994), pp. 204–241.

76   **politics in the 1930s:** This story comes from a speech that Frances Perkins gave at the Social Security Administration on October 23, 1962. It can be found at http://www.ssa.gov/history/perkins5.html.

79   **do-my-best goals:** See G. Richard Shell, *Bargaining for Advantage: Negotiation Strategies for Reasonable People, Second Edition* (New York: Penguin, 2006), pp. 26–39 (treating the literature on setting goals).

79   **idea, issue, or action:** Phil Erwin, *Attitudes and Persuasion* (Hove, UK: Psychology Press, 2001).

80   **early in an idea-selling process:** Penny Coleman, *A Woman Unafraid: The Achievements of Francis Perkins* (New York: Atheneum, 1993), pp. 59–60.

82   **"What convinces is conviction":** Quoted in G. Richard Shell, *Bargaining for Advantage: Negotiation Strategies for Reasonable People, Second Edition* (New York: Penguin, 2006), p. 30.

82   **"importance of his cause":** Quoted in Michiko Kakutani, "The Poet Laureate in the White House," *New York Times,* December 19, 2006, p. D8; Douglas L. Wilson, *Lincoln's Sword: The Presidency and the Power of Words* (New York: Knopf, 2006).

Chapter 4: Build Relationships and Credibility: Trust

85 **"I have relationships":** Quoted in the *Economist* (May 24, 2003), p. 84.

85 **"preach to the pelicans":** Gerry Spence, *How to Argue and Win Every Time* (New York: St. Martin's Griffin, 1995), p. 47.

85 **flight across the Atlantic:** We take most of the story about Charles Lindbergh's famous flight and the planning that preceded it from Lindbergh's own account. See Charles Lindbergh, *The Spirit of St. Louis* (New York: Scribner, 1953), pp. 3–180. We supplemented the story with materials about Charles Levine. See Herb Geduld, "Charlie Levine and his Flying Machine," *Jewish World Review* (June 29, 1998), p. 5.

88 *bestow,* **like friendship:** Richard M. Perloff, *The Dynamics of Persuasion* (Mahwah, NJ: Lawrence Erlbaum Associates, 2003), p. 159; Daniel J. O'Keefe, *Persuasion Theory and Research, Second Edition* (Thousand Oaks, CA: Sage, 2002), p. 181.

90 **skill plays a crucial role in selling ideas:** There are many books on networking and relationships. Harvey Mackay, *Dig Your Well Before You're Thirsty* (New York: Currency Doubleday, 1990).

91 **"with all men as Mr. Lincoln":** Andrew Carnegie, *Autobiography* (Boston: Houghton Mifflin Company, 1920), p. 101.

91 **on the street:** H. W. Brands, *Masters of Enterprise* (Hoboken, NJ: Wiley, 1999), pp. 52–53.

91 **"able to pay them":** Andrew Carnegie, *Autobiography* (Boston: Houghton Mifflin Company, 1920), p. 92.

91 **"customers' kids":** Harvey Mackay, *Dig Your Well Before You're Thirsty* (New York: Currency Doubleday, 1990), p. 27.

92 **feeling positive emotions:** R. F. Bornstein, "Exposure and Affect," *Psychological Bulletin,* Vol. 106 (1989), pp. 265–289; R. F. Bornstein, D. R. Leone, and D. J. Lacey, "The Generalizability of Subliminal Mere Exposure Effects," *Journal of Personality and Social Psychology,* Vol. 53 (1987), pp. 1070–1079.

92 **lifestyle choices:** Arch G. Woodside and J. William Davenport, "The Effect of Salesman Similarity and Expertise on Consumer Purchasing Behavior," *Journal of Marketing Research,* Vol. 11 (May 1974), pp. 198–202.

92 **using a similarity-based gambit:** Connie Bruck, *Master of the Game* (New York: Penguin, 1994), pp. 56–57.

93 **drive through his application:** Donald Trump, *The Art of the Deal* (New York: Random House, 1987), p. 136.

94 **"on an ongoing basis":** Harvey Mackay, *Dig Your Well Before You're Thirsty* (New York: Currency Doubleday, 1990), p. 65.

94 **close friends and family:** Mark S. Granovetter, "The Strength of Weak Ties," *American Journal of Sociology,* Vol. 78 (May 1973), pp. 1360–1380.

94 **important assets a person has:** Eric W. K. Tsang, "Can *Guanxi* Be a Source of Sustained Competitive Advantage for Doing Business in China?" *Academy of Management Executive,* Vol. 12, No. 2 (1998), pp. 64–93.

94 **these favours at opportune times:** Michel Ferrary, "The Gift Exchange in Social Networks of Silicon Valley," *California Management Review*, Vol. 45, No. 4 (2003), pp. 120–138.

95 **who lack these contacts:** Brian Uzzi, "Embeddedness in the Making of Financial Capital: How Social Relations and Networks Benefit Firms Seeking Financing," *American Sociological Review*, Vol. 64 (1999), pp. 481–505.

95 **high-tech economy:** Michel Ferrary, "The Gift Exchange in Social Networks of Silicon Valley," *California Management Review*, Vol. 45, No. 4 (2003), pp. 120–138.

95 **"wait to pick them off":** Hae Hu, "Alternative Bargaining Styles in a Competitive Environment: The Fixed-Income Securities Market." This student paper is on file with G. Richard Shell, the Wharton School.

96 **Reciprocity-Level, and Trust-Level:** Our discussion of the three levels of working relationships was inspired by Daniel Z. Levin, Ellen M. Whitener, and Rob Cross, "Perceived Trustworthiness of Knowledge Sources: The Moderating Impact of Relationship Length," *Journal of Applied Psychology*, Vol. 91, No. 5 (2006), pp. 1163–1171.

97 **choices for building relationships:** A great deal has been written on the perils and promise of various forms of interactions as platforms for persuasion. See, e.g., Ronald B. Adler and Jeanne Marquardt Elmhorst, *Communicating at Work, Eighth Edition* (Boston: McGraw-Hill, 2005), pp. 24–34 (e-mail); ibid. at 282–308 (meetings); Yuri Miyamoto and Norbert Schwarz, "When Conveying a Message That May Hurt a Relationship: Cultural Differences in the Difficulty of Using an Answering Machine," *Journal of Experimental Social Psychology*, Vol. 42 (2006), pp. 540–547 (voice mail); Richard Storey, *The Art of Persuasive Communication* (Stowe, VT: Gower, 1997), pp. 197–204 (telephone); Kim Barnes, *Exercising Influence* (Berkeley, CA: Barnes & Conti, 2000), pp. 121–127 (e-mail); G. Richard Shell, "Electronic Bargaining: The Perils of E-mail and the Promise of Computer-assisted Negotiations," in Stephen J. Hoch and Howard C. Kunreuther, *Wharton on Making Decisions* (Hoboken, NJ: Wiley, 2001), pp. 201–221 (e-mail).

98 **set his sights on Parsons:** Our sources for the story in the text include Ken Auletta, "The Raid," *The New Yorker* (March 20, 2006), p. 132–143; Richard Siklos, "Solving Time Warner," *New York Times* (August 13, 2005), p. D1; Richard Siklos and Andrew Ross Sorkin, "Time Warner and Icahn Reach a Settlement," *New York Times*, February 18, 2006, p. A1.

99 **Pierre Lemieux:** Jared Sandberg, "Yes, Sell My Stocks," *Wall Street Journal* (September 12, 2006), p. B1.

100 **competence, expertise, and trustworthiness:** Elizabeth J. Wilson and Daniel L. Sherrell, "Source Effects in Communication and Persuasion Research: A Meta-Analysis of Effect Size," *Journal of the Academy of Marketing Science*, Vol. 21, No. 2 (1993), pp. 101–112; Herbert Simons, *Persuasion in Society* (Thousand Oaks, CA: Sage, 2001), pp. 333196–198; Ronald B. Adler and Jeanne Marquardt Elmhorst, *Communicating at Work, Eighth Edition* (Boston: McGraw Hill, 2005), pp. 333–334; Jay Conger, *Winning 'em Over* (New York: Simon & Schuster, 1998), pp. 57–73.

100 **Prime Minister Winston Churchill:** Roy Jenkins, *Churchill: A Biography* (New York: Plume, 2002), pp. 790–795.

101 **"would leave it up to me":** Akio Morita, *Made in Japan* (New York: E. P. Dutton, 1986), p. 93.

101 **just one phone call:** Tim Jackson, *Inside Intel* (New York: Plume, 1997), pp. 22–23.

102 **Glasgow factory:** William Grimes, "A Wealth of Notions: Adam Smith's True Legacy," *New York Times* (September 15, 2005), p. E31.

102 **engaging with the staff:** Jim Carlton, *Apple* (New York: HarperBusiness, 1997), pp. 32–33.

103 **"that changes everything":** Stephen M. R. Covey, *The SPEED of Trust: The One Thing That Changes Everything* (New York: Free Press, 2006).

104 **agendas, including their own:** J. Kline Harrison and M. William Clough, "Characteristics of 'State of the Art' Leaders: Productive Narcissism Versus Emotional Intelligence and Level 5 Capabilities," *The Social Science Journal,* Vol. 43 (2006), pp. 287–292.

104 **"he labours for others":** Aristotle is quoted in Peter M. Blau, *Exchange and Power in Social Life* (Hoboken, NJ: Wiley, 1964), p. 199.

104 **the Baldrige Award:** This story, told by Debbie Collard, appears in John P. Kotter, *The Heart of Change* (Boston: Harvard Business School Press, 2002), pp. 73–77. We also exchanged e-mails with Ms. Collard to clarify portions of her story.

106 **"pulled the trigger":** Gerry Spence, *How to Argue and Win Every Time* (New York: St. Martin's Griffin, 1995), p. 44.

106 **without feeling disenfranchised:** The subject of how to use authority with credibility is well covered in the literature. See Peter M. Blau, *Exchange and Power in Social Life* (Hoboken, NJ: Wiley, 1964), pp. 199–223; Howard Gardner, *Changing Minds* (Boston: Harvard Business School Press, 2004), pp. 72–89; Keith Grint, "Problems, Problems, Problems: The Social Construction of 'Leadership,' " *Human Relations,* Vol. 58, No. 11 (2005), pp. 1467–1494; Jan-Willem van Prooijen, Keesvan den Bos, E. Allan Lind, and Henk A. M. Wilke, "How Do People React to Negative Procedures? On the Moderating Role of Authority's Biased Attitudes," *Journal of Experimental Social Psychology,* Vol. 42 (2006), pp. 632–645; Joseph Raz, "Authority and Justification," *Philosophy and Public Affairs,* Vol. 14, No. 1 (1985), pp. 3–29.

107 **"blemishes—but real":** Gerry Spence, *How to Argue and Win Every Time* (New York: St. Martin's Griffin, 1995), p. 47.

## Chapter 5: Respect Their Beliefs: A Common Language

111 **"ordering your words to fit":** Burton Watson, translator, *Han Fei Tzu: Basic Writings* (New York: Columbia University Press, 1964), p. 109.

111 **"and agree with it":** Sir Francis Bacon's quote can be found at http://www.fordham.edu/halsall/mod/bacon-aphor.html.

111 **lead singer Bono:** We take this story from several sources, the chief of which is James Taub, "The Statesman," *New York Times Magazine*

(September 18, 2005), pp. 80–86. Other sources include John Wagner, "In Helms, Bono Finds the Ally He's Looking For," *The Charlotte News and Observer* (September 21, 2000), p. A1; "Persons of the Year," *Time Magazine* (December 26, 2005), p. 33; Jesse Helms, "Bono," *Time Magazine* (April 30, 2006), p. 27.

115  **to the language of inspiration:** Robert T. Oliver, *The Psychology of Persuasive Speech* (New York: David McKay Company, 1957), p. 38.

115  **new Macintosh computer:** Todd D. Jick and Mary Gentile, "Donna Dubinsky and Apply Computer, Inc. (A)," Harvard Business School Case number 9486083 (Feb. 21, 1986).

116  **"include [the] pensions!":** Quoted in Robert T. Oliver, *The Psychology of Persuasive Speech, Second Edition* (New York: David McKay Company, 1957), p. 226.

117  **freshly-minted MBA:** This story is told in Tim Jackson, *Inside Intel* (New York: Plume, 1997), p. 201. According to Mr. Melmon's personal Web site, he left Intel out of frustration that it would not respond to his PC idea and went to work for an advertising agency—a perfect job for a visionary persuader. See http://www.nsv.com/richardmelmon.html.

117  **miscued job application:** Our sources on the Vayner story include Ben McGrath, "Aleksey the Great," *The New Yorker* (October 10, 2006), p. 4; David Enrich and Jamie Levy Pessin, "Yale Student Gets a Lesson on the Power of Video," *Wall Street Journal* (October 14, 2006), p. B3.

119  **major magazine company:** Robert A. Guth, "How Microsoft Is Learning to Love Online Advertising," *Wall Street Journal* (November 16, 2006), p. A1.

121  **"strategic inflection point":** Andrew S. Grove, *Only the Paranoid Survive* (New York: Currency Doubleday, 1999), p. 1–14.

121  **health care system:** Lee Gomes, "Portal: Andy Grove Enters New Post-Intel Role as Active capitalist," *Wall Street Journal* (November 1, 2006), p. B1.

122  **in especially persuasive ways:** For background on why appeals to purpose and meaning are persuasive, see Roy F. Baumeister and Kathleen D. Vohs, "The Pursuit of Meaningfulness in Life," in *Handbook of Positive Psychology,* C. R. Snyder and Shane J. Lopez, editors (New York: Oxford University Press, 2002), pp. 608–618 (the essence of meaning is "connection"); Charles Stangor, Gretchen B. Sechrist, and John T. Jost, "Social and Intergroup Beliefs," in *Social Influence,* Joseph P. Fortas and Kipling D. Willaims, editors (Philadelphia: Psychology Press, 2001), pp. 235–252; Jeffrey D. Ford and William A. Pasmore, "Vision: Friend or Foe During Change?" *Journal of Applied Behavioral Science,* Vol. 42 (2006), pp. 172–176.

123  **faced ruin:** Ray Kroc, *Grinding It Out* (Chicago: Contemporary Books, 1977), pp. 108–109.

124  **(LTCM):** Roger Lowenstein, *When Genius Failed* (New York: Random House, 2000), pp. 214–218.

125  **gains tremendous traction:** For an excellent resource on all the theories mentioned in the text, go to Changing Minds, http://changingminds.org/explanations/theories. In addition, see Daniel Gilbert, "I'm O.K., You're Biased," *New York Times* (April 16, 2006) (Week in Review), p. 12 ("The

human brain knows many tricks that allow it to consider evidence, weigh facts and still reach precisely the conclusion it favours").

125 **from many different cultures:** Sharon Begley, "Science Journal: When Terror Strikes, Liberals and the Right Vote Further Apart," *Wall Street Journal* (October 13, 2006), p. B1 (explaining "worldview defense" phenomenon); Mark Bowden, "The Six-Million Person Question," *Wall Street Journal* (October 4, 2006), p. A14 (discussing Holocaust denial).

125 **complete, accurate map:** David Ewing Duncan, *The Geneticist Who Played Hoops with My DNA* (New York: William Morrow, 2005), pp. 112–114.

126 **he was sure to forget:** This comment about Charles Darwin comes from John Dewey, *How We Think* (Mineola, NY: Dover Publications, 1997), p. 76.

126 **National Aeronautics and Space Administration:** W. Henry Lampbright, *Powering Apollo: James Webb of NASA* (Baltimore: Johns Hopkins University Press, 1995), pp. 47–68.

129 **entry into that market:** Paul Carroll, *Big Blues* (New York: Crown, 1993), pp. 18–25.

129 **prize-winning book:** David McCullough, *1776* (New York: Simon & Schuster, 2005), pp. 284–285.

131 **think about work:** The Best Buy example was the cover story for *Business-Week* magazine on December 11, 2006, Michelle Conlin, "Smashing the Clock," *BusinessWeek* (December 11, 2006), pp. 60–68.

## Chapter 6: Give Them Incentives to Say Yes: Interests and Needs

137 **"can ever be effective":** H. A. Overstreet, *Influencing Human Behavior* (New York: W. W. Norton, 1925), p. 33.

137 **"to promote yours":** This is another quote with an uncertain pedigree. See http://www.tribuneindia.com/2004/20040201/spectrum/book8.htm. The quote can also be found in Robert Green, *The 48 Laws of Power* (New York: Penguin, 1998), p. 100.

137 **write home from college:** Dale Carnegie tells this story in his book, *How to Win Friends and Influence People* (New York: Pocket Books, 1936), p. 32.

137 **"how to get it":** Dale Carnegie, *How to Win Friends and Influence People* (New York: Pocket Books, 1936), p. 31.

138 *I* **from their selling presentations:** Jerry Vass, *Soft Selling in a Hard World, Second Edition* (Philadelphia: Running Press, 1998), pp. 22–23.

139 **than ones that do not:** Peter R. Darke and Shelly Chaiken, "The Pursuit of Self-Interest: Self-Interest Bias in Attitude Judgment and Persuasion," *Journal of Personality and Social Psychology,* Vol. 89 (2005), pp. 864–883.

139 **less persuasive when they stand to lose:** Peter R. Darke and Shelly Chaiken, "The Pursuit of Self-Interest: Self-Interest Bias in Attitude Judgment and Persuasion," *Journal of Personality and Social Psychology,* Vol. 89 (2005), pp. 864–883.

139  **might help them with?:** Jay A. Conger, *Winning 'em Over* (New York: Simon & Schuster, 1998), pp. 74–96.

139  **into the Grand Hyatt:** This story comes from Robert Slater, *No Such Thing as Over-exposure: Inside the Life and Celebrity of Donald Trump* (Upper Saddle River, NJ: Prentice Hall, 2005), pp. 62–65.

140  **an interest they shared:** Steve Wozniak (with Gina Smith), *iWoz* (New York: W. W. Norton, 2006), pp. 171–172.

141  **low-cost trade-offs in such packages:** Jared R. Curan, Hillary Anger Elfenbein, and Heng Xu, "What Do People Value When They Negotiate? Mapping the Domain of Subjective Value in Negotiation," *Journal of Personality and Social Psychology*, Vol. 91 (2006), pp. 493–512.

142  **pet rabbits in the backyard:** This story comes from Andrew Carnegie himself. See Andrew Carnegie, *Autobiography* (New York: Doubleday, 1920), pp. 20–22.

142  **dominant motives in human life:** Dale Carnegie, *How to Win Friends and Influence People* (New York: Pocket Books, 1936), p. 18. See also Morris Rosenberg, *Conceiving the Self* (New York: Basic Books, 1979), pp. 54–57 ("the self-esteem motive is universally and characteristically . . . a dominant motive in the individual's motivational system").

142  **count on stiff resistance:** Robert Kegan and Lisa Laskow Lahey, "The Real Reason People Won't Change," *Harvard Business Review* (November 2001), pp. 85–92 (discussing the concept of "competing commitments" as a method of uncovering why people say "no" and what to do about it).

142  **he faced enormous obstacles:** W. Henry Lambright, *Powering Apollo: James E. Webb of NASA* (Baltimore: Johns Hopkins University Press, 1995), pp. 119–120.

144  ***Bargaining for Advantage:*** G. Richard Shell, *Bargaining for Advantage: Negotiation Strategies for Reasonable People, Second Edition* (New York: Penguin, 2006). The text summarizes both the Six Foundations (chapters 1–6 in *Bargaining for Advantage*) and the four stages of negotiation (chapters 7–10).

145  **Manhattan Project during World War II:** Richard Rhodes, *The Making of the Atomic Bomb* (New York: Simon & Schuster, 1986), pp. 540–546; Kai Bird and Martin J. Sherwin, *The Triumph and Tragedy of J. Robert Oppenheimer* (New York: Random House, 2005), pp. 282–283.

150  **detailed letter of resignation:** Michael Wallis, *Oil Man: The Story of Frank Phillips and the Birth of Phillips Petroleum* (New York: Doubleday, 1988), pp. 320–322.

151  **"It's obvious":** W. Henry Lambright, *Powering Apollo: James E. Webb of NASA* (Baltimore: Johns Hopkins University Press, 1995), pp. 112–113.

156  **for less skilled negotiators:** N. Rackham and J. Carlisle, "The Effective Negotiator—Part 2: Planning for Negotiations," *Journal of European Industrial Training*, Vol. 2, No. 7 (1978), pp. 2–5.

157  **their time to these behaviors:** N. Rackham and J. Carlisle, "The Effective Negotiator—Part 1: The Behavior of Successful Negotiators," *Journal of European Industrial Training*, Vol. 2, No. 6 (1978), pp. 6–11.

Chapter 7: State Your Case: The Proposal

159 **"a problem half solved":** This quote can be found at http://www.thinkex ist.com.

159 **"makes strong actions":** This quote can be found at http://www.quotations page.com.

159 **and nonpolitical:** The story of Marissa Mayer's "office hours" is told in Fara Warner, "How Google Searches Itself," *Fast Company* (June 2002), p. 50. See also Ben Elgin, "Managing Google's Idea Factory," *Business-Week* (October 3, 2005), p. 27.

161 **one of Harvard's libraries:** Ellen Langer, Arthur Blank, and Benzion Chanowitz, "The Mindlessness of Ostensibly Thoughtful Action: The Role of Placebo Information in Interpersonal Interaction," *Journal of Personality and Social Psychology,* Vol. 36, No. 6 (1978), pp. 635–642.

162 *Mindfulness* **in 1989:** Ellen Langer, *Mindfulness* (Boston: Addison Wesley, 1990).

163 **"heuristic" processing:** This terminology comes from the "Elaboration Likelihood Model" utilized in communication and persuasion research. See James B. Stiff, *Persuasive Communication* (New York: Guilford Press, 1994), pp. 175–197; Daniel J. O'Keefe, *Persuasion Theory & Research* (Thousand Oaks, CA: Sage, 2002), pp. 137–167.

163 **heart attacks:** Heather Won Tesoriero, Ilban Brat, Gary Williams and Barbara Martinez, "Merck Loss Jolts Drug Giant, Industry," *Wall Street Journal* (August 22, 2005), p. A1.

165 **"What shall we do?":** The PCAN model is a distilled version of the stock questions that rhetoric and argumentation scholars advise asking to address any kind of policy question or proposal for action. See, e.g., Jeanne Fahnstock and Marie Secor, *A Rhetoric of Argument, Third Edition* (Boston: McGraw-Hill, 2004), pp. 283–313.

165 **Apple CEO Steve Jobs:** Jon Steel, *Perfect Pitch: The Art of Selling Ideas and Winning New Business* (Hoboken, NJ: Wiley, 2007), pp. xi–xvi.

167 **briefly again at the end:** Find out more about the Primacy and Recency Effects by visiting Changing Minds at http://www.changingminds.org/ex planations/theories.

168 **entered World War II:** We took the story of General George C. Marshall's famous "three minutes" with President Roosevelt from two sources. See Leonard Mosley, *Marshall: A Hero for Our Times* (New York: Hearst Books, 1982), pp. 133–139; George C. Marshall, *The Papers of George Catlett Marshall,* Vol. 2, Larry Brand, Editor (Baltimore: Johns Hopkins University Press, 1986), pp. 208–213.

170 **"is the key to persuasion":** Quoted in Denise Bostdorf and Steven Goldzwig, "Idealism and Pragmatism in American Foreign Policy Rhetoric: The Case of John F. Kennedy and Vietnam," *Presidential Studies Quarterly,* Vol. 24 (Summer 1994), p. 515.

171 **"define first and then see":** Walter Lippmann, *Public Opinion* (New York: Free Press, 1997) (reissued edition of 1922 book), p. 81. This is also quoted in Denise Bostdorf and Steven Goldzwig, "Idealism and Pragmatism in

American Foreign Policy Rhetoric: The Case of John F. Kennedy and Viet-nam," *Presidential Studies Quarterly,* Vol. 24 (Summer 1994), p. 515.

171   **the problems of Africa:** James Taub, "The Statesman," *New York Times Magazine* (September 18, 2005), pp. 80–86.

173   **idea-selling campaign:** The story of Ferris's wheel is told in Erik Larson, *The Devil in the White City* (New York: Crown, 2003), pp. 155–160.

174   **"vast body in action":** Robert Graves, "World's Fair, June 28—Special," *The Alleghenian* (July 1, 1893), quoted at http://www.clpgh.org/exhibit/neighborhoods/northside/nor_n105b.html.

175   **"confront the brutal facts":** Jim Collins, *Good to Great* (New York: Random House, 2001), p. 13.

176   **to take him aside:** Michael Useem, *Leading Up: How to Lead Your Boss So You Both Win* (New York: Crown Business, 2003), pp. 48–49.

176   **argue your opponent's case:** See Gerry Spence, *How to Argue and Win Every Time* (New York: St. Martin's Griffin, 1995), p. 131 ("concession coming from your mouth is not nearly as hurtful as an exposure coming from your opponent's"). Research also supports the "stealing thunder" strategy. See Mike Allen, "Comparing the Persuasive Effectiveness of One- and Two-Sided Message," in Mike Allen and Raymond W. Preiss, Editors, *Persuasion: Advances Through Meta-Analysis* (Cresskill, NJ: Hampton Press, 1998), pp. 87–97; Kipling D. Williams and Lara Dolnik, "Revealing the Worst First: Stealing Thunder as a Social Influence Strategy," in *Social Influence,* Joseph P. Forgas and Kipling D. Williams, editors (Philadelphia: Psychology Press, 2001), pp. 213–231; Herbert W. Simons, *Persuasion in Society* (Thousand Oaks, CA: Sage, 2001), pp. 201–202.

179   **when making a policy argument:** For general treatments of the forms of evidence available to support policy arguments about "what to do," see Robert T. Oliver, *The Psychology of Persuasive Speech, Second Edition* (New York: David McKay Company, 1957), pp. 201–221; Herbert W. Simons, *Persuasion in Society* (Thousand Oaks, CA: Sage, 2001), pp. 167–171; Jay A. Conger, *Winning 'em Over* (New York: Simon & Schuster, 1998), pp. 97–109; Richard Perloff, *The Dynamics of Persuasion, Second Edition* (Mahwah, NJ: Lawrence Erlbaum Associates, 2003), pp. 176–185; John C. Reinard, "The Persuasive Effects of Testimonial Assertion Evidence," in Mike Allen and Raymond W. Preiss, editors, *Persuasion: Advances Through Meta-Analysis* (Cresskill, NJ: Hampton Press, 1998), pp. 69–86.

180   **system into a business:** The story of how Yahoo came to accept advertising is told in Karen Angel, *Inside Yahoo!* (Hoboken, NJ: Wiley, 2002), pp. 35–37.

180   **"achieve more easily":** Quoted in Robert T. Oliver, *The Psychology of Persuasive Speech* (New York: David McKay Company, 1957), p. 159.

180   **"is the only thing":** James B. Simpson, *Simpson's Contemporary Quotations, Revised Edition* (New York: HarperCollins, 1997), quotation number 4269. See also http://www.bartleby.com/63/69/4269.html.

181   **it was a demonstration:** Tim Jackson, *Inside Intel* (New York: Plume, 1997), p. 101.

Chapter 8: Make It Memorable: The Personal Touch

185 **"there is California":** We found this quote on http://www.thinkexist.com.

185 **"which reason knows nothing of":** Blaise Pascal, *Pensees,* Pt. 2, art. 17, no. 5 (1660). See also http://www.wisdomquotes.com/cat_reason.html.

185 **delivered in the world every day:** Jared Sandberg, "Tips for PowerPoint: Please Spare Us," *Wall Street Journal* (November, 14, 2006) at B1.

185 **during a recent corporate presentation:** This survey is cited at http://www. businessobjects.com/news/press/press2005/20051031_informersion_survey_comp.asp.

187 **investigated this question in the *New York Times Magazine:*** Stephen J. Dubner and Steven D. Levitt, "Selling Soap: How Do you Get Doctors to Wash Their Hands?" *New York Times Magazine* (September 24, 2006), pp. 22–23.

188 **how an entire industry has been built on this principle:** Robert B. Cialdini, "Systematic Opportunism: An Approach to the Study of Tactical Social Influence," in Joseph P. Forgas and Kipling D. Williams, editors, *Social Influence: Direct and Indirect Processes* (Philadelphia: Psychology Press, 2001), pp. 25–39. For more on vividness in presentations, see H. A. Overstreet, *Influencing Human Behavior* (New York: W. W. Norton, 1925), pp. 50–70.

190 **illustrates the power of a demonstration:** John P. Kotter, *The Heart of Change: Real-life Stories of How People Change Their Organizations* (Boston: Harvard Business School Press, 2002), pp. 29–30.

191 **self-developing film was technically feasible:** This story comes from Victor K. McElheny, *Insisting on the Impossible: The Life of Edwin Land* (Reading, MA: Perseus Books, 1998), pp. 341–349.

191 **more likely to actually adopt that belief:** For a discussion of the "foot in the door" technique, see Robert B. Cialdini, *Influence: Science and Practice, Fourth Edition* (Boston: Allyn and Bacon, 2001), pp. 65–68.

191 **displayed it at an employee retreat:** Kara Swisher, *aol.com* (New York: Times Business Books, 1998), pp. 106–128.

192 **commit the company to the world of Web-based:** Mike Useem tells this story in *Leading Up: How to Lead Your Boss So You Both Win* (New York: Crown, 2001), pp. 63–65.

193 ***this idea should matter to you:*** To review some of the research on this point, go to Marwan Sinaceur and Larissa S. Tiedens, "Get Mad and Get More Than Even: When and Why Anger Expression Is Effective in Negotiations," *Journal of Experimental Social Psychology,* Vol. 42 (2006) pp. 314–322; Gerben A. van Kleef and Carsten K. W. De Dreu, "The Interpersonal Effects of Emotions in Negotiations: A Motivated Information Processing Approach," *Journal of Personality and Social Psychology,* Vol. 87, No. 4 (2004), pp. 510–528.

193 **"you end up making a deal":** Donald J. Trump, *The Art of the Deal* (New York: Random House, 1987), p. 88.

193 **when he relied on emotion:** Col. Harland Sanders, *Life as I Have Known It Has Been Finger Lickin' Good* (Carol Stream, IL: Creation House, 1974), p. 117.

194 **test different forms of persuasion:** This study is cited and explained in Daniel J. O'Keefe, *Persuasion Theory & Research, Second Edition* (Thousand Oaks, CA: Sage, 2002), p. 229. The widespread use of "cases" as teaching tools by business schools also testifies to the power of examples to capture and hold attention—thus persuading. Whether these case studies convey reliable management knowledge is, of course, another matter.

194 **something scholars call *movement*:** H. A. Overstreet, *Influencing Human Behavior* (New York: W. W. Norton, 1925), p. 12.

195 **used a "mystery story" approach:** Tad Friend tells this story about a story in "Creative Differences," *The New Yorker*, August 30, 1999, p. 47.

197 **in *The World Crisis*:** Winston Churchill, *The World Crisis, Abridged and Revised Edition* (New York: Free Press, 2005) (original edition published in 1927), p. 839. You can actually hear Winston Churchill read this passage in its extended form at http://www.nationalarchives.gov.uk/pathways/firstworldwar/audio_accounts/s_churchill.htm.

198 **communicating political views:** The case was *Virginia v. Black* and was heard on December 11, 2002. As reported in *Slate* by Dahlia Lithwick, "Out of nowhere booms the great, surprising 'Luke-I-am-your-father' voice of He Who Never Speaks. Justice Clarence Thomas suddenly asks a question and everyone's head pops up and starts looking madly around, like the Muppets on *Veterinarian Hospital*. 'Aren't you understating the effects . . . of 100 years of lynching?' he booms. 'This was a reign of terror, and the cross was a sign of that. . . . It is unlike any symbol in our society. It was intended to cause fear, terrorize.' " See http://www.slate.com/id/2075301. A transcript of the entire argument can be found at http://www.supremecourtus.gov/oral_arguments/argument_transcripts/01–1107.pdf.

199 **"most effective means of persuasion he possesses":** This quotation from Aristotle's *Rhetoric*, Book 1, Chapter 2 can be found at http://www.americanrhetoric.com/aristotleonrhetoric.htm.

200 **the million-dollar ball:** The case of *Popov v. Hayashi* can be found at http://www.owlnet.rice.edu/~econ438/fall05/popovhayashi121802dec.pdf. The ball ended up selling for only £450,000.

202 **talks with Microsoft to be acquired:** Kara Swisher, *aol.com* (New York: Times Business Books, 1998), p. 82.

203 **destroy the Russian missile sites:** Richard E. Neustadt and Ernest R. May tell this story in *Thinking in Time: The Uses of History for Decision-Makers* (New York: Free Press, 1986), pp. 1–16.

203 **use to advance thinking in their disciplines:** Andrew Abbott provides a detailed description of these moves in chapter 4 of *Methods of Discovery: Heuristics for the Social Sciences* (New York: W. W. Norton, 2004).

Chapter 9: Close the Sale: Commitments and Politics

207 **"pounds of promises":** Look for this quote at http://www.brainyquote.com/quotes/authors/m/mae_west.html.

207 **"by those who are dumber":** We paraphrased this quote slightly. See http://
thinkexist.com/quotation/those_who_are_too_smart_to_engage_in_poli-
tics_are/14463.html.

207 **inventors and engineers:** We took the story of Charles Kettering and his
idea for an air-cooled automobile engine from the following sources.
Alfred P. Sloan Jr., *My Years with General Motors* (New York: Doubleday,
1963), pp. 71–94; Stuart W. Leslie, "Charles F. Kettering and the Copper-
cooled Engine," *Technology and Culture,* Vol. 20, No. 4 (1979), pp. 752–
795; entry for "Charles Kettering" in the Ohio Central online encyclopedia,
http://www.ohiostorycentral.org/entry.php?rec=223.

210 **"status quo" bias:** Daniel Kahneman, Jack L. Knetch, and Richard Thaler,
"Anomalies: The Endowment Effect, Loss Aversion, and Status Quo Bias,"
in Daniel Kahneman and Amos Tversky, editors, *Choices, Values, and
Frames* (New York: Cambridge University Press, 2000), pp. 159–170; William Samuelson and Richard Zeckhauser, "Status Quo Bias in Decision
Making," *Journal of Risk and Uncertainty,* Vol. 1, No. 1 (March 1988),
pp. 7–59.

211 **litigation rights:** E. J. Johnson, J. Hershey, J. Meszaros, and H. Kunreuther,
"Framing, Probability Distortions, and Insurance Decisions," *Journal of
Risk and Uncertainty,* Vol. 7 (1993), pp. 35–51.

212 **people other than you:** A full treatment of the commitment process and its
relationship to the Consistency Principle in social psychology can be found
in Charles A. Kiesler, *The Psychology of Commitment* (New York: Academic Press, 1971). See also Robert B. Cialdini, *Influence: The Psychology
of Persuasion* (New York: William Morrow, 1984), pp. 57–113; Karl E.
Weick, *Sensemaking in Organizations* (Thousand Oaks, CA: Sage, 1995),
pp. 155–162.

212 **foot-in-the-door phenomenon:** For more on this, see Robert B. Cialdini, *Influence: The Psychology of Persuasion* (New York: William Morrow, 1984),
pp. 57–113. The homeowner study discussed in the text can be found at J.
L. Freedman and S. C. Fraser, "Compliance Without Pressure: The Foot-
in-the-Door Technique," *Journal of Personality and Social Psychology,*
Vol. 4 (1966), pp. 195–203. See also Daniel J. O'Keefe, *Persuasion Theory
& Research* (Thousand Oaks, CA: Sage, 2002), pp. 230–240.

214 **"let's do that":** Nancy Griffin and Kim Masters, *Hit and Run: How Jon
Peters and Peter Guber Took Sony for a Ride in Hollywood* (New York:
Simon & Schuster, 1997), p. 75.

217 **his or her turf:** For a good review of the literature on organizational turf
and its effects on politics, see Graham Brown, Thomas B. Lawrence, and
Sandra L. Robinson, "Territoriality in Organizations," *Academy of Management Review,* Vol. 30, No. 3 (July 2005), pp. 577–594.

217 **"power of its officials":** Quoted in N. Frolich and J. Oppenheimer, *Modern
Political Economy* (Upper Saddle River, NJ: Prentice-Hall, 1978), p. 69.

218 **cubicle or a kingdom:** Our small part of this saga is told in James B.
Stewart, *Disney War* (New York: Simon & Schuster, 2005), pp. 216–217.
But read the whole book for a fascinating account of the entire drama.

218  **when she took over HP:** The "thousand tribes" comment appears in Carly Fiorina, *Tough Choices* (New York: Portfolio, 2006), p. 8; the story of her encounter with the CFO appears at p. 178.

219  **bonding behaviors:** See H. Tajfel, "Interindividual and Intergroup Behavior," in H. Tajfel, Editor, *Differentiation Between Social Groups: Studies in the Social Psychology of Intergroup Relations* (London: Academic Press, 1978), pp. 27–60. This is sometimes called the "Granfalloon Technique." See Anthony R. Pratkanis and Elliott Aronson, *Age of Propaganda* (New York: W. H. Freeman, 2001), pp. 216–223.

219  **the scarcity response:** This is well-handled in Robert B. Cialdini, *Influence: The Psychology of Persuasion* (New York: William Morrow, 1984), pp. 237–271.

220  **from the lower prices:** For more on the "losers are louder" political phenomenon, see G. Richard Shell, *Make the Rules or Your Rivals Will* (New York: Crown Business, 2004), pp. 32–56 (on various political influence games) and pp. 157–177 (on how incumbents fight to maintain the status quo).

220  **"ironing out of differences":** Alfred P. Sloan Jr., *My Years with General Motors* (New York: Doubleday, 1963), p. 105.

221  **a broken company in his hands:** Our discussion of the Asda story is based on a Harvard Business School case, which is based—in its turn—on a document prepared by Asda Group PLC called "The Asda Story." Harvard Business School, "Asda, Parts A, A1, B and C" (Cases number 9–498–005, -006, -007, and -008) (May 6, 1998).

223  **low-cost air travel:** Herb Kelleher, "A Culture of Commitment," *Leader to Leader*, Vol. 4 (Spring 1997), pp. 20–24.

224  **addresses an *urgent* need:** John P. Kotter and Dan S. Cohen, *The Heart of Change* (Boston: Harvard Business School Press, 2002), pp. 15–36.

224  **"policy window":** G. Richard Shell, *Make the Rules or Your Rivals Will* (New York: Crown Business, 2004), pp. 44–46.

225  **your idea momentum:** Karl Weeks, "Small Wins," *American Psychologist*, Vol. 39 (1984), pp. 40–49; John P. Kotter and Dan S. Cohen, *The Heart of Change* (Boston: Harvard Business School Press, 2002), p. 18.

226  **bomber in the 1990s:** Eric Schmidt, "U.S. Weapons Makers Intensify Lobbying Efforts as Budgets Fall," *New York Times* (August 6, 1991), p. C1.

226  **appear to be the "extremists":** People's opinions are affected by the social pressure exerted in their social surroundings. See Solomon E. Asch, "Opinions and Social Pressure," *Scientific American*, Vol. 193 (1955), pp. 31–35; Sandra Blakeslee, "What Other People Say May Change What You See," *New York Times* (June 28, 2005), p. E1; Robert B. Cialdini, *Influence: The Psychology of Persuasion* (New York: William Morrow, 1984), pp. 114–166.

226  **television series *Lost*:** Olga Craig, "The man who discovered 'Lost'—and found himself out of a job," *The London Telegraph* (August 14, 2005); http://www.telegraph.co.uk/news/main.jhtml?xml=/news/2005/08/14/wlost14.xml.

227 **"sweep us along":** This is quoted in Robert Green, *The 48 Laws of Power* (New York: Penguin, 1998), p. 243.

229 **a reputation for innovation:** For more on the Matthew Effect, see Robert K. Merton, "The Matthew Effect in Science," *Science*, Vol. 159, No. 3810 (1968), pp. 56–63.

231 *When We Were Kings:* The boxing documentary movie *When We Were Kings,* directed by Leon Gast, was about the heavyweight professional boxing match in Zaire between George Foreman and Muhammad Ali in 1974. The footage was shot in 1974 but was tied up in litigation for nearly twenty-two years, and the film was released in 1996.

## Chapter 10: Woo with Integrity: Character

235 **"glints in every mind":** James C. Humes, *The Wit and Wisdom of Winston Churchill* (New York: HarperPerennial, 1995), p. 364.

235 **"the tree is the real thing":** We found this one at http://www.brainyquote. com/quotes/authors/a/abraham_lincoln.html.

235 **most closely associated with it:** We take our account of the New Era scandal from Joseph T. Wilson, *Frankensteins of Fraud: The 20th Century's Top Ten White-Collar Criminals* (Austin, TX: Obsidian Publishing, 2000). See also Steve Stecklow, "Crumbling Pyramid: Owing £500 Million, New Era Charity Seeks Refuge From Creditors," *Wall Street Journal* (May 16, 1995), p. A1. Finally, our thanks go to David Osgood, a CPA from Northern Virginia with whom we spoke and who has presented numerous talks on the New Era situation, including one attended by an FBI agent who investigated the fraud, and who confirmed the details of Wilson's account. See Osgood's presentation at http://www.auditforum.org/. . ./mid%20atlan tic%2006%202006/Handouts%20for%20Dave%20Cotton%20Session. pdf.

243 **"Crush Your Enemy Totally":** The laws mentioned in the text are, respectively, Laws number 7, number 12, and number 15 in Robert Green, *The 48 Laws of Power* (New York: Penguin, 1998), pp. 34–78. There is, of course, much, much more to be said about the ethics of persuasion in business than we have touched on with our practical, down-to-earth advice. For those who seek more information, see, e.g., Harvard Business Review, *Ethics in Practice: Managing the Moral Corporation*, Kenneth R. Andrews, Editor (Boston: Harvard Business School Press, 1987); John M. Darley, David M. Messick, and Tom R. Tyler, editors, *Social Influences on Ethical Behavior in Organizations* (Mahwah, NJ: Lawrence Erlbaum Associates, 2001); Stephen M. R. Covey, *The SPEED of Trust: The One Thing That Changes Everything* (New York: Free Press, 2006); Marvin T. Brown, *Corporate Integrity: Rethinking Organizational Ethics and Leadership* (New York: Cambridge University Press, 2005); Joseph L. Badaracco, *Defining Moments: When Managers Must Decide Between Right and Right* (Boston: Harvard Business School Press, 1997).

248 **defined pedestrian crossings:** Hans Monderman and his traffic philosophy can be investigated in Sarah Lyall, "A Path to Road Safety with No Signposts," *New York Times* (January 22, 2005), p. A4. See also Malcolm Gladwell, "Blowup," *The New Yorker* (January 22, 1996), pp. 32–36 ("Why are more pedestrians killed crossing the street at marked crosswalks than at unmarked crosswalks?").

# Topical Bibliography

## Argumentation and Rhetoric

Abbott, Andrew. *Methods of Discovery: Heuristics for the Social Sciences.* New York: W. W. Norton & Company, 2004.

Aristotle. *Rhetoric.* Mineola, NY: Dover, 2004.

Burke, Kenneth. *A Rhetoric of Motives.* Berkeley: University of California Press, 1969.

Fahnstock, Jeanne, and Marie Secor. *A Rhetoric of Argument, Third Edition.* Boston: McGraw-Hill, 2004.

Garver, Eugene. *For the Sake of Argument.* Chicago: University of Chicago Press, 2004.

Killingsworth, M. Jimmie. *Appeals in Modern Rhetoric.* Carbondale: Southern Illinois University Press, 2005.

Spence, Gerry. *How to Argue and Win Every Time.* New York: St. Martin's Griffin, 1995.

Toulmin, Stephen E. *An Examination of the Place of Reason in Ethics.* Cambridge: Cambridge University Press, 1961.

———. *The Uses of Argument.* Cambridge: Cambridge University Press, 2003.

Walton, D. N. *One-Sided Arguments: A Dialectical Analysis of Bias.* Albany: State University of New York Press, 1999.

## Biographies and Industry Studies

Angel, Karen. *Inside Yahoo!* Hoboken, NJ: Wiley, 2002.

Bird, Kai, and Martin J. Sherwin. *The Triumph and Tragedy of J. Robert Oppenheimer.* New York: Random House, 2005.

Brand, Larry, ed. *The Papers of George Catlett Marshall, Volume 2.* Baltimore: Johns Hopkins University Press, 1986.

Brands, H. W. *Masters of Enterprise.* Hoboken, NJ: Wiley, 1999.

Brown, Marvin T. *Corporate Integrity: Rethinking Organizational Ethics and Leadership.* Cambridge: Cambridge University Press, 2005.

Bruck, Connie. *Master of the Game*. New York: Penguin, 1994.

Bunnell, David. *Making the Cisco Connection*. Hoboken, NJ: Wiley, 2003.

Burrows, Peter. *Backfire*. Hoboken, NJ: Wiley, 2003.

Carlton, Jim. *Apple*. New York: Harper Business, 1997.

Carnegie, Andrew. *Autobiography*. Boston: Houghton Mifflin, 1920.

Carroll, Paul. *Big Blues: The Unmaking of IBM*. New York: Crown, 1993.

Cassidy, John. *Dot.Con*. New York: HarperCollins, 2002.

Chernow, Ron. *The House of Morgan*. New York: Simon & Schuster, 1990.

———. *Titan: The Life of John D. Rockefeller, Sr*. New York: Random House, 1998.

Coleman, Penny. *A Woman Unafraid: The Achievements of Frances Perkins*. New York: Atheneum Books, 1993.

DeGeorge, Gail. *The Making of Blockbuster*. Hoboken, NJ: Wiley, 1996.

Duncan, David E. *The Geneticist Who Played Hoops with My DNA*. New York: HarperCollins, 2005.

Fiorina, Carly. *Tough Choices*. New York: Portfolio, 2006.

Garin, Kristoffer A. *Devils on the Deep Blue Sea*. New York: Penguin, 2005.

Goodwin, Doris Kearns. *Team of Rivals: The Political Genius of Abraham Lincoln*. New York: Simon & Schuster, 2005.

Goulder, Grace. *John D. Rockefeller: The Cleveland Years*. Cleveland, OH: Western Reserve Historical Society, 1972.

Griffin, Nancy, and Kim Masters. *Hit and Run*. New York: Simon & Schuster, 1996.

Grove, Andrew S. *Only the Paranoid Survive*. New York: Currency Doubleday, 1999.

Hamlin, Charles Eugene. *The Life and Times of Hannibal Hamlin, Volume 2*. Whitefish, MT: Kessinger Publishing, 2006.

Hays, Constance L. *The Real Thing: Truth and Power at the Coca-Cola Company*. New York: Random House, 2005.

Humes, James C. *The Wit and Wisdom of Winston Churchill*. New York: Harper Perennial, 1995.

Issacson, Walter, ed. *A Benjamin Franklin Reader*. New York: Simon & Schuster, 2003.

Jackson, Tim. *Inside Intel: Andy Grove and the Rise of the World's Most Powerful Chip Company*. New York: Plume, 1998.

Jenkins, Roy. *Churchill: A Biography*. New York: Plume, 2002.

Keegan, John. *Winston Churchill*. New York: Lipper/Viking Adult, 2002.

Kipnis, David. *The Powerholders*. Chicago: University of Chicago Press, 1976.

Klein, Maury. *The Life and Legend of Jay Gould*. Baltimore: Johns Hopkins University Press, 1986.

Kroc, Ray. *Grinding It Out*. Chicago: Contemporary Books, 1977.

Lampbright, W. Henry. *Powering Apollo: James Webb of NASA*. Baltimore: Johns Hopkins University Press, 1995.

Larson, Erik. *The Devil in the White City*. New York: Crown, 2003.

Lewis, Michael. *Liar's Poker*. New York: Penguin, 1989.

Lewis, Reginald F., and Blair S. Walker. *Why Should White Guys Have All the Fun?* Hoboken, NJ: Wiley, 1995.

Lincoln, Abraham, and Roy P. Basler. *Collected Works of Abraham Lincoln, Volume 4*. New Brunswick, NJ: Rutgers University Press, 1953.

Lindbergh, Charles. *The Spirit of St. Louis*. New York: Scribner, 1953.

Love, John F. *McDonald's*. New York: Bantam Books, 1995.

Lowenstein, Roger. *When Genius Failed*. New York: Random House, 2000.

McCullough, David. *1776*. New York: Simon & Schuster, 2005.

McElheny, Victor K. *Insisting on the Impossible: The Life of Edwin Land*. Reading, MA: Perseus Books, 1998.

McLean, Bethany, and Peter Elkind. *The Smartest Guys in the Room*. New York: Penguin, 2003.

Mandela, Nelson. *Long Walk to Freedom*. Boston: Little, Brown & Company, 1994.

Manes, Stephen, and Paul Andrews. *Gates*. New York: Doubleday, 1993.

May, Ernest R., and Philip D. Zelikow. *The Kennedy Tapes*. Cambridge, MA: Belknap, 1997.

May, James M. *Trials of Character*. Chapel Hill: North Carolina University Press, 1988.

Morgan, Ted. *FDR: A Biography*. New York: Simon & Schuster, 1985.

Morita, Akio, Edwin M. Reingold, and Mitsuko Shimomura. *Made in Japan: Akio Morita and Sony*. New York: E. P. Dutton, 1986.

Moseley, Leonard. *Marshall: A Hero for Our Times*. New York: Hearst Books, 1982.

Nasaw, David. *Andrew Carnegie*. New York: Penguin Press, 2006.

Neustadt, Richard E. *Report to JFK*. Ithaca, NY: Cornell University Press, 1999.

Packard, David. *The HP Way*. New York: Harper Business, 1995.

Rhodes, Richard. *The Making of the Atomic Bomb*. New York: Simon & Schuster, 1986.

Sampson, Anthony. *Mandela*. New York: Random House, 1999.

Sanders, Col. Hartland. *Life As I Have Known It Has Been Finger Lickin' Good*. Carol Stream, IL: Creation House, 1974.

Slater, Robert. *No Such Thing as Over-Exposure: Inside the Life and Celebrity of Donald Trump*. Upper Saddle River, NJ: Prentice Hall, 2005.

Sloan, Alfred P., Jr. *My Years with General Motors*. New York: Doubleday, 1963.

Spedding, James, Robert Leslie Ellis, and Douglas Denon Heath (eds.). *The Works of Francis Bacon*. London: Longman, 1857–74.

Stewart, James B. *Disney War*. New York: Simon & Schuster, 2005.

Swisher, Kara. *aol.com*. New York: Random House, 1998.

Tedlow, Richard S. *Andy Grove: The Life and Times of an American*. New York: Portfolio, 2006.

————.*Giants of Enterprise: Seven Business Innovators and the Empires They Built.* New York: Harper Business, 2001.

————. *The Watson Dynasty.* New York: HarperCollins, 2003.

Temin, Peter, with Louis Galambos. *The Fall of the Bell System.* Cambridge: Cambridge University Press, 1987.

Vise, David A., and Mark Malseed. *The Google Story.* New York: Delacorte Press, 2005.

Wallis, Michael. *Oil Man: The Story of Frank Phillips and the Birth of Phillips Petroleum.* New York: Doubleday, 1988.

Walton, Sam, with John Huey. *Made in America: My Story.* New York: Doubleday, 1992.

Wilson, Douglas L. *Lincoln's Sword: The Presidency and the Power of Words.* New York: Alfred A. Knopf, 2006

Wozniak, Steve, with Gina Smith. *iWoz.* New York: W. W. Norton & Company, 2006.

## Decision Making

Allison, Graham, and Philip Zelikow. *Essence of Decision.* New York: Addison Wesley Longman Publishers, 1999.

Dewey, John. *How We Think.* Mineola, NY: Dover, 1997.

Follott, Mary P. *Creative Experience.* New York: Longmans, 1924.

Gladwell, Malcolm. *Blink: The Power of Thinking Without Thinking.* Boston: Little, Brown & Company, 2005.

Hoch, Stephen J., and Howard C. Kunreuther. *Wharton on Making Decisions.* Hoboken, NJ: Wiley, 2001.

Kahneman, Daniel, and Amos Tversky (eds.). *Choices, Values, and Frames.* New York: Cambridge University Press, 2000.

Kiesler, Charles A. *The Psychology of Commitment.* New York: Academic Press, 1971.

Langer, Ellen. *Mindfulness.* Boston: Addison Wesley, 1990.

Neustadt, Richard E., and Ernest R. May. *Thinking in Time.* New York: Free Press, 1986.

## Ethics

Andrews, Kenneth R., ed. *Ethics in Practice: Managing the Moral Corporation.* Boston: Harvard Business School Press, 1987.

Badaracco, Joseph L. *Defining Moments: When Managers Must Decide Between Right and Right.* Boston: Harvard Business School Press, 1997.

Darley, John M., David M. Messick, and Tom R. Tyler, eds. *Social Influences on Ethical Behavior in Organizations.* Mahwah, NJ: Lawrence Erlbaum Associates, 2001.

Wilson, Joseph T. *Frankensteins of Fraud: The 20th Century's Top Ten White-Collar Criminals.* Austin, TX: Obsidian Publishing, 2000.

### Influence, Persuasion, and Negotiation

Adler, Ronald B., and Jeanne Marquardt Elmhorst. *Communicating at Work.* New York: McGraw-Hill, 2005.

Allen, Mike, and Raymond W. Preiss. *Persuasion: Advances Through Meta-Analysis.* Cresskill, NJ: Hampton Press, 1998.

Anderson, Erling S., Kristoffer V. Grude, and Tor Haug. *Goal Directed Project Management.* Sterling, VA: Kogan Page, 2004.

Barnes, B. Kim. *Exercising Influence.* Berkeley, CA: Barnes & Conti Associates, Inc., 2000.

Bauer, Joel, and Mark Levy. *How to Persuade People Who Don't Want to be Persuaded.* Hoboken, NJ: Wiley, 2004.

Brembeck, Winston L. *Persuasion: A Means of Social Influence.* Upper Saddle River, NJ: Prentice-Hall, 1976.

Canary, Daniel J., Michael J. Cody, and Valerie L. Manusov. *Interpersonal Communication.* Boston: Bedford/St. Martin's, 2003.

Carnegie, Dale. *How to Win Friends and Influence People.* New York: Pocket Books, 1981.

Cialdini, Robert B. *Influence: The Psychology of Persuasion.* New York: William Morrow, 1984.

———. *Influence: Science and Practice.* Boston: Allyn & Bacon, 2001.

Conger, Jay A. *Winning 'em Over.* New York: Simon & Schuster, 1998.

Erwin, Phil. *Attitudes and Persuasion.* Hove, UK: Psychology Press, 2001.

Fisher, Roger, and Daniel Shapiro. *Beyond Reason.* New York: Viking, 2005.

Forgas, Joseph P., and Kipling D. Williams. *Social Influence: Direct and Indirect Processes.* Philadelphia: Psychology Press, 2001.

Gardner, Howard. *Changing Minds.* Boston: Harvard Business School Press, 2004.

Heath, Chip, and Dan Heath. *Made to Stick: Why Some Ideas Survive and Others Die.* New York: Random House, 2007.

Hogan, Kevin. *The Science of Influence: How to Get Anyone to Say Yes in 8 Minutes or Less.* Hoboken, NJ: Wiley, 2005.

Hogan, Kevin, and James Speakman. *Covert Persuasion: Psychological Tactics and Tricks to Win the Game.* Hoboken, NJ: Wiley, 2006.

Kolb, Deborah M., Ph.D, and Judith Williams, Ph.D. *The Shadow Negotiation.* New York: Simon & Schuster, 2000.

Kotter, John P. *Power and Influence: Beyond Formal Authority.* New York: Free Press, 1985.

Lakhani, Dave. *Persuasion: The Art of Getting What You Want.* Hoboken, NJ: Wiley, 2005.

Lax, David A., and James Sebenius. *The Manager as Negotiator*. New York: Free Press, 1986.

Miller, Robert B., and Gary A. Williams, with Alden M. Hayashi. *The 5 Paths to Persuasion*. New York: Warner Business Books, 2004.

Mortensen, Kurt W. *Maximum Influence*. New York: AMACOM, 2004.

O'Keefe, Daniel J. *Persuasion Theory and Research, Second Edition*. Thousand Oaks, CA: Sage, 2002.

Oliver, Robert T. *The Psychology of Persuasive Speech, Second Edition*. New York: David McKay Company, 1957.

Overstreet, H.A. *Influencing Human Behavior*. New York: W. W. Norton & Company, 1925.

Patterson, Kerry, Joseph Grenny, Ron McMillan, and Al Switzler. *Crucial Conversations*. New York: McGraw-Hill, 2002.

Perloff, Richard M. *The Dynamics of Persuasion*. Mahwah, NJ: Lawrence Erlbaum Associates, 2003.

Pratkanis, Anthony, and Elliot Aronson. *Age of Propaganda*. New York: W. H. Freeman and Company, 2000.

Puhn, Laurie, J.D. *Instant Persuasion*. New York: Penguin, 2005.

Raudsepp, Eugene. *What the Executive Should Know About Creating and Selling Ideas*. Larchmont, NY: American Research Council, 1966.

Reardon, Kathleen K. *Persuasion in Practice*. Newbury Park, CA: Sage, 1991.

Scott, Susan. *Fierce Conversations*. New York: Berkley Books, 2002.

Shell, G. Richard. *Bargaining for Advantage: Negotiation Strategies for Reasonable People, Second Edition*. New York: Penguin, 2006.

————. *Make the Rules or Your Rivals Will*. New York: Crown Business, 2004.

Simons, Herbert W., with Joanne Morreale and Bruce Gronbeck. *Persuasion in Society*. Thousand Oaks, CA: Sage Publications, 2001.

Steel, Jon. *Perfect Pitch: The Art of Selling Ideas and Winning New Business*. Hoboken, NJ: Wiley, 2007.

Stiff, James B. *Persuasive Communication*. New York: Guilford Press, 1994.

Storey, Richard. *The Art of Persuasive Communication*. Stowe, VT: Gower, 1997.

Trump, Donald. *The Art of the Deal*. New York: Random House, 1987.

Vass, Jerry. *Soft Selling in a Hard World, Second Edition*. Philadelphia: Running Press, 1998.

Vengel, Alan A. *The Influence Edge*. San Francisco: Berrett-Koehler, 2000.

## Leadership

Collins, Jim. *Good to Great*. New York: Random House, 2001.

Covey, Stephen R. *The SPEED of Trust: The One Thing That Changes Everything*. New York: Free Press, 2006.

Doig, Jameson W., and Erwin C. Hargrove. *Leadership and Innovation.* Baltimore: Johns Hopkins University Press, 1987.

Hesselbein, Frances, and Paul M. Cohen. *Leader to Leader.* San Francisco: Jossey-Bass, 1999.

Kotter, John P., and Dan S. Cohen. *The Heart of Change: Real-life Stories of How People Change Their Organization.* Boston: Harvard Business School Press, 2002.

Metcalf, Henry C., and L. Urwick. *Dynamic Administration: The Collected Papers of Mary Parker Follett.* New York: Harper, 1940.

Sawyer, Ralph D. *Sun-Tzu: The Art of War.* Boulder, CO: Westview Press, 1994.

Turner, J. Rodney, Kristoffer V. Grude, and Lynn Thurloway. *The Project Manager as Change Agent.* London: McGraw-Hill, 1996.

Useem, Michael. *Leading Up.* New York: Crown Business, 2001.

## Organizational Politics and Culture

Bacharach, S. B., and E. J. Lawler. *Power and Politics in Organizations.* San Francisco: Jossey-Bass, 1981.

Bailey, F. G. *The Tactical Uses of Passion: An Essay on Power, Reason, and Reality.* Ithaca, NY: Cornell University Press, 1983.

Bellman, Geoffrey M. *Getting Things Done When You Are Not in Charge.* New York: Simon & Schuster, 1992.

Blau, Peter M. *Exchange and Power in Social Life.* Hoboken, NJ: Wiley, 1964.

Brandon, Rick, and Marty Seldman. *Survival of the Savvy.* New York: Free Press, 2004.

Cohen, Allan R., and David L. Bradford. *Influence Without Authority.* Hoboken, NJ: Wiley, 1990.

DeLuca, Joel R., Ph.D. *Political Savvy.* Berwyn, PA: Evergreen Business Group, 1999.

de Waal, Frans. *Chimpanzee Politics: Power and Sex Among the Apes, Revised Edition.* Baltimore: Johns Hopkins University Press, 1998.

Dobson, Michael S., and Deborah S. Dobson. *Enlightened Office Politics.* New York: AMACOM, 2001.

Downs, Anthony. *Inside Bureaucracy.* Prospect Heights, IL: Waveland Press, 1994.

DuBrin, Andrew. *Winning Office Politics.* Upper Saddle River, NJ: Prentice Hall, 1990.

Frank, Jill. *Surviving in the Jungle of Office Politics.* Dallas, TX: Sterling Communications, 1998.

Frolich, N., and J. Oppenheimer. *Modern Political Economy.* Upper Saddle River, NJ: Prentice-Hall, 1978.

Greene, Robert. *The 48 Laws of Power.* New York: Penguin, 1998.

Hawley, Casey. *100+ Tactics for Office Politics*. Hauppauge, NY: Barron's Educational Series, 2001.

Kramer, Roderick M., and Tom R. Tyler. *Trust in Organizations*. Thousand Oaks, CA: Sage, 1996.

Lippmann, Walter. *Public Opinion*. New York: Free Press, 1997 (reprint edition).

Mackay, Harvey. *Dig Your Well Before You're Thirsty*. New York: Currency Doubleday, 1990.

McIntyre, Marie G. *Secrets to Winning at Office Politics*. New York: St. Martin's Griffin, 2005.

Pfeffer, Jeffrey. *Managing with Power*. Boston: Harvard Business School Press, 1992.

Porter, Lyman W., Harold L. Angle, and Robert W. Allen. *Organizational Influence Processes*. Armonk, NY: M. E. Sharpe, Inc., 2003.

Reardon, Kathleen Kelley. *It's All Politics*. New York: Random House, 2005.

———. *The Secret Handshake*. New York: Random House, 2000.

Rozakis, Laurie, and Bob Rozakis. *The Complete Idiot's Guide to Office Politics*. Indianapolis: Alpha Books, 1998.

Schein, Edgar H. *The Corporate Culture*. San Francisco: Wiley, 1999.

———. *Organizational Culture and Leadership*. San Francisco: Jossey-Bass, 1985.

Simon, Herbert A. *Administrative Behavior*. New York: Free Press, 1945.

Smith, Kenwyn K. *Groups in Conflict*. Dubuque, IA: Kendall/Hunt Publishing Company, 1982.

Tajfel, H., ed. *Differentiation Between Social Groups: Studies in the Social Psychology of Intergroup Relations*. London: Academic Press, 1978.

Tannen, Deborah. *Talking from 9 to 5*. New York: Avon Books, 1994.

Weick, Karl E. *Sensemaking in Organizations*. Thousand Oaks, CA: Sage, 1995.

Wilson, James Q. *Bureaucracy*. New York: Basic Books, 2000.

## Personality Psychology and Personal Effectiveness

Alessandra, Tony, and M. J. O'Connor. *The Platinum Rule: Discover the Four Basic Business Personalities and How They Can Lead You to Success*. New York: Warner Books, 1996.

Buckingham, Marcus, and Donald O. Clifton. *Now, Discover Your Strengths*. New York: Free Press, 2001.

Covey, Stephen R. *The 7 Habits of Highly Effective People*. New York: Free Press, 1989.

———. *The 8th Habit: From Effectiveness to Greatness*. New York: Free Press, 2004.

Maher, Brendan A., ed. *Progress in Experimental Personality Research, Volume 2*. New York: Academic Press, 1965.

Miller, William I. *Faking It.* Cambridge: Cambridge University Press, 2003.

Rosenberg, Morris. *Conceiving the Self.* New York: Basic Books, 1979.

Simonton, Dean Keith. *Who Makes History and Why.* New York: Guilford Press, 1994.

Snyder, C. R., and Shane J. Lopez, eds. *Handbook of Positive Psychology.* Oxford: Oxford University Press, 2002.

Snyder, Mark. *Public Appearances, Private Realities: The Psychology of Self-Monitoring.* New York: W. H. Freeman, 1987.

Wilson, Timothy D. *Strangers to Ourselves.* Cambridge, MA: Belknap, 2002.

Wood, Karen Ginsburg. *Don't Sabotage Your Success!* Oakland, CA: Enlightened Concepts Publishing, 2001.

Young, James Webb. *A Technique for Producing Ideas.* Chicago: NTC Contemporary Publishing, 1975 (reprint edition).


Social Networking

Burt, Ronald S. *Brokerage & Closure.* Oxford: Oxford University Press, 2005.

Cross, Rob, and Andrew Parker. *The Hidden Power of Social Networks: Understanding How Work Really Gets Done in Organizations.* Boston: Harvard Business School Press, 2004.

Darling, Diane. *The Networking Survival Guide: Get the Success You Want by Tapping into the People You Know.* New York: McGraw-Hill, 2003.

Ferrazzi, Keith. *Never Eat Alone: And Other Secrets to Success, One Relationship at a Time.* New York: Currency Doubleday, 2005.

Misner, I. R., and D. Morgan. *Masters of Networking: Building Relationships for Your Pocketbook and Soul.* Atlanta: Brad Press, 2000.

Putman, Robert D. *Bowling Alone.* New York: Simon & Schuster, 2000.

Watts, Duncan. *Six Degrees: The Science of a Connected Age.* New York: W. W. Norton, 2003.

# Index